Contemporary Democracies

Contemporary Democracies

Participation, Stability, and Violence

G. BINGHAM POWELL, JR.

Harvard University Press
Cambridge, Massachusetts, and London, England

Library of Congress Cataloguing in Publication Data
Powell, G. Bingham.
    Contemporary democracies.
    Includes Bibliographical references and index.
    1. Comparative government.   2. Democracy.
I. Title.
JF51.P66   321.8   82-2890
ISBN 0-674-16687-6 (paper)   AACR2

Acknowledgments

In the long course of research on a problem one accumulates debts of many kinds. I am glad to acknowledge some of them here. The University of Rochester gave me a semester's sabbatical leave in the spring of 1977, during which I collected most of the data described in Chapter 2 and the Appendix; it also provided computer time for the subsequent analysis and a tremendously stimulating environment in its Department of Political Science. Students in my undergraduate and graduate courses called "Issues in Democracy" and "Problems in Comparative Politics" helped me work through many of the ideas developed in the book. Their questions and their interest encouraged my research. Janice Brown, Donna French, and Claire Sundeen typed parts of successive versions of the manuscript. Gabriel Almond, Norman Nie, William Riker, and Sidney Tarrow encouraged me with their reactions to a much earlier version of the manuscript. Raymond Duch, Harold Stanley, and particularly, Bruce D. Berkowitz made useful comments on several chapters. Aida Donald of Harvard University Press offered both encouragement and a thoughtful review of the penultimate version. Jorge Domínguez wrote a detailed and extremely helpful review for the Press. Camille Smith contributed meticulous editing. Above all I am indebted to Sidney Verba and to Lynda W. Powell for emotional, intellectual, and technical assistance on many versions and aspects of the manuscript and the analysis. I can only ascribe remaining difficulties and errors to my own fallibility—and to the intractable nature of some important problems.

The question of political performance in democracies has attracted the attention of many distinguished scholars. My work builds upon their thought and research. Where I am aware of such intellectual debts, I have tried to acknowledge them in the notes. Inevitably, many indirect influences have not been acknowledged. I have attempted to repay these scholarly debts in the most appropriate coin by writing the best book I can at this time. I dedicate it to all those who have tried to enhance our understanding of democratic political performance.

Contents

Tables

Figures

Contemporary Democracies

Introduction /
Democracy, Parties, and Performance

1

About thirty contemporary nations might reasonably claim to be working political democracies. Citizens of these countries are able to organize and vote in competitive elections. The national political leaders are held accountable to their citizens through electoral means. In some of these nations the political process seems to work quite well: citizens participate actively in elections, stable governments are formed, discontent is expressed through democratic competition rather than through violent conflict. In other nations the process works less successfully. Citizens' political involvement is characterized by turmoil rather than by electoral participation. Governments are unstable, unresponsive, or both. Violence is widespread. The life expectancy of democracy itself is a matter of constant calculation.

Why does the political process work more successfully in some democracies than in others? It is likely that a nation's social and economic environment, its political institutions and organizations, and the beliefs and strategies of its political leaders help shape political performance. The system of political parties also is likely to play a key role.

Numerous scholars, including some of the most influential figures in comtemporary political science, have studied various aspects of political performance in democracies.[1] Theoretical argument, analysis of specific countries, and selection of compelling examples have all been brought to bear. Despite these studies, much uncertainty remains. Most studies have focused on only one or two factors at a time and not attempted to assess their simultaneous effects. Some of the best have dealt with a few countries or even a single nation. The best comparative studies of a large number of countries have attempted to explain levels of violence, without examining internal democratic processes.[2] Perhaps because of these limitations, considerable disagreement exists about the specific advantages and problems of different types of constitutional arrange-

1

ments and party systems, as well as about the compatibility of different elements of political performance.

I shall consider the effects of environmental, institutional, and party-system conditions on political performance in the full set of contemporary democracies. This analysis contributes to our understanding of some intensely debated questions. Do political party systems that appeal to narrow groups of citizens, rather than to broad electoral majorities, encourage the legitimate channeling of competition, or do they tend to foster political discontent and violence? Do high levels of political participation by citizens help or hinder the achievement of government stability and the control of violence? Upon such questions the scholarly community is sharply divided.

The era since the Second World War has been the largest experiment with democracy in human history. Before 1900 only a handful of nations might have been considered democracies.[3] Their number increased to about twenty after 1920, but the events surrounding the Great Depression overwhelmed several of these (including Weimar Germany, Austria, and Estonia). Since the early 1950s, however, new opportunities have been offered for the study of democracy. The greater number of democracies, the long period without a general international war, and the appearance of sophisticated techniques of research and analysis have made it possible to develop and test new theories of the political process and its consequences in democratic settings.[4] I shall compare and analyze the political process across the thirty-odd contemporary democratic political systems. I shall examine political performance in these nations from the late 1950s, after the postwar reconstruction had been assimilated, through two decades. I shall focus on the role of political party systems in shaping political performance within the context of their social and cultural environment. Considering the full set of democratic countries, offers perspective on those aspects of democracy with which we are familiar and provides variation in the factors believed to shape political performance.

The Contemporary Democracies

In order to test theories about political performance in democracies we need to identify a set of countries that qualify as working democratic systems. Some of the disagreements emerging from previous studies originate in the different sets of countries examined. One danger in deciding which countries to include is that some democracies may be omitted and their relevant experiences neglected. If these countries are located in particular geographic regions or share particular types of party systems, the conclusions of the analysis will be biased by their exclusion. A second danger is that countries may be included that do not share the common defining properties of a democracy. If a nation's elections and parties do not shape the choice of leaders and policies, if they are merely a facade for a military junta or one-party rule, then including that nation will also distort conclusions about political processes in a democratic context. Consequently, the initial selection of the set of countries to study is important and requires some justification.

If the term "democracy" is restricted to political systems in which all citizens participate in day-to-day policymaking, then there are no democracies among the nations of the world. It is doubtful if a unit as large as a nation can work as a pure democracy. The relevant national experiences today are found in political systems where representative leaders are chosen through competitive elections. The competitive electoral context, with several political parties organizing the alternatives that face the voters, is the identifying property of the contemporary democratic process. To study political performance in democratic systems among today's nations means to study political performance in those nations characterized by competitive elections in which most citizens are eligible to participate.[5]

More explicitly, to identify the set of contemporary national democracies, I looked for political systems meeting *all* of the following criteria:

1. The legitimacy of the government rests on a claim to represent the desires of its citizens. That is, the claim of the government to obedience to its laws is based on the government's assertion to be doing what the people want it to do.[6]
2. The organized arrangement that regulates this bargain of legitimacy is the competitive political election. Leaders are elected at regular intervals, and voters can choose among alternative candidates. In practice, at least two political parties that have a chance of winning are needed to make such choices meaningful.
3. Most adults can participate in the electoral process, both as voters and as candidates for important political office.
4. Citizens' votes are secret and not coerced.
5. Citizens and leaders enjoy basic freedom of speech, press, assembly, and organization. Both established parties and new ones can work to gain members and voters.

In selecting a set of countries meeting these criteria, I built on the work of other scholars who have attempted similar tasks. The approach closest to my own definition of representative democracy is Robert Dahl's study of "polyarchy." Dahl rates 114 countries by their levels of participation and contestation in 1969, and designates 35 of them as at least "near polyarchies."[7] Several years earlier Dankwart Rustow had offered a list of countries that had had three or more consecutive, popular, and competitive elections as of early 1967.[8] Most comprehensive in coverage, although not oriented to democracy as such, was Arthur Banks's coding of political characteristics of all nations each year from 1815, or their date of independence, to 1966.[9] Countries designated by Banks as having fully effective legislatures chosen through electoral processes seem to be possible democracies. More recently, David Butler, Howard Penniman, and Austin Ranney identified 28 nations that had "democratic general elections" in at least a "partly free" setting in the late 1970s.[10] Despite substantial differences in their objectives, these four studies show considerable agreement. Twenty-one countries appear on all four lists, and comments suggest that five others fail to make a given list only because of the date of the study.

Despite important variations in the degree of democracy, the distinction between contemporary nations meeting most of the above criteria most of the time and those failing to do so is fairly clear. In the 1970s, well over a third of the nations of the world were ruled by military governments or (in a few cases) traditional monarchies that prohibited or completely subordinated all political parties. In another third of the nations, competition among parties was legally or practically prohibited, although the degree of dissent permitted within a single-party framework ranged from rather monolithic control, as in the USSR, to substantial intraparty competition in Tanzania.[11] These countries do not appear in the various lists of democracies.

The major uncertainties regarding inclusion in the present study stemmed from questions about the reality of competition and the role of political parties. An associated problem concerned countries that tasted democracy, so to speak, but did not remain democratic long enough to provide evidence about the democratic process in action. I eliminated countries where military intervention or other events prevented a democracy from reaching its fifth consecutive birthday. For simple reasons of lack of data I also had to eliminate likely democracies with fewer than one million citizens: Botswana, Iceland, Luxembourg, and Trinidad and Tobago were casualties of this lack of information.

Table 1.1 shows the countries that are included in this study. As

Table 1.1   The Contemporary Democracies: Nations with democratic regimes for at least five years, 1958–1976.[a]

Democratic regime continuous 1958–1976

Australia	West Germany	Norway
Austria	Ireland	Sweden
Belgium	Israel	Switzerland
Canada	Italy	United Kingdom
Costa Rica	Japan	United States
Denmark	Netherlands	Venezuela[b]
Finland	New Zealand	

Democratic regime seriously limited or suspended

France (1958)	Sri Lanka[d] (1971–76)
India (1975–76)	Turkey (1960–61) (1971–72)
Jamaica[c] (1976)	

Democratic regime definitely replaced

Chile (1973–)	Philippines (1972–)
Greece (1967–74)	Uruguay (1973–)

a. Only nations with a population of 1 million or more are included.

b. A democratic regime was established in Venezuela in 1959; but periodic emergencies and terrorism limited democratic freedoms in the early 1960s.

c. Jamaica became independent in 1962. A state of emergency was declared in 1976, but elections were subsequently held late that year, and the emergency later lifted.

d. The name of Ceylon was changed to Sri Lanka in 1971. Following massive guerrilla attacks in 1971, the government imposed restrictions on freedom of press and assembly that made the country's status as a democracy under our definition doubtful until 1977, although elections continued to be held.

noted, 21 of these appeared in all four earlier lists of democracies: Australia, Austria, Belgium, Canada, Costa Rica, Denmark, Finland, France, West Germany, India, Ireland, Israel, Italy, Japan, the Netherlands, New Zealand, Norway, Sweden, Switzerland, the United Kingdom, and the United States. Five more—Chile, Greece, Jamaica, the Philippines, and Uruguay—appear on three lists and are absent from one only because of the timing of their democratic period. The scholarly consensus seems fairly well established in considering these 26 nations as being working democracies for at least five years in the 1958–1976 period.[12] To them, I have added Ceylon, (Sri Lanka), Turkey, and Venezuela. Each of these appears on three lists, and my own examination of various studies of their politics leads me to agree with the majority and include them as democracies for at least a substantial part of the time.

In addition to their appearance on lists compiled by other scholars, the 29 countries[13] were subjected to another test: Did the competitive electoral process result in a change in the party or party coalition controlling the chief executive during these two decades? Although it is definitionally possible to have a democratic context in which power did not change hands (because of continuing support of the incumbents by a majority of citizens), such power changes seem a clear indication of importance of competitive elections. Their absence calls for closer scrutiny. In 22 countries there was clear evidence of elections leading directly to a transfer of a party power. In another 4 countries (Finland, Israel, Italy, and the Netherlands), elections did lead to some sort of complex re-forming of coalitions, although the connections to the election were not always very clear-cut. Only in India, Switzerland, and Japan were there no transfers of power following elections between 1958 and 1976. In 1977 clear transitions did take place in Israel and India, following opposition election victories. Only in Japan and Switzerland, then, must one rely on subjective judgment that sharp changes in citizen support would have led to changes in party control of the executive, despite the fact that in the 1960s and 1970s such transitions did not occur. In general, the case for calling these 29 nations democracies appears quite strong.

A comment on some countries not included is in order. Six countries were mentioned in only one study: Brazil (until 1963), Malaysia, Mexico, Portugal, South Africa, and Spain. Spain and Portugal were authoritarian regimes until 1975, at least, and thus do not fall into our time period, although a future study might include them. South Africa's disenfranchisement of the black majority disqualifies it as a democracy. Various studies suggest that in Mexico and Malaysia the opportunities for victory available to the opposition were much more symbolic than realistic. Brazil's experience with democratic politics in the late 1950s and early 1960s did not last long enough to provide a comparable case for analysis.[14]

Three countries appear on two lists, and a case can be made for inclusion of each of them: the Dominican Republic, Colombia, and Lebanon. In each case, the decision to delete was based on limits on the role of party and electoral politics in a political system with important democratic aspects. These limits were indicated by such events as the opposition boycott and later need for external pressure in elections in the Dominican Republic, the pact limiting presidential election competition in Colombia, and the fact that the majority of legislators in Lebanon were not members of any political party.[15] Moreover, in none of these countries did competitive elections lead to a transfer of power during the period of the study.

Table 1.1 also indicates the continuity of the democratic process in the 29 countries. In nearly a third of them, democracy was seriously suspended at one time or another. In 4 countries democracy was definitely replaced, at least temporarily, by military or executive dictatorship. These attributions refer only to the national level, ignoring local states of emergency, such as those in Canada in 1969 and in Northern Ireland (in the United Kingdom), in the 1970s. Such events suggest the potential fragility of the democratic process. Despite the vulnerability of some of the democracies, however, violence and regime changes seem no more likely to have taken place in the democracies than in the monarchies, military regimes, and single-party governments of the period.[16]

Political Parties and the Democratic Order

Scholars and commentators assert that a strong system of political parties is essential for a strong democracy.[17] The party system shapes citizen participation through the electoral process. The stability of political leadership depends on party activities in the electoral and legislative arenas. The dynamics of the party system may either inhibit or exacerbate turmoil and violence. The strategies and commitments of party leaders can be critical for the support of the democratic regime in time of crisis.

I shall look at the role of parties from two major perspectives. First, the system of political parties constitutes an important linkage between the social, economic, and constitutional setting on the one hand and political performance patterns on the other. Examining citizen partisanship, party strategies, and election outcomes helps us to understand, for example, how economic development affects voter participation, or the ways election laws affect government stability. Not all effects of environmental conditions operate through the party system, but many of them do so. Tracing those links is a step toward understanding the process.

Second, political party systems have autonomous influence of their own. The configurations of memory, organization, and perception that they represent have independent effects once they are established. A large body of scholarship purports to predict or explain these effects, but the literature abounds in often contradictory assertions. I shall endeavor to resolve some of these arguments. Is it majoritarian systems or multiparty minority systems that discourage citizen turmoil? What are the implications of support for extremist parties for different types of performance? Are strong linkages between groups and parties favorable or unfavorable for strong democratic performance?

I shall look at party systems both as linkages and as independent factors. It is also likely that some social and cultural variables affect party systems and political performance simultaneously. It will be important to model carefully the relationships among environmental conditions, party systems, and political performance. Despite the large literature on party systems, their direct and linking effects have seldom been examined systematically.

Standards of Political Performance

This analysis focuses on three dimensions of political performance: citizen electoral participation, government stability, and political order. These broad standards of political performance are evoked by many, if not most, contemporary regimes, both democracies and nondemocracies. They have much in common with the general criteria developed by Harry Eckstein, Ted Robert Gurr, and their colleagues for evaluating the performance of all political systems: durability, civil order, legitimacy and decisional efficiency.[18]

Citizen electoral participation is seen as critically significant by many students of democracy. Although it is not the only important form of participation, electoral activity may play the essential role in forcing elites to respond to other forms of citizen involvement.[19] Moreover, the formal participation of citizens in the national political process through elections is an important symbol of legitimacy in most modern societies. With the increased secularization of the political culture in most parts of the world, support for political systems by citizens has come increasingly to depend upon the claim either to respond to citizens' preferences, as in liberal democracies, or to act in their ultimate interests.[20] Whether the level of citizen participation is in fact related to the legitimacy of the chosen policies in democracies, and hence to the ease of enforcing policies and maintaining political order, is a question that I shall address in later chapters. The opinions of scholars and commentators are divided: some believe participation enhances legitimacy, and hence order; others believe it exerts disruptive pressures on political stability. (see Chapter 2).

Government stability and, more vaguely, effectiveness have been a major theme in the debates about constitutional arrangements and party systems in democracies. At least implicitly, the presence of short-lived governments is taken as evidence of poor performance in democracies and in other systems as well. Eckstein, Gurr, and their colleagues make the stable allocation of top political officials in roles of political authority a major criterion of performance.[21] Dahl suggests that unstable governments may well stimulate "a loss of confidence in representative democracy," and even argues that, "In any country where competitive politics is accompanied by a highly fractionalized party system (which in a parliamentary system is likely also to produce a weak executive) the chances for a shift toward hegemonic regime are rather high."[22] The empirical relationships among fractionalized party systems, government instability, and regime durability within democracies are matters for investigation. In fact, my conclusions are quite different from Dahl's in this respect, as later chapters will make clear. But the choice of government stability as a standard of performance follows a long tradition of political analysis.

Political order means the absence of turmoil and violence and the maintenance of the basic forms of the democratic regime. Almost all regimes, and certainly the democratic ones, seek to limit violence and disorder and to sustain their own existence. Widespread violence is generally accepted as a sign of failure of the democratic process. To observe disorder is not, of course, to assign responsibility for failure. The breakdown of democratic order may reflect policy failures of the regime, bargaining intransigence by either policymakers or minorities, or efforts by a minority to undermine democratic values. But democracies that are able to avoid such disorder, while still remaining competitive and free democratic systems, are better performers than those that are dominated by violence or that restrict freedom in the name of order. At a later point I shall distinguish among several types of disorder, but at present it is enough to indicate order as a general criterion of political performance.

Two general points should be made about the use of participation, government stability, and order as criteria of political performance. First, these are dimensions of the processes of political systems, not of the policies they adopt and try to implement. Examination of the policy performance of different democratic systems would call for a major study in its own right, linking the needs and policy preferences of citizens to governmental efforts and outcomes in different countries. The interaction of political, economic, and international factors in shaping such outcomes as economic growth, equality, inflation, and unemployment would be a major concern. To use language developed elsewhere, I concentrate in this book on system and process performance, not on policy performance.[23] Of course, the dimensions of participation, stability, and order may be relevant for policy performance. Certainly, failures of stability and order may hinder the effectiveness of policies. In addition to their intrinsic desirability in contemporary culture,[24] stability and order are valued for such instrumental reasons. But process performance is not the same as policy performance, and no claim is made here to incorporate the latter.

A second point is that democracies do embody values that are specially linked to their nature as democratic systems. While participation, stability, and order are goals sought by most contemporary political systems, including authoritarian regimes, the democratic political system promises other values as well. These are closely associated with the defining democratic properties mentioned earlier: responsiveness to citizen preferences, competition, meaningful opportunities for participation, and civil and political freedoms. Each of the countries chosen for this study claimed to embody these values and did so to some degree. Consequently, these standards of democratic performance are not easily studied within the democratic systems. While gross abuses can be used to disqualify a nation from the list of democracies, systematic evaluations of smaller differences in responsiveness or competition are more difficult. In Chapter 9 I shall examine specifically democratic elements of performance in some depth, attempting at least to point the way toward further comparative study. But the bulk of my analysis focuses on the three general performance dimensions: participation, government stability, and order.

Early in the development of this study, it became clear that few efforts had been made to collect and analyze comparable data on political performance across the full set of contemporary democracies. In Chapter 2 I shall describe the measures that I developed for each of the three performance dimensions and introduce the comparative data for the 29 countries. The controversy concerning the relationships among the three performance dimensions, a continuing theme, will then be provisionally explored and the way prepared for its analysis in a multivariate context in later chapters.

Chapter 3 introduces and tests some widely held expectations about the effects of social and economic conditions on political performance. The effects are of interest in their own right and establish the background for subsequent examination of political processes. Chapter 4 takes a similar look at the ways contitutional and cultural factors influence political performance. The constitutional analysis is developed in the context of another theoretical theme: the controversy between those who favor strong executives with legislative majorities, on the one hand, and those who favor the mobilization of diverse citizen interests into a legislative arena where all can take part in bargaining and policymaking, on the other.

Chapter 5 treats alternative theories about the role of party systems, introducing both conflicting arguments about the desirable attributes of party systems and empirical measures that make it possible to test these arguments against contemporary democratic experience. As party systems themselves reflect social conditions and constitutional arrangements, yet also exhibit autonomous continuity, the chapter analyzes the relationships of party systems with their social, economic, and constitutional environments before describing the patterns of performance that are associated with various contemporary party systems. In their support for theorists favoring multiparty, nonmajoritarian party systems with strong linkages between groups and parties, the latter results are among the most surprising in the book. No constitutional or party system, however, is without its disadvantages.

Chapters 6, 7, and 8 combine theories about democratic processes with statistical modeling to trace the linkages among environment, party, and the three dimensions of political performance. Chapter 9 gives some attention to particularly democratic performance values. The concluding chapter, Chapter 10, summarizes what has been learned, returning to the question of the relationships among performance dimensions and the implications of alternative constitutional and party-system strategies. The analysis in the later chapters also suggests that creative political leadership can surmount the constraints and incentives of the regular processes to enhance (or diminish) democratic political performance.

Political Performance /
The Initial Comparison

2

This chapter introduces the measures of performance that describe the relative successes of the contemporary democracies in mobilizing voters, forming stable governments, and maintaining order between 1958 and 1976.[1] I shall first examine the performance of the different democratic countries on each measure, providing some descriptive background to give the reader a sense of events leading to these outcomes. Then it will be possible to look at the relationships among the performance measures and to answer some of the questions about their apparent compatibility raised by democratic theorists.

Citizen Voting Participation

Participation by citizens in competitive elections is a distinctive feature of democratic politics. Most democratic theorists assert that without significant citizen involvement the democratic process falls short of its goals.[2] It has also been suggested that citizen involvement has important effects—either positive or negative—on other aspects of political performance. Defenders of popular participation argue that substantial citizen involvement in meaningful elections both reflects and encourages a sense of democratic legitimacy that will help contain violence and channel it into regular competition.[3] The "democratic elitists," by contrast, suggest that the involvement of citizens should be minimized to keep the system in the hands of those who are better informed and more supportive of its values.[4] Before joining in this complex debate we need some basic information about the working of citizen electoral participation in practice. Unfortunately, in the past little effort has been made to compile these basic facts.

The Amount of Voting Participation The amount of citizen participation in elections is easier to ascertain than the meaningfulness of that participation to the citizens or to the working of the political system. Table 2.1 presents some descriptive information that casts light on the subject: it shows the average percentage of citizen participation in the national legislative elections (presidential elections in strong presidential systems) between 1958 and 1976.[5] These percentages are the average number of voters divided by the number of citizens of voting age.[6] That is, they are percentages of eligible voters as usually shown for U.S. election turnouts, not percentages of those registered. (The latter measure would be highly misleading because of different registration laws.) Turnout levels are relatively consistent within most countries from election to election, despite the decline in the United States in the 1960s and 1970s.[7]

Five countries stand out as having quite low citizen participation in general elections: In India, Jamaica, Switzerland, Turkey, and the United States only about two-thirds of the eligible electorate voted in the average national election. In another group of nine countries, including Chile, Canada, Japan, France, and Britain, the turnout averaged between 70 and 75 percent, and in seven countries the average turnout was in the high 70s or low 80s. The highest turnout—averaging over 85 percent—occurred in Australia, Austria, Belgium, Denmark, Italy, the Netherlands, and Sweden. In several of these countries, as I discuss more fully in Chapter 6, turnout is encouraged by penalties for not voting, and in some cases this compulsory turnout results in substantial numbers of spoiled ballots (around 7 percent in Belgium, for example). Nonetheless, the range of citizen participation is quite substantial—a difference of over 25 percent of the citizens between the most and least participatory countries. By the late 1970s turnout in, say, Austria was nearly double that in the United States.

Voting turnout is only one form of participation in the political process. Citizens also participate through discussion of issues, efforts to mobilize others in election campaigns, involvement in groups that try to influence policy choices, and direct contacts with incumbent officials. Many of these actions are more complex and more individually influential than voting participation. Comparative studies of participation, especially by Sidney Verba, Norman Nie, and their associates, have shown voting participation to be relatively weakly related to the propensity of individuals to engage in other political acts.[8] For example, the level of participation in national elections in the United States is obviously very low in comparative perspective, but such comparative data as have been gathered show Americans very active in groups and in

Table 2.1 National voting turnout and government change in response to election outcomes, 1958–1976.

Country	Elections included	Average turnout (Percentage of Citizens of eligible age)[a]	Elections at which gov't had changed in response to an election in the preceding decade
Switzerland	1963, 67, 71, 75	53%	None
United States	1960, 64, 68, 72, 76	59	All
India	1962, 67, 71, 77	60	None
Jamaica	1962, 67, 72	61	All
Turkey	1965, 69, 73	62	All
France	1962, 67, 68, 73, 78	70	Some
Canada	1962, 63, 65, 68, 72, 74	71	Some
Chile	1964, 70	71	All
Japan	1960, 63, 67, 69, 72, 76	71	None
Uruguay	1958, 62, 66, 71	71	Some
Ceylon (Sri Lanka)	1960, 60, 65, 70	72	All
Costa Rica	1962, 66, 70, 78	73	All
United Kingdom	1964, 66, 70, 74, 74	74	All
Ireland	1961, 65, 69, 73, 77	75	Some
Philippines	1957, 61, 65	77	All
Venezuela	1958, 63, 68, 73	80	Some
Israel	1961, 65, 69, 73, 77	81	Some/Complex
New Zealand	1960, 63, 66, 69, 72, 75	81	All
Norway	1961, 65, 69, 73, 77	82	Some
Finland	1962, 66, 70, 72, 75	84	Some/Complex
West Germany	1961, 65, 69, 72, 76	84	All
Greece	1963, 64, 74, 78	85	Some
Australia	1961, 63, 66, 69, 72, 75	86	Some
Sweden	1960, 64, 68, 70, 73, 76	86	Some/Complex
Denmark	1960, 64, 66, 68, 71, 73, 75, 77	87	Some
Belgium	1961, 65, 68, 71, 74, 77	88	Some
Austria	1962, 66, 70, 71, 75	89	All
Netherlands	1959, 63, 67, (71, 72, 77)	90	Some/Complex
Italy	1963, 68, 72, 76	94	Some/Complex

Sources: See note 6 to this chapter.

a. In Philippines and pre-1970 Chile, eligibles exclude illiterates. In Ceylon eligibles exclude Indian Tamils. Average for the Netherlands is for pre-1971 period, when compulsory voting was in effect. Presidential elections only in Chile, Philippines, United States, and 1971 Uruguay. A few elections are excluded because of difficulty in locating reliable data for those years.

campaign work. Americans also are typically faced with a greater variety of national, state, and local elections and referenda than are citizens in many other nations.[9]

Still, the data in table 2.1 remain a significant measure of a major form of citizen involvement. National elections provide the principal opportunity for citizens to express their collective will and shape national politics. Voting turnout is the best comparative measure we have of citizen participation in these elections. Studies of other forms of participation remain confined to a relatively small number of countries. Moreover, as suggested by the great efforts made to get citizens to the polls in many authoritarian regimes where their votes have no impact on the choice of leaders and policies, electoral participation has important symbolic meaning, as an affirmation of the legitimacy of the regime. A number of individual-level studies of citizen attitudes in democracies also suggest this connection.[10]

Meaningfulness   Determining how meaningful citizens perceive partici-pation to be is not possible without surveys of individual opinions. The criteria for "spoiled ballots" are too dissimilar across nations for the number of such ballots to be useful as a measure of citizens' negative attitudes toward the meaningfulness of elections. The last column of table 2.1 lists a different indication of meaningfulness: whether election outcomes had led to a change in the party controlling the chief executive, either directly or as part of a governing coalition, in at least one election in the previous decade.[11] In most countries elections did lead to such transfers of power, at least occasionally. In the United States, presidential elections saw frequent changes from Democratic to Republican administrations or vice versa. Such alterations also took place frequently in the presidential systems of Costa Rica, Chile, Venezuela, and the Philippines. Parliamentary systems, in which the chief executive is chosen by the parliament and dependent upon its support for tenure in office, also frequently saw changes in direct response to electoral outcomes. Some of these occurred when a single party won a majority, as in Britain in 1964 and 1970 and in New Zealand and Australia in 1972. Others occurred when a preelectoral coalition of parties won a victory, as in Ireland in 1973 and Australia in 1975. Yet others occurred when the new parliament formed a government with a new base in response to changed electoral outcomes, as in Germany in 1961 and Denmark in 1968. In these countries voters had good reason to perceive that election outcomes did make a difference, at least in selecting key government personnel.

In a few countries the connection between elections and executive control was difficult to see or unusual. The best examples here are Italy, the Netherlands, and Finland. In each of these countries the complicated multiparty system occasionally resulted in parties that were repudiated by the electorate being brought into the government, and vice versa. In each of them, some impact of electoral trends can be found in some of the postelectoral bargaining, as in the "opening to the left" in Italy in 1963, when the gradual deterioration of the Christian Democrats led them to change their basis of government support. But the connections are not easy to determine, and are sometimes incomprehensible.

In three countries only were there no examples of electoral consequences for the control of the chief executive between 1958 and 1976. In Switzerland the four largest parties all provided proportionate representation to a collective "chief executive" with rotating chairmanship. Election outcomes varied little; the shared control of the government varied not at all. In Japan the Liberal Democratic party retained an absolute control of the legislature—limited by its own factions—from its unification in 1955 through the period studied. In India the Congress party dominated national poltics until the suspension of democracy in 1975 and the dramatic victory of the new Janata party, a coalition of old oppositions and some old Congress party elements, in the next free election in 1977.

This does not necessarily mean that electoral participation is not meaningful in this last set of countries. In Switzerland the use of national referenda, and the importance of cantonal-level politics gave more life to democratic participation than might be apparent from national legislative results alone.[12] In India there were changes of government in vigorous state-level politics in many areas, and the national election in 1971 helped settle an important dispute between factions of the Congress party, resulting in an overwhelming victory for Mrs. Gandhi's faction over her opponents. In 1977 a major transition of power did occur, when the new Janata party won a surprising victory and (temporarily) drove the Congress party from office.

These examples of change of government in response to elections do not, of course, settle the question of the meaningfulness of involvement among those who voted. Failure to change government, as in Japan, certainly partly reflected the voters' continuing satisfaction with Japan's remarkable postwar growth. Frequent changes in voters' preferences, as in Britain and Jamaica, may partly reflect dissatisfaction with all parties and a propensity to punish the incumbents. Moreover, the assessment of meaningfulness should eventually take account of the range of choices offered to citizens, the relationship between those alternatives and citizen preferences, and the problem of permanent exclusion of some groups and parties from postelection power. I shall address some of these themes in Chapter 9, after more detailed consideration of different representational systems. In most of the democracies all major parties did achieve some share of governing power in the 1960s or 1970s. The evidence gives some solid support to the idea that in most of the democracies citizens do play a critical part in the political process.

Stable and Effective Government

Determining what is a stable and effective government is a troubling task. Citizens frequently disagree about public policies; such disagreement is a major reason for having a democratic political process in the first place. Hence, citizens often disagree about whether or not they are well governed. Even determining what is a stable government, apart from questions of violence and coercion, is not easy. Observers tend to characterize such countries as Italy and Finland, in which the life of a prime minister and his cabinet is short, as having unstable governments. From one perspective this characterization is apt, and scholarly research has demonstrated the difficulty of controlling the bureaucracy and of implementing policies in a country such as Italy or the France of the Fourth Republic. Yet it is also true that in the period studied Italy's government always included the Christian Democratic party as the predominant element, and manifested great and consistent continuity of (conservative) policies.[13] By contrast, presidential systems, such as the United States and Venezuela, can have chief executives who serve their full term yet face a hostile legislature and find it extremely difficult to get their policies implemented.

Table 2.2 offers two indicators of government performance in the 1967–1976 decade. The left side of the table shows the average durability of the chief executive during this period. The first government considered was usually the one in office in 1967, although it might have assumed power earlier. The last government considered was the latest to have the majority of its tenure fall into this time period, although it might have endured on into 1977. The maximum time shown in the table is 36 months, as that is the shortest duration in the democracies between regularly scheduled elections (New Zealand and Sweden). Executives remaining in office that long or longer are given the maximum durability score in this analysis.

A parliamentary government is here defined as "enduring" as long as it has the same composition of political parties holding cabinet positions and the individual prime minister has not been forced from office involuntarily. A presidential government endures as long as the same individual (or his successor, if he dies or retires voluntarily), remains in office, regardless of the composition of the cabinet. (Differences between presidential and parliamentary government are discussed in Chapter 4.) Any type of government is defined as ending, however, when a national election is held, even if the same parties return to power or the same individual is reelected. A parliamentary government also ends when a new party is added to or an old party deleted from the government. Any major change in constitutional power, such as the assumption of control by the military or a dictatorial chief executive, also implies a new government, even if the personnel are unchanged.

The second column of table 2.2 shows a rough indicator of government effectiveness: the maintenance of concurrent legislative majorities by the party or coalition in control of the executive. For simplicity's sake, I define this control as existing whenever the party or coalition of parties represented in the cabinet of the government also holds a parliamentary majority. Obviously, because of lack of party discipline, this measure may overstate government effectiveness in some cases—as in the typical Democratic majority and presidential control in the United States. Because of outside party support for a minority parliamentary government, the measure may also understate effective government in some countries. But in general this measure is a fair first approximation of the ability of the executive to deal with the legislature.

As a crude approximation of effectiveness, the table indicates whether the government held a legislative majority for 75 percent of the decade (90 months). Thus Japan and New Zealand, where the chief executives represented parties with legislative majorities, get maximum effectiveness scores. Belgium and the Netherlands also display substantial legislative effectiveness, as their coalition governments commanded legislative majorities, although some of them were not very durable. On the other hand, neither the United States, with the long period of the Republican minority presidency, nor Denmark, with its frequent minority-party cabinets, qualifies as very effective.

Table 2.2 Stability and effectiveness of government, 1967–1976.

Country	Stability: Average durability of governments or presidents	Effectiveness: Did government have a legislative majority 75% of decade?
Italy	7 months	No
Finland	16	Yes
Turkey	16	No
Belgium	20	Yes
Denmark	22	No
Netherlands	22	Yes
Ceylon (Sri Lanka)	23	Yes
Norway	24	No
Uruguay	25[a]	Yes
Australia	27	Yes
India	28	Yes
United Kingdom	29	Yes
Austria	30	Yes
Canada	30	Yes
U.S.A.	30[b]	No
Chile	36[c]	No
Costa Rica	36	No
France	36	No
Germany	36	Yes
Ireland	36	Yes
Jamaica	36	Yes
Japan	36	Yes
New Zealand	36	Yes
Philippines	36	Yes
Sweden	36	No
Venezuela	36	No
Switzerland	36	Yes

a. Uruguay includes two presidencies. The first, from 1966 to 1971, ran the full term. In the second, the president held office for only 14 months before the military intervened and made him subject to their programs and authority. His democratic tenure is here considered to have ended at that point.

b. This figure for the United States includes Nixon's shortened second term (19 months), and the somewhat shortened Ford presidency (29 months), as well as Johnson's full second term and Nixon's full first term.

c. I use 36 months as the maximum for comparative purposes; the average durability of the government in many of these countries is actually longer than 36 months.

The difference between the two measures is particularly interesting in relation to the different constitutional designs within the democracies, a theme I shall discuss in more detail in Chapter 4. The presidential systems typically use the electoral process directly to aggregate citizens' votes into the powerful resources given to the presidential incumbent. At the same time the electoral process separately aggregates citizens' votes into legislative representation. It is difficult to force an elected president from office—the case of Nixon in 1974 is a remarkable exception—and durability of the chief executive is quite great. But the differences in selection and resources of legislature and executive frequently result in one party controlling the former and another the latter. Hence, executive effectiveness depends on complex and difficult cross-party dealing between the two branches (see Chapter 7). The parliamentary systems, by contrast, make it rather difficult for a party or group of parties to hold the executive without also controlling the legislature. Hence, the two measures are much more closely related to each other in the parliamentary systems.

Maintaining Political Order

Democracies have a very special relationship to political conflict. Most other types of regimes either forbid any expressions of serious disagreement or allow them only from a very few powerful leaders. Legitimate efforts to influence policy by those outside the ruling circle are limited to petitions and suggestions. If these fail, discontent must be repressed or expressed through violence. Democracies provide every citizen with a basic political resource and the freedom to use and expand it by organizing and mobilizing other citizens. Democracy is, from this perspective, a gamble that discontent can be channeled through the legitimate electoral channels. An outbreak of serious, collective violence in a democratic society is manifest evidence that the regime is not performing well.

Of course, to be concerned about violence is not to pass moral judgment upon groups who use violence. Groups and individuals who see themselves as permanently excluded from real power, despite apparent electoral resources, may become desperate, especially if the powers of government are used to disadvantage them. But the presence of major violence suggests some failure in the gamble that is democracy, some inability to find ways to give some satisfaction to all groups through the democratic process.

Indicators of the Failure of Order   Table 2.3 shows three different indicators: riots, deaths resulting from political violence, and the suspension or replacement of the national regime. These three are not the same events. Riots and deaths represent, respectively, the different dimensions of mass violence Douglas Hibbs characterizes as "protest" and "internal war."[14] Riots are defined as large numbers of citizens acting out of control in an unplanned and disorganized fashion, and destroying property. Deaths by political violence sometimes result from rioting, usually as the police restore order, but are more frequently the outcome of systematic armed attacks by terrorists. (Legal executions are not included, nor are nonpolitical murders.) The suspension or replacement of national democracy comes about, usually, through actions of the military or the chief executive, rather than through the simple degeneration of order into armed conflict. Events have ranged from the temporary but intensive suspension of political activities and many civil rights throughout Jamaica in the last half of 1976 to the clear replacement of democracy by ongoing authoritarian rule in the Philippines, Chile, and Uruguay.

A substantial debate has arisen over whether the number of riots and deaths should be taken at face value or presented on a per capita basis. On the one hand, it seems clear that an intensive burst of rioting, such as that which shook France in 1968, counts in some absolute sense, and should not be buried by being divided by population size. On the other hand, it seems plausible that 27 riots in tiny Uruguay do indicate more severe discontent, a more serious failure of democratic performance, than the similar numbers of riots in Japan and France.

In making simple evaluations and comparisons there is no obvious answer to this problem. Both absolute and per capita figures have some claim to attention. In table 2.3 I present the absolute numbers; see note d to the table for the differences that would appear if per capita data were used. The reader who is interested in the full set of per capita comparisons can easily calculate them from the population data in table 3.1 below and the violence statistics in the Appendix.

Population size must be considered in attempts to explain the different levels of violence in the democracies. It is an important national characteristic that does tend to be associated with the frequency of violent events, particularly riots and protests, as we shall see in Chapter 3. Thus although both absolute and per capita measures of violence are useful in simple comparisons, any theoretical explanation of violence must take account of population size in order to avoid bias.

Table 2.3 Indications of the failure of political order: 1958–1967, 1967–1976.[a]

Conflict	1958–1967[c]		1967–1976[c]	
Regime suspended or replaced	France, Greece, Turkey		Ceylon, Chile, India, Philippines, Turkey, Uruguay, Jamaica	
Deaths from political violence: Average over 10 per year while democratic	India	320.3	Philippines	332.7
	Philippines	37.5	India	328.4
	Ceylon	31.5	Ceylon	302.8
	U.S.A.	29.0	U.K. (Northern Ireland)	160.0
	Turkey	11.9	Chile	87.3
	France	10.1	U.S.A.	20.7
			Uruguay	18.2
			Turkey	18.1
			Jamaica	17.9
Riots: Average over 2.5 per year while democratic	U.S.A.	62.8	India	56.8
	India	33.0	U.S.A.	42.7
	Italy	9.3	U.K.	11.7
	Japan	7.0	Italy	7.4
	U.K.	6.5	Venezuela	4.5
	Ceylon	3.8	Turkey	4.4
	West Germany	3.1	France	3.3
	Belgium	3.0	Japan	2.9
	Turkey	3.0	Uruguay	2.7
	Greece	2.7		
Less severe conflict[b]	Australia, Austria, Canada, Chile, Costa Rica, Denmark, Finland, Ireland, Netherlands, New Zealand, Norway, Uruguay		Australia, Austria, Canada, Belgium, Costa Rica, Denmark, Finland, West Germany, Ireland, Netherlands, New Zealand, Norway, Sweden, Switzerland	

Sources: Data for the first decade from Taylor and Hudson, *World Handbook*. Data for the second decade compiled by the author. One-year overlap in decades designed for source comparability. See Appendix for complete 1967–1976 data and a comparison with a recently published alternative source.

a. Greece is excluded as nondemocratic in most of the second decade; Jamaica and Venezuela are added in the second decade. Israel is excluded because of data incomparability; especially after 1967 the distinction between internal and external violence is extremely blurred.

b. If the deaths and riots are divided by population size to obtain a per capita measure, Austria, Canada, Chile, and Uruguay are in the topmost group in the first decade, Chile and Jamaica in the second. No countries are added to the high-death group in the first decade, but Ireland and Venezuela are added in the second.

c. The numbers in these columns represent the total number of riots or deaths suffered while the country remained a democracy, divided by the years democratic in the decade.

Issues and Actions of Violent Conflict In general, the details of a particular episode of violent conflict are beyond the scope of this study. I shall be looking at patterns and relationships across countries, with an occasional focus on events in a particular country. It is worthwhile at this point to take a very brief look at the events behind some of the second-decade conflicts summarized in table 2.3.[15]

Among the most severe conflicts in any of our democracies, in terms of lives lost, were those in India, where more than 2500 people were killed in the eight years before Mrs. Gandhi suspended democratic freedoms and elections in 1975. A variety of separate conflicts were involved, the deadliest of which were the armed clashes between government troops and separatist guerrillas and other terrorists. Many hundreds of citizens were also killed in rioting between Hindu and Moslem ethnic groups and as police restored order in a range of riots associated with language issues, food shortages, and political clashes. Clashes between supporters of opposing political parties at election time also caused substantial numbers of deaths. The suspension of democratic government was not a direct outcome of the political violence, but was justified by the government in terms of its fear that opposition leaders would call upon the army to intervene.

In the Philippines the deadliest conflict was associated with the Moro (Moslem) guerrilla movement and its demand for a separate homeland. Clashes occurred between Moslem and Christian communities and between Moslem guerrillas and government troops. There was also severe fighting between extreme leftist (Huk) guerrillas and government troops. Moreover, the elections in 1967 and 1969 saw more than one hundred people killed in armed attacks and bombings. Democratic government was suspended by President Marcos, who proclaimed martial law in September 1972, after substantial urban turmoil and intense partisan and factional disputes between the president and his political opponents.

In Ceylon (Sri Lanka) the major conflict was an assault on police stations and other government centers by a leftist guerrilla organization in 1971. Continuing tensions between Ceylon's Tamil and Sinhalese communities did not erupt in violent conflict of any magnitude. The guerrilla assault was launched by a youth-oriented leftist group, demanding faster and more vigorous action by the new leftist government to deal with unemployment and other grievances. Some 1200 persons were reported killed in the upheaval, and the government imposed censorship and various restrictions on freedom of movement for a number of years afterward, although elections continued to be held.

Of similar cost in human lives was the strife in Northern Ireland. The civil rights movement of the Catholic minority, demanding both political equality and economic improvements, met stubborn resistance and violent assaults on demonstrators. Terrorists on both sides soon turned to bombings and assassinations, and the death toll passed 1600 by the decade's end. Democratic self-rule in Northern Ireland was a casualty along the way, although the United Kingdom as a whole continued to function as a democracy.

In Chile the pattern of deadly strife was somewhat different. Many of the deaths occurred in the military coup against the government of Marxist President Salvador Allende in 1973. However, the mounting tensions between political groups were evident long before that, with an average of about ten deaths a year in terrorist bombings, election clashes, attempts to take over land, and the like in the late 1960s and early 1970s. The efforts of the new government, and more extreme groups to its left, to introduce fundamental changes into social and political life in Chile intensified the strife between political groups.

In the United States most of the deaths by political violence occurred in the racial riots that broke out in the mid-1960s and continued through the early 1970s in American cities. (Most of the deaths were the result of the use of force by authorities in restoring order.) A number of black leftist groups, such as the Black Panthers, also suffered fatalities in clashes with or assaults by the police.

In Uruguay the major confrontation occurred between government military forces and the Tupamaro guerrilla movement, whose initially peaceful and spectacular escapades gave way to more violent clashes. The determination of military leaders to take control of the antiguerrilla campaign was a major factor in the replacement of the civilian government by a military-dominated one.

In Turkey guerrilla terrorist attacks, associated with high tension between regular political parties, also led to military intervention in the form of ultimatums to the government in 1971–1972. Although the army later returned control to civilian authorities, deaths from election clashes and terrorist bombings and snipings continued to occur, and became more frequent in the late 1970s. (Another military coup took place in 1980.)

Most of the other deaths by political violence in the democracies resulted from terrorist actions, although none of these were associated with the major suspension of democratic government. In Italy mounting terrorist attacks from both right and left extremist groups resulted in about 90 deaths in the 1967–1976 decade, and an even more severe rate in 1978. In Venezuela terrorist attacks caused about 60 deaths in the late 1960s and early 1970s. In the Republic of Ireland and in West Germany attacks by terrorists (of the Irish Republican Army, seeking Irish intervention in Ulster, in the former and of the far-left Bader-Meinhof group in the latter), brought 40 and 27 deaths respectively and, in both cases, substantial government suspension of individual rights on a temporary basis. Similar incidents of a smaller scale were reported in Japan, France, and Canada.

The violence in Jamaica was of a different and more serious kind. Clashes between armed extremist supporters of the two major political parties resulted in nearly 200 deaths, and the imposition of a state of emergency, in 1976. Although elections were held virtually on schedule in 1976 (and again in 1980), the high interparty tensions jeopardized the future of democracy in that small island nation.

A number of nations experienced substantial riots and turmoil without such high costs in human life. Most spectacular is the case of France, with its popular uprising, including many riots, in 1968. These riots were associated with a national strike, which brought the society to a temporary standstill and had important consequences for policy. Japan also experienced a number of riots, many of them associated with political demonstrations by parties or student groups, and Italy had far more of a similar kind. But in these countries, unlike the American and Indian experiences, riots were usually brought under control with minimum loss of life, as was also true of the language rioting in Belgium in 1968 and the religious clashes in Belgium in the 1950s. The different bases and consequences of the various forms of violence will be discussed in more detail in Chapter 8.

Compatibility of the Performance Dimensions

I have already referred to the controversy among democratic theorists about the relationships between dimensions of political performance. One line of thought assumes that all of the dimensions tend to accompany and support each other.[16] Participation enhances legitimacy, which improves stability and inhibits violence; stable and ordered democracies are accorded more legitimacy, which encourages more participation. A very different view of democracy expects high citizen involvement to put a serious strain on the ability of democracies to govern effectively and to make the policies needed to support democratic government in the long run. Either because of the suspicion that the average citizen is not strongly committed to democracy,[17] or because of fear of the "overloading" of a system faced with too many demands,[18] theorists who hold this view expect poor stability and substantial turmoil in democracies with very involved citizens.

Government stability is another subject of controversy. The common view has been that government stability strengthens democracy, at least by offering citizens a reassuring symbol of continuity. Critics such as Karl Bracher have suggested that the overthrow of democracy in Weimar Germany and the collapse of the French Fourth Republic "are to be ascribed in no small way to discontent about the discontinuity of parliamentary state politics."[19] But an alternative view sees a serious potential for abuse of power by party governments that command stable and unshared control of the national legislature and executive, and there is concern that minorities faced by such strong governments are more likely to turn to violence.[20]

Remarkably enough, the diverging speculations about the compatibility of the performance dimensions have not been subjected to serious comparative investigation. Rather, intuitively plausible conjectures (such as the supportive roles of all three dimensions for and by the legitimacy of the regime), or well-known cases (such as the conjunction of active participation, cabinet instability, violence, and the overthrow of the regime in Weimar Germany), are made to serve the purposes of argument.

Evidence does exist on how, in fact, the dimensions relate to one another. It can be examined by various statistical techniques, and the conclusions are remarkably robust and consistent.[21] The countries with high voting turnout had on average the least violence, in both the 1958–1967 and 1967–1976 decades. Countries with low voting participation had the most violence. The Pearson correlation coefficients between voting turnout and riots are $-.27$ for 1958–1967 and $-.32$ for 1967–1976; for riots per capita the figures are $-.05$ and $-.39$. Similarly, voting turnout correlates negatively with deaths and deaths per capita: $-.45$, $-.42$; $-.21$, $-.28$. All of these correlations except one are significant at the .05 level or more.[22] Moreover, although for technical reasons it is not fully appropriate to compare these correlations with those computed on a dichotomous variable, we can note that voting turnout was also sharply negatively related to likelihood of the overthrow or suspension of the democratic regime. The correlation is −.46 with whether or not the country experienced such an event in 1967–1976 (as shown in table 2.3).

Nearly as striking, however, is the fact that participation was associated with government *instability*. All good things did not go together in the performance measures. Voting turnout correlates at −.36 with the durability of the chief executive. Looking carefully at the subgroups suggests that the negative relationship is particularly a consequence of low average stability of government in the countries with the very highest turnout levels. The median durability of the chief executive in the seven countries with highest participation was only 22 months, as compared to 30 months among the full set of democracies. Thus participation does seem to have negative associations, as some have expected, but only with executive durability, not with public disorder. Executive stability itself is only weakly related to any performance measure other than participation. Finally, across the full set of countries the government-effectiveness measure—the same parties controlling both legislature and executive—is not much related to either participation or deadly violence, or even to executive durability.

The patterns can be presented quite clearly in a factor analysis, as shown in table 2.4. Because of the diverging expectations about relationships among the performance dimensions, an oblique rotation was used, allowing the dimensions to emerge as correlated. But in fact the three political dimensions are virtually unrelated to one another. Rioting and deaths appear strongly (negatively) related to the first dimension, which I have called political order. Executive durability is the major item on the second dimension, and executive control is the major variable relating to the third. As already suggested by the correlation, voting turnout is strongly positively associated with political order, but strongly negatively related to government stability. Otherwise, the variables are quite cleanly associated with the particular dimensions, although there is a weak loading of rioting on the stability and effectiveness dimensions. Basically the same patterns emerge, whether we use oblique or orthogonal rotation, absolute or per capita measures of violence, truncated or logged violence scores. The "democratic replacement or suspension" variable, when added to the factor analysis, loads heavily and negatively on the first factor and is trivially related to the other two, supporting the idea that the first dimension does measure political order. Among the individual variables, deaths by

Table 2.4 Factor analysis of relationships between measures of democratic performance.

	Loadings on rotated factors[a]		
Performance Measures	Factor 1: political order	Factor 2: government stability	Factor 3: government control
Voting turnout 1960–1977	+.53	−.50	−.07
Executive durability 1967–1976	+.09	+.73	−.05
Executive control of legislature, 1967–1976	+.01	−.04	+.58
Rioting 1967–1976[b]	−.82	−.21	+.30
Deaths by violence 1967–1976[b]	−.69	+.02	−.12

a. These loadings are the factor patterns from an oblique rotation. (The factor "structure" is very similar.) The factors themselves are essentially uncorrelated (−.11, −.08, −.16), so varimax rotation produces very similar results. The three factors have eigenvalues of 1.0 or more. The factor analysis uses the SPSS Factor Analysis program, with default options. See Norman H. Nie, et al., *SPSS: Statistical Package for the Social Sciences* (New York: McGraw-Hill, 1978 ed.), ch. 25. The analysis uses the 27 nations that were democracies for five years or more in the decade 1967–1976 (excluding Israel because of problems of data comparability).

b. These are absolute numbers, but using per capita riots and deaths yields similar results. As in all correlation and regression in this book, extreme cases (absolute or per capita) are truncated to the ninetieth percentile values to prevent bias. Log transformed riots and deaths also yield a similar pattern.

violence relate most strongly to the suspension of national democracy.

These patterns bear clearly on the arguments about compatibility of dimensions. The evidence suggests above all the danger of drawing strong inferences from a few well-known cases, such as Germany in the 1920s (where participation, instability, and disorder converged). The total set of patterns supports neither those who suspect that participation has a negative effect on democratic order nor those who see the three dimensions as reinforcing. Rather, it suggests a positive role for participation as an agent of legitimate involvement and an inhibitor of disorder, but it also suggests a cost of participation in the realm of government stability. Between government stability and political order themselves very little net relationship appears. Rioting does show a weak negative relationship to government stability and a positive one to government majorities.

In this examination of the compatibility of the performance dimensions, I have merely described patterns of association; I have not tested theories about causes. There are theoretical reasons to expect that environmental conditions, such as level of economic development, will affect each dimension of performance. So should the system of political parties. In the following chapters I shall test various theories about the causes of participation, stability, and order.

The Social and Economic Environment

3

Some countries seem to be much more difficult to govern than others. They fall short, time and again, of the levels of participation, stability, and containment of violence attained by other nations. Since the ancient Greeks, philosophers and social scientists have explained such persistent differences by pointing to aspects of the social and economic environment of the society.[1] Conditions of wealth or scarcity, equality or disparity, shared cultural values or disputed ones have been seen as the sources of variation in political performance. In some cases elaborate theories have been proposed to link, say, the level of economic development with the extensiveness of political participation. In other cases assertions that, for instance, smaller nations are easier to rule, seem to be based on common sense or simple observation.

In this chapter I shall set forth, briefly, some of the most widely accepted hypotheses about the effects of environmental conditions on democratic performance, and see how they fare in explaining the events of the two decades under consideration. My first objective is simple description: is it the case, for example, as often assumed, that small countries have higher levels of voting participation and less violence than larger ones? As the evidence has usually not been examined for the full set of democracies, it is useful to try to get our bearings by finding out if the general descriptive ideas are correct. My second objective is to provide an initial test of the credibility of the underlying theory about the impact of environment on democratic performance. Only hypotheses with reasonably sound and plausible theoretical credentials are examined. The data could be searched endlessly for patterns, and through chance some would emerge. But such an open-ended search is not my objective here. I use a single plausible measure for each of the major independent variables, such as GNP per capita as a measure of level of modernization, rather than using complex indices.[2] Other measures will be discussed in text or notes, but I have chosen a single measure for most analysis, and I present an initial table showing the score of each country on the measure, so that the reader can check the relationship between the scores on that measure and the scores on various performance measures presented in Chapter 2. Similarly, to provide a descriptive picture the data are initially presented in the form of a simple comparison of medians, looking directly at the independent and dependent variables in question. Only after this first look at the relevant relationships is some multivariate analysis undertaken to determine the strength of the variables when considered simultaneously.

Population Size

As table 3.1 reveals, the contemporary democracies vary tremendously in population. India and the United States have a hundred or more times as many residents as Israel and Jamaica. Both common sense and previous crossnational studies tell us that these great differences in population size are likely to have substantial effects on democratic performance. Despite a tradition of speculation about ideal population size, however, there have been few efforts to develop sophisticated theory linking numbers of citizens to participation, government stability, or violence. We have rather clear-cut expectations about the directions of effects of population size, but not well-developed notions about the processes involved.[3]

Population Size and Participation   Most theorizing about population size and participation has built from the likelihood that in a large political environment an individual cannot have much personal influence on politics. Various studies of individual information, efficacy, and political concern suggest that, other things being equal, these participation-enhancing attitudes are more likely to flourish in a political environment that is small and proximate to the individual.[4] Given such a government with important power to make policies, it is indeed likely that small size does encourage involvement. On the other hand, even the smallest of the nation-states is very large from the point of view of the average individual, who is literally one in a million. Such attitudes seem to be less relevant to voting participation, the admittedly imperfect measure of citizen participation we have used in this study, than to more difficult participatory acts.[5]

A somewhat different view of the relationship between population and participation focuses on the organizational difficulties of creating

Table 3.1 Population size and democratic performance.

Country	1965 population (millions)	Median voting turnout	Median executive durability	Median riots/year 1958–1967	Median riots/year 1967–1976	Median deaths/year by political violence 1958–1967	Median deaths/year by political violence 1967–1976
Costa Rica	1.4						
Jamaica	1.8						
Israel	2.6						
New Zealand	2.6						
Uruguay	2.7	81%	31 months	.1	.2	.1	0
Ireland	2.9						
Norway	3.7						
Finland	4.6						
Denmark	4.8						
Switzerland	5.9						
Austria	7.3						
Sweden	7.7						
Greece	8.6						
Chile	8.6						
Venezuela	8.7	86%	30 months	1.8	.3	.1	.1
Belgium	9.5						
Ceylon	11.2						
Australia	11.3						
Netherlands	12.3						
Canada	19.6						
Turkey	31.1						
Philippines	32.3						
France	48.9						
Italy	51.6						
United Kingdom	54.6	71%	30 months	4.8	3.9	6.4	13.5
West Germany	59.0						
Japan	98.0						
U.S.	194.6						
India	486.7						

Sources: Population data from Taylor and Hudson, *World Handbook;* performance data from Chapter 2.

unified party systems and of mobilizing large numbers of citizens at election time in very large countries.[6] In this version, it is not so much the perception of citizens that they can have little influence in national politics, but the difficulty encountered by political leaders in building organizations to involve citizens that gives an advantage to the smaller nations in getting their citizens to the polls.

The data in table 3.1 suggest that while voting turnout is, on average, greater in the smaller nations, the relationship is weak and statistically not significant. The two largest nations, India and the United States, do have a low turnout, but so do the small countries of Jamaica and Switzerland, while the highest turnout is found in Italy, one of the larger countries. When other factors are taken into account, the impact of population size on voting participation is further reduced (see table 4.4).

Population Size and Government Performance   In discussing the success of some of the smaller European democracies in developing stable governments in the face of internal conflict, and the failure of such nations as France and Italy to do so, Val Lorwin commented that the small countries may be advantaged by their more intimate politics, the opportunity of leaders to know each other and their citizens more closely.[7] But table 3.1 does not show much relationship between size and either stability or effectiveness. In simple descriptive terms, it does not seem to be true that the small countries are better able to generate effective governments. However, both common sense and evidence to come in the next chapter remind us that government performance can be powerfully affected by a nation's constitutional arrangements, and any conclusions about the impact of population size on performance must take these arrangements into consideration. Doing so will show that Lorwin's suggestion may not be ill-founded.

Population Size and Containing Violence   Various scholars have suggested that order should be easier to maintain in smaller nations.[8] One line of thought emphasizes the "natural" propensity for human interaction to result in a certain amount of friction. The more friction that occurs in a given locale, the more likely it is that violence will break out. In a large nation, the number of sites for such friction is greater; by chance alone, such a nation will have more violence; some of that violence will be political. Another explanation is more explicitly related to governing. In a small nation it is easier for authorities to perceive when discontent is smoldering and to act to prevent its outbreak, either through suppression or by alleviating its causes. In large nations, the information processes work less well, and control is more difficult; hence, outbursts are more likely.

In a careful analysis of mass political violence in more than a hundred nations, Douglas Hibbs found population size to be strongly related to the number of incidents of "collective protest," including both peaceful demonstrations and rioting, but not to organized armed attacks or number of deaths caused by political violence.[9] The experience of the democracies in both decades is fairly consistent with these findings. Table 3.1 shows clearly that the larger democracies have more riots. The large nations are also likely to have more deaths from political violence, although this relationship conceals wide variability, especially in the second decade. Subsequent analysis will show that population size remains the most important predictor of rioting across the democratic countries regardless of what other features of environment or political process are explored. Its effect on the amount of deadly violence, though sharply reduced, also remains significant (see table 3.6).

Whatever the reason for the link between population size and violence, it is clear that population size is a factor to keep in mind in attempting to compare and understand political violence across nations. For this reason, the subsequent tables in this chapter will compare riots and deaths on a per capita basis.

Modernization and Economic Development

Much recent writing on the impact of environmental conditions on political performance focuses on social modernization and economic development.[10] The countries with modernized social structures and developed, industrial economies are expected to have higher levels of political participation, more stable and effective governments, and less political violence than countries with more traditional social structures and preindustrial economies.

Hypotheses based on emphasizing specific components of the social structure are difficult to test in this body of theory, because contemporary nations at different levels of economic development differ from each other in a host of closely intertwined ways. The nations with higher worker productivity also have, on average, more educated populations, smaller agricultural sectors, more extensive communications and transportation networks, better health and medical care, more diversified export sectors in their economies, and so forth.[11] These various attributes are not accidentally related, but are to a large degree part of a broader process of modernization. Moreover, for historical reasons, the nations at similar levels of development often also share similar cultural heritages and degrees of independent political experience. Students of the consequences of modernization have focused on different elements of it, and have predicted various political outcomes dependent on specific combinations of factors, such as the ratio of economic development to social mobilization, or the level of economic development attained at the time of introducing political competition.[12] But it is difficult to test these predictions clearly, because of the rather small number of less economically developed democracies and, often, because of rather poor specification of the elements in the theory itself.

Table 3.2 shows the level of modernization and economic development in the democratic regimes, according to several commonly accepted indicators. It is clear that in 1965 per capita GNP, literacy, employment in nonagricultural occupations, and export diversification were all strongly related to each other.[13] Moreover, as shown by the 1972 GNP per capita figures, the earlier rankings were difficult to alter, with only Japan making a clear leap from the poorer to the wealthier nations; and even in 1965 Japan had had a highly literate population, a large nonagricultural sector with diversified exports, and higher economic productivity than most other non-Western nations.

Thus we shall have to be content with rather broad hypotheses about the political consequences of modernization and economic development. First, modernization is associated with much greater economic and governmental capacity. As seen in table 3.2, yearly per capita income typically is more than ten times as high in the advanced economies as in the less advanced economies. Although special circumstances, such as discovery of oil, can alter this pattern of income in the short run, the pattern usually means that the more developed nations have much more wealth with which to meet citizen demands than do the less developed ones. Moreover, in the more productive and wealthier nations governments typically can extract greater proportions of income from the society.[14] Where most of the population lives on subsistence farming, there is not much extra income to extract for collective political purposes. Generally low levels of training and communication in less modernized societies also make it difficult to establish effective revenue-collection systems.

Wealth does not guarantee political success. Many social problems are vast and intractable; individual aspirations may rise faster than available income, however great; the government's need for funds may outrun its collection of them. But large amounts of new income generated each year create important capabilities that may be used by creative leaders for dealing with political problems.

Economic development has momentous political consequences of a second kind. In an economically primitive nation the majority of the population is made up of peasants or agricultural workers, engaged in subsistence farming in a few crops. In a highly economically developed

Table 3.2 Economic development in democratic regimes.

Country	1965 GNP per capita	1972 GNP per capita	Average year's real GNP growth, 1965–1972	Literate adults	Agricultural employees[a]	Export concentration[a]
U.S.	$4810	$5590	2.0%	99%	8%	.08
Sweden	3441	4480	2.5	100	18	.09
Canada	3327	4440	3.2	99	12	.08
Switzerland	3139	3940	2.9	100	15	.11
Denmark	2853	3670	3.7	100	23	.10
Australia	2694	2980	3.1	98	(13)	.14
New Zealand	2664	2560	1.8	99	18	.22
France	2589	3620	4.8	99	25	.06
West Germany	2558	3390	4.1	99	8	.10
Norway	2543	3340	3.8	100	24	.08
Belgium	2427	3210	4.6	99	7	—
U.K.	2446	2600	2.0	99	5	.09
Finland	2354	2810	4.9	100	38	.16
Netherlands	2091	2840	4.3	99	13	.06
Israel	1940	2480	7.1	90	13	.20
Austria	1732	2410	5.0	98	18	.07
Italy	1485	1960	4.3	92	24	.07
Ireland	1319	1510	3.7	96	42	.11
Venezuela	1187	1260	1.1	80	(38)	—
Japan	1159	2320	9.7	98	21	.09
Greece	927	1460	—	82	48	.21
Uruguay	771	760	.4	90	23	—
Chile	760	800	2.2	84	34	.46
Jamaica	669	800	3.9	85	52	.29
Costa Rica	556	630	4.1	84	58	.27
Turkey	379	370	4.3	46	58	.17
Philippines	215	220	2.4	72	67	.15
Ceylon (Sri Lanka)	193	188	2.0	75	46	.46
India	136	110	1.4	28	68	.17

Sources: 1965 GNP per capita from Taylor and Hudson, *World Handbook,* with figures multiplied by 1.35 to convert to the value of 1972 U.S. dollars. 1972 GNP per capita from *World Bank Atlas,* 1974. Yearly growth from *World Bank Atlas,* 1975. Literacy, agricultural employees, and export concentration from Taylor and Hudson, *World Handbook.*

a. Agricultural employees measure is the percentage of adult males employed in agriculture; dubious data shown in parentheses. The export concentration measure is an index ranging from .01, or less, to 1.0. The small numbers imply that export revenues derive from export of many different commodities; large numbers imply domination of export revenue by a few commodities. In the extreme case, approaching 1.0, virtually all revenues derive from a single commodity.

nation, the population is made up of many specialized groups and subgroups, with a diversity of interests, skills, organizations, and resources. Greater education and literacy are necessary for economic development, because greater skills and specialization are needed. Hence, the population becomes more diversified, but also more interdependent and linked together by mutual needs and awareness. Specialized interest groups and secondary organizations usually emerge to express and cater to these special needs: workers' trade unions, business and professional associations, and the like.

This aspect of modernization increases the potential for mobilizing citizens into the political process. Political involvement is encouraged by the increased individual and group skills, the improved information networks, the greater involvement of the government in everyday life. Mobilization is also encouraged by exposure to the idea, pervasive in modern culture, that human fate can be altered through conscious and deliberate action. For a variety of reasons, then, economic development and modernization are expected to be associated with a citizenry more easily engaged in the political process.[15]

Modernization and Participation   Many scholars have suggested that the human development that accompanies modernization should enhance political participation. Some of these theorists have explicitly emphasized the greater information and psychological involvement of citizens in the more modernized societies. Higher levels of political awareness and involvement should facilitate higher levels of participation, especially participation in the more difficult forms of political action. Other theorists have been more concerned with the transformation of group relationships, especially those of secondary groups and political parties, in the more modernized societies. More extensive and specialized group structures, and party systems more effectively organized to mobilize them, should draw more individuals into the political arena through collective action. These are not mutually exclusive predictions: each leads us to expect more participation in the more modernized societies.[16]

Despite the large body of speculative analysis, and some fine studies of one or a few countries, the only published studies of the relationship between economic development and voting turnout across a large set of nations draw upon the data presented in the *World Handbook of Political and Social Indicators* in 1964.[17] In the *World Handbook* the authors report a strong (Pearson) correlation of .47 between economic development and voting participation of citizens in enfranchised age-groups for a single election. However, the majority of the countries covered are not democracies, and the meaning of the act of voting varies sharply from country to country, as do inducements and penalties for participation.

My analysis of the average turnout of eligible voters in national elections from 1960 to 1977 across the full set of democracies (reported in Chapter 2) supports the expectation that turnout will be greater in the more economically developed nations. Table 3.3 shows that median voting turnout increases sharply from the predominantly traditional countries to the modern ones, although it levels off once substantial modernization is achieved. The simple (Pearson) correlation between log GNP per capita and turnout is .35, substantially lower than the finding of the authors of the *World Handbook,* but still statistically significant at the .05 level. Other measures of modernization such as literacy level ($r = .40$) and percentage employed in nonagricultural occupations ($r = .36$) yield very similar results. To look at it a bit differently, considering only the countries without penalties for not voting, turnout is about 11 percent higher in the countries with GNP per capita over $1000 in 1965 than in those with GNP per capita below that figure.

Across the full set of democracies, the poorer nations are slightly more likely to compel their citizens to go the polls. Hence, the effect of such laws is to diminish the apparent effect of economic development on turnout. A striking example is Venezuela, which has very harsh penalties for not voting, and a high turnout that has increased as more citizens have been registered. Enrique Baloyra reports survey results showing that about 40 percent of the citizens claim that they would not vote if the penalties were removed.[18] The relationship between per capita GNP and turnout increases if we control for registration laws and compulsory voting. (These legal provisions are discussed more completely in Chapter 6.) Clearly, the general expectation that economic development and modernization should be associated with higher democratic participation is supported by the evidence.

Modernization and Government Performance Little systematic thought has been given to the question of how economic development affects government performance. In general it would seem reasonable to expect that the greater capacity of government in the more modernized societies would enhance executive stability and effec-

Table 3.3 Modernization and political performance.

Country	Modernization level (1965)	Median turnout	Median executive durability	Median yearly riots/million		Median yearly deaths/million	
				1958–1967	1967–1976	1958–1967	1967–1976
India Ceylon Philippines Turkey Costa Rica Jamaica	Predominantly traditional	67%	32 months	.07	.11	.66	4.5
Chile Uruguay Greece Japan Venezuela Ireland	Mixed traditional and modern	71%	36 months	.23	.15	.04	1.3
Italy Austria Finland Norway France Denmark	Modern with traditional sector	86%	23 months	.07	.01	.03	0
Netherlands U.K. Belgium West Germany New Zealand Australia Switzerland Canada Sweden U.S.	Predominantly modern	83%	30 months	.06	.03	.01	0

tiveness.[19] In fact there is little empirical relationship between either the durability of the chief executive or the frequency of executive control of the legislature and the degree of economic development and modernization. The next chapter will show that constitutional arrangements have important influences on government performance, but even taking these into account, level of economic development is not associated with these measures of more stable and effective democratic government. As we shall see in Chapters 7 and 9, the level of development has conflicting impacts on the electoral and legislative party processes. Complex effects emerge that deny any simple relationship. The "obvious" expectation simply turns out to be wrong. Table 3.3 shows the median durability of executives of different developmental levels; the less modernized countries actually have the more durable executives.

Modernization and Violence   The theories of modernization lead to highly pessimistic expectations about the ability to control violence and sustain democracy in societies that are beginning to undergo the process of development. A number of theorists argue that in the early and early middle stages of development the aspirations of individuals and groups will outrun the society's ability to respond to them, with frustrating and destabilizing consequences.[20] The process of modernization may be especially difficult in the democracies, because their open political structure offers incentives for leaders to arouse expectations, and their freedom allows opposition to organize its assaults on the established order.

Generally, this expectation is strongly supported by the data. The democratic regimes were replaced or seriously suspended in nine of the democracies between 1958 and 1976. Of those nine nations, only France can be characterized as a modernized nation. On the other side of the coin, among the less developed democracies, only Costa Rica, Japan, Jamaica, and Venezuela escaped a serious threat to the democratic regime. And Jamaica seemed in serious trouble because of intense interparty violence in 1976. Japan achieved impressive economic growth, and moved into the set of modernized nations by the second decade.

Suspension of democracy was usually associated with armed attacks and deaths by political violence, which tended to occur more often in the less developed nations. Table 3.3 divides the democracies into four groups according to their level of modernization in 1965. The distinction is primarily on the basis of GNP per capita, but among the modernized nations the presence of a substantial agrarian sector is also used to divide the countries. The table makes it obvious that deaths by violence are concentrated in the least modern nations, although they are also present to a substantial extent in the modernizing ones, especially in the second decade.

Two other points are worth noting. First, the data on deadly violence show little evidence of "curvilinear" effects, in which the middle levels of modernization are more difficult to handle because political awareness outruns capacity. Among the democracies, it is the poorest nations that are most likely to experience major violence and overthrow of the regime.[21] It may well be that the democratic system itself is responsible for this fact, as it encourages substantial mobilization of at least the more literate groups, even in the relatively undeveloped societies. We must also recognize that all of the countries here are somewhat more modernized, at least in substantial pockets (as in India), than are the world's very poorest countries.

The second point is that rioting, the more mass-involved form of violence, is less clearly related to modernization than is armed violence. In the first decade, the mixed traditional and modern nations stand out as most riot-prone. Possibly some tendency for the population's demands to outrun society's capacity is at work here. The same pattern shows up in the second decade, if we shift Japan and Ireland down a category, as their growth makes reasonable. Insofar as there is evidence of a curvilinear effect of modernization on violence, it is seen in the impact on rioting, not on more organized violence. The poorest nations, especially in the first decade where the data are more complete and reliable, show little more rioting than the more modernized ones. I shall return to the puzzle of the weak relationship between modernization and rioting in later chapters. The working of the political system itself, its capacity to mobilize citizens through legitimate channels and to win their support, must be taken into account.

Needless to say, the level of modernization is not all-determining. The comparison of medians in table 3.3 obscures the fact that a few modern nations—such as Britain and the United States—had quite high levels of deaths and attacks. But it is obvious that the level of modernization and its accompanying economic and social features have a major impact on violence. Insofar as containment of violence is a measure of democratic performance, the poorer nations seem to be much more difficult to govern as democracies.

Social Cleavages

If everyone had the same political preferences, the task of making policy would be much easier. Politics would be a matter of discovering the policy everyone preferred and then implementing it. But preferences vary. These variations may be based on fundamentally different beliefs about the way society should be run, as when different religious groups have different ideas about the relationship between church and state. Or they may be based on similar social tastes but different social and economic positions, as when different class groups prefer tax and redistribution policies that favor the economic positions of their respective members. These variations across groups of individuals may be the basis for large-scale mobilization and organization of the resources of many individuals, and hence may be potentially convertible into political power.

A set of attitudes that divides the nation's citizens into major political groups is called a political cleavage. Sometimes political cleavages develop that are "purely" political: they reflect opinions about policies and are developed, sustained, and organized by political leaders committed to such policies. They divide families, friends, and neighbors as each individual responds differently to the problem, or they are built upon local networks of communication and organization, depending upon who is the first to seize these. But more frequently the alignment of large groups is based upon deep social, economic, and cultural divisions in the fabric of the society itself. Differences of occupation, religion, language, race, custom, and geography provide a natural base for political leaders who seek to mobilize support. Because such divisions typically also help to shape and organize the networks of communication and contact in a society, it is easier to build organizations and campaign for support along the lines of social divisions than across them. And once such a socially distinct "cleavage group," such as urban factory workers or highly religious farmers, is politically organized and provided with political symbols, its members' support is likely to be highly reliable.[22]

Political theorists often distinguish between two major types of social cleavages: economic cleavages and cultural cleavages. One line of thought, whose origins can be found in the writings of the Greeks and whose most powerful modern statement is the work of Marx, argues that economic differences are at the heart of politic disputes. Another line of thought contends that cultural ("ethnic") differences, such as language, race, tribe, and religion, are far more serious and fundamental social divisions than economic ones.

Subcultural Cleavages   I follow common practice by including language, race, caste, tribe, and religion, as well as distinctive regional custom, as possible demarcations of subcultures. This generous application of the term "subcultures" (or "ethnicity") raises two problems. One is deciding when a social division is sufficiently marked to have potential political significance—a problem shared by politicians and political scientists alike. A second problem is determining whether conflict in a given case actually grows out of subcultural cleavage, or whether it instead reflects the economic deprivation of certain subcultures. A case can be made that ostensibly cultural differences that spill over into serious political conflicts do reduce in the end to economics— that the conflicts of religion in Northern Ireland, or of language in Belgium, or of race in the United States, are based in the relative wealth or poverty of the contending communities. There does seem to be something distinctive about severe ethnic conflicts, however, and they seem particularly hard to resolve within purely democratic bounds.

One problem is that many ethnic conflicts involve issues that are difficult to compromise. To compromise on a political issue requires each side to give a bit. In wage disputes, for example, or issues of taxation or social welfare, compromises may be reached by increasing benefits or costs by some moderate fraction. In growing economies, especially, a wide range of solutions may be available for constructive bargainers. But in ethnic issues, such compromises may be more difficult to discover, either because the benefits are indivisible, or because compromise would involve intense costs to one or the other party. If religious parades are important to citizens of one religion and directly offensive to citizens of the other, it is difficult to achieve a compromise policy on parades if both groups live in the same area. (In the Netherlands, such a compromise allows religious parades in predominantly Catholic areas and forbids them in Protestant areas.) It is possible to have two languages taught in the school system, but children brought up in one language will find the other more difficult in classroom use. Many faiths may consider religious instruction an essential part of a child's education, but it may become a subject of great dispute when children of different faiths attend the same schools. Various scholars have argued that this inherently greater difficulty in "bargainability," in finding reasonable compromises, is what makes ethnic differences so politically serious.[23]

Subcultural differences are also serious politically because they create, almost by definition, a sense of distance between factions. Where a strong sense of difference exists, it is easy for real and fancied grievances to be exaggerated, for distance to become transformed into fear, distrust, and hostility.[24] Moreover, it may well be that matters of language, religion, and custom that are learned in early childhood are integral to the individual's sense of his own identity.[25] A threat to these values becomes a threat to the individual's selfhood, a threat which must be resisted at all costs. Racial discrimination may involve a similar threat at the personal and inescapable level, putting even normally uninvolved persons into a situation of personal fear and anger. A threatened ethnic group may well prefer to see democracy limited rather than be subjected to the whims of a hostile majority group. In any case, such fear and hostility will complicate bargaining over concrete issues, make coalitions across ethnic lines difficult to organize and sustain, and perhaps increase citizens' willingness to use or condone destructive tactics. Political leaders may also persuade discontented citizens to blame all of their troubles on minority scapegoats, as a means of mobilizing support in crises.[26]

Ethnic Division and Democratic Performance Table 3.4 uses a measure of ethnic division called the Index of Ethnic Fractionalization. The Russian Atlas *Nordov Mira* identified linguistic, tribal, and cultural groups in the nations of the world. Based upon that analysis, Taylor and Hudson, in the *World Handbook,* developed an index of fractionalization, which measures the probability that any two citizens, chosen at random, will be of different ethnic groups. The index ranges from zero, where all citizens share the same ethnic characteristics, to a potential high of 1.0, where every citizen is of a different ethnic group. In practice, the ethnic fractionalization of the democracies ranges from .02 in extremely homogeneous Japan to .89 in extremely heterogeneous India. Taylor and Hudson's index does not include religious divisions. In countries with major religious divisions, as between Christian and Moslem, I have calculated an index of religious fractionalization.[27] But in none of the democracies is it higher than the index of ethnic fractionalization. Table 3.4 shows the fractionalization index for each country and the median levels of democratic performance for the groups of countries that ranked low, moderate, and high, on ethnic fractionalization.

The theories of subcultural division lead us to expect more violence in the ethnically divided countries, because of the greater difficulty in bargaining and the greater sense of distance between groups. Expectations about the effect of ethnic fractionalization on voting participation are much less obvious. It could be argued either that ethnic divisions would be a ready source of participatory mobilization or that the explosive nature of ethnic conflicts would make them difficult to channel into the regular political arena. In fact, as table 3.4 clearly shows, voting turnout is lower in the ethnically divided countries. Multivariate analysis will show that this relationship does not vanish when we control for the level of economic development.

We might expect less executive stability in the ethnically divided

Table 3.4 Ethnic division and political performance.

Country	Ethnic fractional-ization index[a]	Median voting turnout	Median executive durability	Median yearly riots/million		Median yearly deaths/million	
				1958–1967	1967–1976	1958–1967	1967–1976
Japan	.02						
West Germany	.03						
Ireland	.04						
Italy	.04						
Jamaica	.04						
Norway	.04						
Denmark	.05	84%	36 months	.04	.03	.01	.02
Costa Rica	.07						
Sweden	.08						
Greece	.10						
Netherlands	.10						
Venezuela	.11						
Austria	.13						
Chile	.14						
Finland	.16						
Uruguay	.20						
Turkey	.25						
France	.26	77%	30 months	.10	.09	.04	.25
Australia	.32						
United Kingdom	.37						
New Zealand	.37						
Ceylon (Sri Lanka)	.47						
Switzerland	.50						
U.S.	.50						
Belgium	.55						
Philippines	.74	71%	30 months	.12	.05	.15	.10
Canada	.75						
India	.89						

a. From Taylor and Hudson, *World Handbook*. The index measures the probability that two randomly drawn citizens will be of different ethnic or linguistic groups.

countries, given the problem of issue bargainability. There is clear evidence for such a relationship. The median durability in the very homogeneous countries is the 36-month limit of our measure, although instability does not increase steadily with heterogeneity. Multivariate analysis supports the presence of a relationship between ethnic divisions and government instability, after taking account of constitutional factors. (See tables 4.4 and 10.1.)

It is moreover, quite clear from table 3.4 that ethnically divided nations experienced many more deaths by violence than did homogeneous ones in both decades.[28] Specific events in the democracies confirm this observation. In Ceylon and India violence between linguistic and religious groups resulted in numerous deaths, caused by mob violence and by poice efforts to restore order. The conflicts in India were particularly bloody. In the Philippines the Moro independence movement waged a costly guerrilla war. In the United States the urban race riots of the late 1960s and early 1970s, in particular, led to substantial loss of life, largely in the course of official efforts to restore order. Canada and Belgium also experienced rioting and terrorist attacks grounded in ethnic issues, although on a much smaller scale, and there were even some bombings and minor clashes over linguistic issues in Switzerland.

The division between Catholics and Protestants in Northern Ireland was not used to increase the ethnic fractionalization score of the United Kingdom, but certainly the estrangement of religious groups there has most of the properties of ethnic conflict, and it resulted in great loss of life in the 1970s. Moreover, much of the loss of life in France in the first decade came from conflict over Algeria; if Algeria had been included as part of France, which it was legally up to 1958, France in the 1950s would qualify as highly ethnically fractionalized.

The relationship between ethnicity and rioting is much less powerful than that between ethnicity and deaths by political violence.[29] Ethnic riots do take place. A number of the democratic nations in each time period saw violence involving either disorganized clashes between ethnic groups or outbursts expressing ethnic grievances. But all of the larger countries did experience substantial rioting, and only some of those riots were based on ethnic groups or ethnic issues. Table 3.4 suggests that in the first decade the more ethnically fractionalized countries had higher rates of rioting per capita, but the correlation is only +.14. In the second decade the relationship is virtually nonexistent: a number of ethnically divided countries, such as Canada and Switzerland, had few riots, while some homogeneous countries, such as France, Uruguay, and Italy, had many. We must not confuse the probability that in ethnically divided countries mass turmoil will be affected by the ethnic makeup of the population, with the propensity of ethnicity as such to generate rioting. This propensity is, at best, weak and uncertain in any given time span.

One property of ethnic rioting is evident across both decades, and in both individual studies of riots and statistical analysis of riot-troubled countries: in ethnically diverse countries, rioting is more frequently deadly.[30] Clashes between groups seem to be more likely to result in deaths if the groups are ethnically distinct, as we might expect from the theories of interpersonal distance and stereotyping. Examination of individual riots suggests that police are more likely to use deadly force in quelling ethnically based riots. While countries with more riots are likely to have more deaths by violence, regardless of ethnicity, the relationship is much more pronounced in the ethnically divided nations. Rioting is not much more common, on a per capita basis, in the ethnically divided nations, but when it occurs it is more serious and more deadly.

Economic Divisions

Aristotle argued more than two thousand years ago that sharp divisions between the poor and the rich create problems for maintaining a stable political system. He advocated creating a large middle class as a solution. Advice in a similar vein runs through the writings of many political theorists. There can be little doubt that economic interest is a major basis of political cleavage. Citizens in at least half of the democracies, for example, gave at least a quarter of their vote to a Labor, Socialist, or Communist party.

But as in the case of subcultural cleavages, we do not fully understand the processes by which economic inequality comes to be perceived as a severe political problem. There is little doubt that occupational divisions and the inequalities that usually accompany them are a convenient basis for constructing political organizations. But it is less obvious how the large inequalities that typically are tolerated in traditional societies become matters of intense disagreement in modernizing ones. It is a matter of perception, rather than absolute hardship, that brings economic inequality to the fore. Peasants in a traditional society may have far less income and live objectively a far harder life than the nobility. As long as they define their proper rights in terms that accept such differences, and as long as survival is possible, they remain quiescent. It was usually the abrogation of traditional rights and privileges, not the awareness of income inequality or occupational immobility, that sparked the great peasant rebellions.[31]

Table 3.5 shows the relationship between income inequality and political performance in the democracies for which income data are available.[32] The measure shown here, one of several roughly equivalent indices, is the share of income going to the wealthiest 20 percent of income earners in a year. The measure includes transfer payments, such as social security and welfare payments. (The effects of taxes are not included, because of lack of data.)[33] The most equitable countries, by these measures, are Australia, Canada, the United States, the Scandina-

Table 3.5 Income inequality and political performance.

Country	Income share to top 20%	Median voting turnout	Median executive durability	Median yearly riots/million		Median yearly deaths/million	
				1958–1967	1967–1976	1958–1967	1967–1976
Australia	39%						
Canada	40						
U.S.	40						
Norway	41						
New Zealand	42						
Sweden	44	78%	30 months	.07	.01	.00	.00
United Kingdom	44						
Japan	46						
Denmark	48						
Italy	48						
Uruguay	48						
Finland	49						
Netherlands	49						
Greece	50	84%	23 months	.08	.03	.05	.04
Ceylon	52						
India	52						
West Germany	53						
France	54						
Philippines	56						
Chile	57						
Costa Rica	60						
Turkey	61	72%	36 months	.06	.13	.30	4.53
Jamaica	62						
Venezuela	65						

Sources: Hollis Chenery et al., *Redistribution with Growth* (New York: Oxford University Press, 1974), pp. 8–9; Felix Paukert, "Income Distribution at Different Levels of Development," *International Labour Review*, 108 (Aug.–Sept. 1973):97–128.

vian nations, New Zealand, and Japan. The least equitable, with the top 20 percent receiving over 60 percent of the income, are the Latin American democracies of Venezuela, Jamaica, and Costa Rica, along with the Philippines and Turkey.

Keeping in mind that income equality, more significantly than population size, modernity, or ethnicity, can be a consequence as well as a cause of political events, we would nonetheless expect less equality to be associated with less stability and more violence, because of the difficulty of meeting redistributive demands from "have-not" groups in the population. Table 3.5 lends some limited support to this idea. The highly inequitable nations had somewhat less voting participation, but the middle-level countries had the highest turnout. Contrary to expectation, executive stability was *higher* in the least equal countries, but both participation and stability show a curvilinear relationship to inequality. As with other environmental effects, aside from population size, rioting is also erratically or insignificantly related to income inequality.

However, the table shows a reasonably strong relationship between inequality and death by violence in both decades. Examination of some specific present and historical conflicts also testifies to the association of inequality with violent conflict. Demands for the redistribution of land and wealth, and government policies attempting to bring about such redistribution were at the heart of the bitter political conflict in Chile after leftist President Salvador Allende was elected in 1970. This conflict, associated with political clashes and terrorist bombings, played a critical part in the overthrow of Chilean democracy through a military coup in 1973. Historically, the exclusion of the new working class from social and political life in Germany and Austria left a heritage of organizational and ideological division that cost both nations dearly in the crises of the early 1930s.[34]

It is important, in a consideration of inequality and violence, to recognize that modernization itself is associated with greater equality.[35] It is obvious from table 3.5 that the least equitable countries are also mostly those at low or middle levels of economic development. In this set of countries, in fact, the association between inequality and development level is about − .60. Multivariate analysis will be necessary to disentangle the effects of inequality and modernization.

A Brief Multivariate Consideration

The various environmental factors that make political performance difficult are to some degree associated with one another. Although the very poorest nations are somewhat less inequitable than the transitional ones, the general association between modernity and equality is rather strong. The more modernized nations are also on average more ethnically homogeneous and slightly smaller than their less developed counterparts. Thus, although there is no doubt that inequality, lower levels of modernization, and ethnicity have all led to intense conflict in specific countries, and although each is associated with more deaths by political violence, it is quite possible from the evidence presented so far that some of these relationships are spurious. That is, they may be descriptively correct but caused by the effects of other variables.

Table 3.6 shows the results of a multivariate regression analysis of the effects of the four major environmental conditions on the amount of political violence.[36] We expect small population size, higher economic development, ethnic homogeneity, and income equality to be advantageous for maintaining political order. Thus, we have theoretical reasons to expect the signs of the coefficients to be positive. For each dependent variable, the table reports both the simple correlations and the standardized regression coefficients that correspond to them. Comparing these reveals how simultaneous consideration of the other environmental conditions reduces or enhances the effects attributable to the variable in question. As population size is entered directly in the equation, all the dependent variables are absolute, not per capita, measures.[37] (The per capita correlations, which can be compared with tables 3.3 to 3.5, are presented in the note to the table.)

The implications of the analysis are quite straightforward. In the explanation of rioting, only population size has consistent and significant effects when all the environmental advantages are considered simultaneously. In both decades the correlations are large, and become even larger, as well as very significant, in the regression equations. Level of economic development is positively related to lower levels of rioting in both decades; it is significant in the first decade, but in the second decade the coefficient is small. Some effects of economic development cannot be fully discounted, and I shall be exploring some of the complexities of the middle levels of development later. Ethnic homogeneity, by contrast, has positive simple correlations in both decades, but these become negative in the regressions. Despite the occurrence of some ethnic riots, ethnic homogeneity does not systematically affect the probability of rioting across the full set of democracies. Similarly, the effects of income equality are in the wrong direction, trivial, or both, across the full time period.

Table 3.6 Environmental advantages and political order: correlation and regression analysis.[a]

| Measure of political order[b] | Environmental advantages in democracies | | | |
	Small population	Economic development (GNP/capita)	Ethnic homogeneity	Income equality
Low rioting, 1958–1967				
Simple correlation	+.83	+.17	+.27	−.08
Regression	+.90**	+.38**	−.30	−.35
Low rioting, 1967–1976				
Simple correlation	+.76	+.15	+.33	−.00
Regression	+.79**	+.09	−.09	+.03
Low deaths, 1958–1967				
Simple correlation	+.55	+.65	+.75	+.25
Regression	+.29*	+.40**	+.46**	+.02
Low deaths, 1967–1976				
Simple correlation	+.35	+.70	+.52	+.25
Regression	+.23*	+.71**	+.08	−.12

a. Correlation coefficients are Pearson r. Regression coefficients are standardized regression coefficients in simultaneous regression equation, with all four independent variables. Because population size is in the regression equation, the violence variables use absolute, not per capita, measures. Simple correlations with per capita riots and deaths because of political violence, with GNP/capita (log), ethnic homogeneity, and equality are as follows: +.11, +.14, −.03; +.27, −.11, +.46; +.71, +.51, +.54; +.72, +.19, +.51. Population size and GNP/capita variables are logged. Twenty-six cases are used in 1958–1967; 27 in 1967–1976.

b. To prevent extreme outliers from biasing the coefficients, the extreme values on riots and deaths are truncated back to the ninetieth-percentile values, a procedure followed throughout the book. A log transformation of the dependent variable yields similar results.

* = F level over 1.7 (significant at .10).

** = F level over 3.0 (significant at .05).

In explaining deaths caused by political violence, the most powerful factor across both decades is level of economic development. The more developed countries have significantly fewer deaths in both periods, at the .05 level or more. The coefficients for population size are much smaller, but remain significant at least at the .10 level in both decades. Ethnic homogeneity is the strongest explainer of low numbers of deaths in the first decade, and the coefficient is at least in the correct direction in the second. Clearly, ethnic homogeneity is a factor in explaining deadly violence. In the second decade, the emergence of serious violence in Chile and Uruguay and the better containment of ethnic violence in several countries seem responsible for the changing explanatory power of development level and ethnic homogeneity. Income inequality, by contrast, shows moderately positive simple correlations, but these become very small or negative in the multiple regression. Whatever the attractiveness of the theories associated with it, the measures of income equality simply do not help to explain differences in either form of violence across the democracies.

A brief technical note is in order here. These regressions are shown for only 21 or 23 cases, depending on the decade, because of missing data for income inequality in a few democracies. Regression equations for the other three variables, run on the full set of cases, shown in table 4.4 below, do not greatly change the present conclusions. Because income inequality has not proved to be a significant environmental feature, and because of the missing data, it is not included in the analyses in subsequent chapters. As throughout this study, the riot and death variables were constrained to the ninetieth percentile values, to prevent a few extreme outliers from biasing the correlation and regression results. Another approach to that problem is to use a log transformation of the dependent variable.[38] The log transformation yields results that are very similar to those in the table.

While the multivariate analysis of effects of environmental advantages on political order is useful at this point, and is not markedly changed by additional variables considered later, the analysis of voting and government stability can more appropriately wait until the constitutional variables have been taken into account in chapter 4. But we can note here that income inequality, despite the plausibility of the argument that it makes governing more difficult, is insignificantly related to executive stability (and in the wrong direction, theoretically). The incorporation of a control for presidential executive does not change these conclusions.

The initial assumption that certain features of the social and economic environment would make good political performance more difficult to achieve in some democracies than in others is certainly supported by the analysis in this chapter. Large countries had more riots and more deaths by political violence. Countries at lower levels of economic development and wealth suffered far more deadly violence (even taking account of population size), had lower voting participation, and were much more likely to experience a serious threat to the democratic regime. However, their levels of rioting were less clearly related to modernization, and, at least in simple comparisons, their chief executives were no less durable than those of the rest of the democracies. Ethnically divided countries, too, experienced lower voting turnout and more deadly violence, although not less government stability; these effects remained in multivariate analysis.

Perhaps the most surprising discovery is the failure of differences in income inequality to survive the multivariate analysis of deaths and riots. The less equitable countries were more violent, in a descriptive comparison. But the relationships became insignificant once population size and, especially, level of economic development were controlled. It is obvious that inequality is a major issue in some democracies. But across the full set of democratic systems, differences in income distribution are not a significant factor, once other environmental variables are controlled.

Most of the findings of this chapter serve as a reconfirmation of previous theorizing about the impact of environmental conditions on political conflict. We expected to find that small size, higher levels of development, and ethnic homogeneity make democracies easier to govern. At least in terms of encouraging voter participation, inhibiting deadly violence, and, to some extent, limiting turmoil, they do. However, the environmental effects on executive stability and majority control turned out to be either trivial or opposite from our expectations. To understand these findings we must analyze the basic constitutional rules by which political leaders are chosen and authoritative decisions are made.

The Constitutional Setting

4

In recent decades the study of constitutions has been out of fashion in comparative politics. This neglect is unfortunate. Elements in constitutional design have a substantial impact on democratic performance. Some of this impact is relatively direct: the political resources of the chief executive affect government stability. Some of the impact is indirect: constitutional arrangements help shape the properties of party systems, which in turn affect participation, stability, and violence. The task of this chapter is to lay the groundwork for examination of the direct and indirect effects of the constitutional setting on democratic performance.

Constitutional Design

Each of the 29 democracies has a unique constitution, a complex set of written and unwritten rules about how leaders are chosen and authoritative decisions are made. I use the term "constitution" to refer to these rules for making political decisions, not to any particular type of document or legal code.[1] Such constitutions have emerged from diverse conditions and they represent efforts to embody the cherished values of a particular society. Typically, the constitutional arrangements also reflect special advantages sought and bargains arrived at by the individuals and groups involved in constitution-making.

Three properties of constitutional arrangements have been particularly the focus of theories of democratic performance: executive-legislative relations, rules of legislative representation, and federalism. These three properties by no means exhaust the list of major constitutional characteristics. Provisions for the protection of individual rights, the scrutiny of governmental decisions, group consultation, substantive obligations of governmental officials, autonomous legal adjudication of disputes in implementing policies, and so forth, can be of great interest and importance. But for this examination of participation, stability, and violence the major theoretical lines of argument seem to focus on those three properties. In this chapter I shall analyze executive-legislative relations and rules of representation. (For a brief discussion of federalism, see Chapter 10, note 9.)

Executive-Legislative Relations   One line of constitutional thought about executive-legislative relations emphasizes an independent chief executive, who is responsible for the execution of national policies and who can initiate policy, yet who is checked and supervised by an independent legislature.[2] The prototype is the American president and the separate but interdependent powers of the president and Congress.[3]

In the "strong presidential" systems, the chief executive is chosen for some fixed term, usually in a direct national election, and can be removed from office before the end of that term only under special circumstances of abuse of office and by extraordinary legislative or judicial action. The president has significant independent authority, such as a veto over legislative bills or the responsibility for initiating budgetary legislation, foreign treaties, or other special policies. He or she appoints major executive officials, perhaps with the consent of the legislature, and can dismiss them at will. Various emergency and war powers also reside in the presidential office. The separation of election bases and the assignment of separate but interdependent powers to legislative and executive is designed to prevent either from engaging in unconstitutional or hasty abuse of power. In a number of presidential systems, concern about abuse of power by the president is underlined by constitutional provisions prohibiting or limiting presidential reelection; for example, the American president can serve only two elected terms, and the Venezuelan and Costa Rican presidents cannot serve two terms in immediate succession (as was also true in democratic Chile).

The other major executive-legislative arrangement is the "parliamentary" system, in which the individual chief executive is chosen by and simply accountable to the national legislature. The prime minister and the cabinet officers, individually or collectively, are subject at all times to removal by the legislature if they cannot maintain majority support. The details of the parliamentary arrangements vary from country to country. In some cases the prime minister is formally nominated by a monarch (as in Britain) or a weak president (as in Italy), who is official head of state and performs most ceremonial functions. In some nations the prime minister can call for immediate elections if rejected by the legislature, or even may be required to do so, while in other constitutions (such as Norway's) there is no provision for elections between fixed terms. In the West German system the requirement for a "constructive" vote of no confidence implies that the prime minister (or chancellor) can be replaced only when a legislative majority supports his successor, while in many parliamentary systems the government can be forced to resign without either a new election or a chosen successor.[4] Moreover, even with similar formal arrangements, customs vary as to the circumstances under which governments resign if defeated on important legislation they have proposed.[5] These practices are further complicated by different relations between chief executives and the two houses of bicameral legislatures.

Such nuances can be extremely important for understanding political events in particular countries. It is difficult to understand the party maneuvering in Ceylon in the 1960s without knowing that the prime minister, after getting a majority backing by the legislature, was allowed to appoint additional legislators to consolidate his or her ability to govern. The complex struggle between parties in Australia in the mid-1970s was greatly shaped by the role of the two legislative houses and the residual constitutional powers of the governor-general. Examples can be multiplied indefinitely. Nonetheless, the parliamentary systems have much in common with one another. For the most part it is quite clear whether a given constitutional system is primarily presidential or parliamentary. Parliamentary systems share above all the daily dependence of the government upon its legislative majority for continuation in office, a fact that has great significance for disciplined party voting in the legislature[6] and for the stability of governments under varying party conditions. The complete list of presidential and parliamentary systems among the democracies appears in table 4.1.

Several mixed arrangements should be noted. The French Fifth Republic is characterized by strong presidential executives that have major decisionmaking authority of their own and are not easily removed from office during their term. Yet they must appoint prime ministers who are subject to legislative confidence, binding the government more closely to the legislature than in most presidential systems. By contrast, the Finnish system is very much like the standard parliamentary system in domestic affairs, but the directly elected president has special authority in foreign policy. Most distinctive of all is the Swiss "collective executive" system, which was also used in Uruguay until 1967. In the Swiss system the "chief executive" is a seven-person council chosen from the national legislature to represent proportionally the major political parties. The chairmanship of the council rotates. Although formally subject to legislative control, the council cannot be simply removed between terms, and in this sense it acts almost as a multiparty presidency.

Theoretical expectations vary about the impact of executive-legislative arrangements on democratic performance. The only clear expectation is that presidential systems should be more stable—as measured by the tenure of the chief executive—than ministerial ones. The greater and more autonomous presidential resources make such stability likely. They do not, however, ensure party or policy compatibility between legislature and executive.

Expectations about effects on participation are less clear-cut. On the one hand, direct participation of citizens in the election of a strong chief executive might encourage citizen involvement. On the other hand, the separate electoral bases of president and legislature may weaken the national party systems, as the organizing and coordinating power of parties is not needed to choose a prime minister; individual candidates may be more important than party labels; weaker party organizations may mean lower turnout. Finally, a single major prize in the presidential contest may encourage party alliances and consolidation, with unknown consequences for participation.

Expectations about violence are also conflicting. The presidential system's stability and concentration of emergency powers may make it easier to clamp down on violent outbreaks, but the divided legislative-executive relations may make it more difficult to respond quickly and positively to policy demands from citizens. Moreover, the independently elected single executive, often with limited individual reelection possibilities, lends itself to less accommodative reactions to discontent.

Bases of Legislative Representation A well-developed body of theory exists to link the constitutional bases of legislative representation to party-system configurations and indirectly to government performance. It was long argued that elections using proportional representation and multimember electoral districts would encourage multiparty systems, while plurality elections and single-member districts (as in the United States and Britain) would encourage two-party systems. Eventually known as Duverger's Law, because of the forceful statement of it by Maurice Duverger in 1954, this argument was given an elegant test by Douglas Rae's empirical study of the political consequences of electoral laws in 1967.[7] I shall be examining the full connections between electoral laws, party-system configurations, and government stability in Chapters 5 and 7. But for our purposes here the inference seems reasonably clear that the proportional representation (PR) systems with multimember districts would be expected to lead to less stability and fewer situations of government control of the legislature, because they encourage the existence of more than two political parties.

A classification of legislative representation can build upon the work of Duverger and Rae. Rae argues that many special features of electoral laws, such as voters' ability to designate second party preferences or candidate preferences within a party, have little influence on the translation of party votes into legislative representation or the support of small parties. (Such features may, however, have important impact upon party cohesiveness and within-party competition, as suggested by Giovanni Sartori, Alan Zuckerman, and others.)[8] The critical distinction, according to Rae, is the number of representatives per district and the use of some proportional scheme for allocating seats if there is more than one member per district.[9] In the single-member system, only one representative can be elected from each district, and parties that accumulate a goodly total of votes by finishing second or third in many districts can be shut out of the legislature entirely. This system, found in purest form in the United States, Britain, Canada, India, Jamaica, the Philippines, and New Zealand, contrasts markedly with the proportional representation systems of most of continental Europe, which elect at least six members per district and use various allocative schemes that permit smaller parties to gain a legislative voice.[10]

Within each major type—plurality single-member districts and proportional multimember districts—is found a range of variations. Duverger and Rae differ rather sharply on whether the French Fifth Republic system with one member per district, but a requirement of a second (runoff) ballot if no party receives a majority on the first round, encourages party consolidation (Rae) or multiparty competition (Duverger). The Australian majority system seems to behave much like the usual single-member-district arrangement, but may sustain some degree of multiple party alliances. Within the multimember PR systems, some methods of calculation give purer representational outcomes than others, as do larger constituencies.[11] Various cut-off rules for party representation, as well as differing rules for elections to the two legislative houses, can also make some difference.

Some electoral representation systems are mixtures of the more clear-cut types. Most notable is the West German system, with half the representatives elected from single-member districts and half from large districts (nationally at-large since 1956). The requirement that a party win 5 percent of the national vote or three individual seats has meant that the Bundestag gives quite proportionate representation, but only to larger parties. A party meeting the minimum 5 percent requirement has its share of the national vote accurately converted into legislative seats by adding the appropriate number of at-large seats to those won in the individual constituencies. Small parties are shut out. The Irish system, with rather small constituencies and a complex preferential ballot for utilizing voters' second-choice preferences, falls toward the PR side of the continuum, but is less encouraging to small parties than most. The small, multimember, but quite inequitably districted Japanese districts tend to favor the largest party, rather than proportional representation of all parties.[12]

Expectations about aspects of democratic performance other than government stability are mixed or conflicting. Supporters of PR tend to believe that the inherently more equitable system of representation will encourage legitimate participation and limit violence. In a broader analysis of conflict and its regulation, Eric Nordlinger argues explicitly that "an exclusive reliance upon majoritarian institutions and practices does not facilitate conflict regulation and may even contribute to conflict exacerbations."[13] Proponents of single-member districts, by contrast, believe that the propensity of such systems to create clear-cut elected majorities will encourage voter involvement, because the choice of the government is more directly shaped by the election returns. Strong majorities may also be better able to deal with citizen discontent. Following the language of the literature on this subject, I shall use the term "election laws" to refer to the legislative rules of representation.

Constitutional Design and Political Performance

The Constitutional Types Expectations about the two major dimensions can be combined into a single typology with resultant predictions. As the only unambiguous theoretical predictions have to do with government stability, and as these emphasize the presidential resources first, followed by the impact of electoral systems on legislative majorities and multipartyism (where legislatures are important for stability), the typology combines all the presidential systems. Regardless of the legislative or party fractionalization, we expect government stability where we find presidential executives. But majority control of the legislature is more doubtful. It depends on simultaneous election of party majorities from different electoral bases in the presidential systems. Within the parliamentary systems the constitutional arrangements emphasizing single-member districts, or at least a few members per district and perhaps cut-off exclusion of small parties, are expected to be more stable than their fully proportional counterparts. (We shall see in Chapter 7 why this assumption may be wrong under some conditions, but the present argument is certainly the common one in the literature.) From these expectations, the parliamentary systems with single or a few representatives per district are designated "majoritarian parliamentary systems," while the others are designated "representational parliamentary systems."

In subsequent chapters I shall use these same terms in discussing the constitutional types. However, in the multivariate tests and in the analyses of party processes, I shall often look separately at the two constitutional dimensions of legislative-executive relations and the bases of electoral representation. By doing so, I can avoid the problem of varying legislative bases within types of presidential systems. I can also treat the intermediate representational types, such as West Germany, as intermediate and not have to force them into a dichotomy for presentation.

Constitution and Performance   We can now classify the democracies by their constitutional features.[14] The seven presidential systems are listed at the top of table 4.1. Six of them were presidential throughout the period of this study, while Uruguay adopted a presidential constitution in a referendum in 1966 and chose its first contemporary president in 1967, at the beginning of the second decade of our analysis. The lower two groupings of countries distinguish the majoritarian and representational parliamentary systems. In parentheses after the name of each country appears the number of representatives per legislative district in the popular legislative chamber, which is the primary basis for distinguishing among the types. As suggested by F.A. Hermans, I have not classified a system as having a fully representational constitution unless it has at least five representatives per district.[15] As mentioned above, West Germany, Ireland, and Japan also have other less representational features accompanying their two to four representatives per district. Here they are shown in the majoritarian group, but in multivariate

Table 4.1 Constitutional types[a] and political performance.

Country	Representatives per district[b]	Median voting turnout	Median executive durability	Median majority control	Measures of political performance			
					Median yearly riots/million		Median yearly deaths/million	
					1958–1967	1967–1976	1958–1967	1967–1976
Presidential systems								
Chile	6							
Costa Rica	8							
France	1	71%	36 months	72%	.14	.15	.18	.53
Philippines	1							
U.S.	1							
Uruguay	5							
Venezuela	9							
Majoritarian-parliamentary systems								
Australia	1							
Canada	1							
Ceylon	1							
West Germany	2							
India	1	73%	33 months	94%	.07	.03	.01	.30
Ireland	4							
Jamaica	1							
Japan	4							
New Zealand	1							
U.K.	1							

Table 4.1 Constitutional types[a] and political performance. (Cont.)

Country	Representatives per district[b]	Median voting turnout	Median executive durability	Median majority control	Median yearly riots/million		Median yearly deaths/million	
					1958–1967	1967–1976	1958–1967	1967–1976
Representational-parliamentary systems								
Austria	6							
Belgium	7							
Denmark	10							
Finland	13							
Italy	19	87%	22 months	64%	.10	.02	.03	.00
Netherlands	150							
Norway	8							
Sweden	8							
Turkey	7							

Sources: Rae, *Electoral Laws*; Banks, *Political Handbook*; Herman, *Parliaments*: Mackie and Rose, *International Almanac of Electoral History*.

a. Switzerland's unique constitutional arrangements exclude it from this analysis. Uruguay became presidential in 1967. Greece and Israel would be classified as representational parliamentary, but are not shown as data are not available for the second decade. Executive durability and majority control are for 1967–1976 only.

b. These are the number of legislators in the popular house of the legislature, divided by the number of electoral districts, in the late 1960s. In 1971 Austria decreased the number of districts, increasing the number of representatives per district to nearly 20. Sweden increased to 12 after 1970.

analysis they will be assigned an intermediate status. The unique Swiss multiparty, strong, collective executive does not appear in the table.

Despite the concern about constitutional complexities, we can see in the table that the expectations about government performance are realized quite effectively. The presidential systems are designed to produce executive stability, and they do so. In fact, only in the United States was a president (Nixon in 1974) forced from office by political pressures in less than three years. In Chile and Uruguay military intervention did remove an incumbent or render him largely powerless before his term expired. But certainly the presidential systems provided more executive stability than either of the other designs. At the same time, the separate election of the president and the legislature often led to minority presidents; a majority of the presidential systems faced a divided legislative/executive situation for over two years in the decade. Moreover, as in the United States, the quite different constituencies to which president and legislature were responsible often made for difficult collaboration between the president and his own legislative party when it was in the majority. (On the positive side, these blurrings of constituencies may have eased executive-legislative relations in the frequent minority-party presidencies; see Chapter 7.) The presidential systems also were characterized by rather low levels of citizen electoral involvement, another respect in which the United States is typical of presidential systems.

Table 4.1 shows that the majoritarian parliamentary constitutions were the most effective at avoiding minority governments, with half of them experiencing less than seven months of minority prime ministers, and were quite effective in generating executive stability. The median duration of the cabinet in such systems, before either being defeated or having to call an election, was around 33 months of the 36-month maximum. The representational parliamentary systems, by contrast, experienced considerable problems with both stability and effective majorities. The average tenure of their chief executives was only around 22 months, and minority governments were quite common.

The representational systems did mobilize very high levels of voting turnout. As we shall see in Chapter 5, these systems also translated voter preference into legislative representation very faithfully and encouraged the formation of new political parties.

While the nature of the constitutional design yields fairly clear expectations about government stability and effectiveness, the implications for the containment of violence are not so obvious. On the one hand, the presidential and majoritarian parliamentary systems should have chief executives capable of dealing vigorously with violence. On the other hand, the representational systems are designed to allow discontented citizens easy access into the political system, thus perhaps taking the pressure off suppressed grievances. Table 4.1 shows the median riots and deaths per capita for the different constitutional types.

Although we cannot reach any final conclusions before we look at environmental factors, the data in table 4.1 speak well for the representational strategy. Rioting was most frequent (per capita) in the presidential systems, although not very strongly related to constitutional types. Deaths by violence were much more clearly associated with constitutional arrangements, with the presidential systems manifesting the most deaths and the representational ones the fewest. This pattern is very clear in both time periods. Given the frequently expressed doubts about the general stability of representational systems—doubts generated by the breakdown of civil order in Austria and Germany in the 1930s and reinforced by terrorism in Italy and Turkey in the late 1970s—the broad cross-system finding that representational systems had the least average violence is worth emphasizing.

Constitutional Types and Performance Dimensions   In Chapter 2 I discussed the question of the relationship between dimensions of political performance. Based on the experience of a few countries, theorists disagree over whether participation is incompatible with government stability and the containment of violence or should support them. Most assume, however, that stability and lack of violence should go together. My findings are quite different. The analysis supports the positive compatibility of participation and political order. But executive stability is a performance dimension quite distinct from maintaining order: I find that voting participation is negatively related to executive stability. Majority control of the legislature forms a third dimension of its own.

The fact that the presidential systems have substantial violence, lower participation, and very high executive stability raises the question of whether the earlier analysis of compatibility of dimensions was shaped primarily by the constitutional settings. Indeed, both common sense and the subsequent analysis of legislative processes suggest that the processes of government formation and lawmaking work quite differently in the presidential and parliamentary systems. Removing the presidential systems (and Switzerland) from the set of democracies makes it possible to replicate the earlier factor analysis to examine the compatibility of dimensions within the parliamentary regimes.

Table 4.2 presents the results of a factor analysis exactly comparable to that presented in table 2.4, but conducted only on the parliamentary systems. There are too few presidential systems for the comparable analysis for them to be worth presenting. (As in table 2.4, absolute rather than per capita measures of riots and deaths are used, although the extreme values are, as usual, constrained to the ninetieth percentile to prevent bias. Since population size is not significantly related to the voting and governmental variables, it is not misleading to use the absolute values of the violence measures. Using the per capita variables yields rather similar results in most respects, although it involves potential technical problems.)[16]

In the parliamentary systems, including both the representational and majoritarian types, the factor analysis produces only two major dimensions (using the usual criterion of eliminating dimensions whose eigenvalue is less than 1.0).[17] These dimensions correspond closely to the dimensions of political order and government stability discussed in

Table 4.2 Factor analysis of the relationships between measures of political performance in parliamentary democracies, 1967–1976.[a]

	Loadings on Rotated Factors[b]	
Performance Measures	Factor 1: Political order	Factor 2: Government stability
Voting turnout	+.47	−.55
Executive durability	+.30	+.74
Executive control of the legislature	−.11	+.29
Riots[c]	−.76	−.15
Deaths by political violence[c]	−.94	+.17

Source: Tables 2.1, 2.2, 2.3.

a. The presidential systems shown in table 4.1 are excluded, as is Switzerland, leaving 19 parliamentary cases in 1967–1976.

b. The loadings are a factor pattern matrix from oblique rotation. The factor "structure" is similar. In the analysis only the first two factors have eigenvalues of 1.0 or more. If a third factor is forced out, it correlates +.56 with Factor 2, and is essentially an executive control factor. Program from Nie et al., *SPSS*.

c. Extreme values of rioting and deaths are truncated to the ninetieth-percentile values to prevent extreme cases from biasing the correlations. Log transformed riots and deaths yield a very similar pattern.

Chapter 2. The first dimension reflects primarily the levels of rioting and deaths from political violence. The second dimension is most heavily weighted by executive stability. Majority control of executive and legislature, which appeared as a separate dimension in the analysis that included the presidential systems, is now positively related to executive stability on the second dimension. If we force the factor analysis to produce a third dimension, majority control does pull away to form that dimension. But the dimension itself is strongly positively correlated with the stability dimension (+ .56). Executive stability and majority control are far from identical in the parliamentary systems, but they do fall, quite clearly, on the same performance dimension.

A second notable, but less powerful and robust, finding from the factor analysis in the parliamentary systems is that executive durability does load positively on the political order dimension. We see here something closer to the expectation by some theorists that all "good" performance measures would support each other. The political order dimension shows fewer deaths by political violence, fewer riots, higher voting turnouts, and more durable chief executives. This finding cannot be pushed too far, however, because the second dimension, which captures the major loading of executive durability and also reflects some degree of legislative control, is weakly negatively related to the first. Moreover, just as in the earlier analysis of the full set of democracies, voting participation is positively related to the general political order dimension, but loads sharply negatively with the government stability dimension.

The major effect of examining compatibility within the parliamentary systems, then, is to find the two measures of government performance more closely related. This analysis reinforces the earlier conclusions favoring the association of more citizen involvement with lower levels of violence, and the distinctiveness of political order and government stability.

Constitution and Culture

Constitutions are man-made designs. These designs reflect the constitution-makers' values, their expectations of the consequences of various arrangements, their often laboriously negotiated compromises.[18] Insofar as constitution-makers have tried to make their constitutions responsive to local needs and conditions, and to avoid negative consequences, associations between constitutional type and democratic performance may reflect those initial efforts, rather than reflect ongoing consequences of the incentives and costs created by the constitution itself. Insofar as the constitution embodies values widely held in a society, both constitutional type and performance pattern may be products of political culture—the configuration of attitudes and beliefs held by citizens and elites in a society[19]—rather than one being a cause of the other.

The inability to measure political culture directly is a grievous limitation of a statistical analysis such as this one. But table 4.3 shows

Table 4.3 Culture and constitutional arrangements.

Cultural influence	Predominate constitution type	Countries fitting type	Exceptions or mixed
American or American-dominated	Presidential executive and majoritarian legislature	U.S. Philippines	West Germany Japan
British or British-dominated or educated	Parliamentary and majoritarian legislature	U.K. Australia Canada Ceylon India Jamaica New Zealand	Ireland
Continental Western Europe and Scandinavia	Parliamentary and representational legislature	Austria Belgium Denmark Finland Israel Italy Netherlands Norway Sweden	France Switzerland
Latin America	Presidential executive and representational legislature	Chile Costa Rica Uruguay Venezuela	(Pre-1967 Uruguay)
Other	Parliamentary and representational legislature	Greece Turkey	

how powerful the relationship is between general culture and constitutional type.

Clearly the fit between cultural background and constitutional type is very strong. Britain and seven of its ex-colonies are marked by the majoritarian parliamentary type, with Ireland, as a country once part of Britain, the only (partial) exception through the period covered by the study. The Latin American countries are all characterized by presidential executives and representational legislatures, except for pre-1967 Uruguay (a collective executive representation system). The United States and its long-time colony the Philippines have presidential systems and single-member-district legislatures. The nations of Western Europe and Scandinavia, as well as Israel whose initial leaders were primarily continental Europeans from the early days of the Zionist movement, typically have parliamentary systems with proportional representation and large multimember legislative districts. France—where DeGaulle installed a presidential system in 1958 to improve stability—and collective executive Switzerland are the exceptions. Japan and West Germany, whose constitutions reflect both some indigenous traditions and American or Anglo-American influence during post–World War II reconstruction, are, appropriately, hybrids of representational and majoritarian patterns.

The individual constitutional histories in these nations include complex bargaining and the emergence of constitutions from elite calculations of party advantage.[20] Despite these idiosyncratic historical events, many of which are indeed reflected in various constitutional provisions, and despite nuances that respond to many local traditions, the general pattern of orientation to representatives and executive control seems very powerfully linked to culture.[21] Indeed, these patterns are so strong that we cannot determine whether constitution-makers' attempts to deal with special environmental problems are playing much of a general role or not. It is true, for example, that the larger and the more ethnically divided countries are more likely to have majoritarian legislatures— usually with single-member districts—than proportional representation. But the cultural background overwhelms all such characteristics in any multivariate considerations, although historical accounts suggest that they played a role in some cases.

Moreover, we cannot be sure whether constitutions affect performance because of the incentives they provide for competition in the political process or because of the cultural values they reflect. Where cultural patterns and constitutional structures seem so closely interwoven, no statistical procedure can adequately disentangle them. In Chapters 5 through 7 I shall try to trace the impact of constitutional arrangements through the intermediate electoral and legislative processes. Where we cannot trace intermediate processes, we cannot determine whether constitutional relationships with performance indicate the effects of certain cultural heritages or the effects of certain decisional arrangements.

Socioeconomic and Constitutional Effects

In the last chapter we saw that size, level of economic development, and ethnic homogeneity all had significant effects on some aspects of democratic performance. As some types of constitutional arrangements are found more frequently in countries with more favorable environmental conditions, we need to examine the association between constitutional types and performance while controlling for the environmental advantages enjoyed by some of the democracies. Some of the associations found so far in this chapter may be spurious effects of environment.

Table 4.4 presents the results of a multivariate regression analysis of environmental advantages and constitutional arrangements. For each measure of performance the table lists the variance explained and then the standardized regression coefficients for the variables of population size, level of economic development, and ethnic homogeneity. These coefficients correspond to those shown in table 3.6 for riots and deaths, except that inequality is eliminated as a variable and consequently more cases can be used. (No data are missing on these variables.) Immediately below the first row of regression coefficients appear the coefficients that emerge when variables for constitutional arrangements are added to the simultaneous regression equation. Comparing the variance explained by the two equations shows how much additional explanatory power is added by considering constitutional differences.

The coefficients for presidential executives and majoritarian representation laws indicate how these relate to each performance measure and how powerful they are. I should point out that the analysis uses the constitutional properties, not a strict dummy variable analysis of the types of constitutions. This approach allows us to see more clearly the separate effects of executive arrangements and legislative election laws, and to make finer distinctions than is possible with the threefold typology.

Table 4.4 Regression analysis of environmental advantages, constitutional arrangements, and political performance (standardized regression coefficients).[a]

Performance dimension	Variance explained	Environmental advantages[b]			Constitutional arrangements[c]		
		Small population	Economic development	Ethnic homogeneity	Presidential executive	Majority electoral laws	Switzerland dummy
Voting participation, 1958–1976	21%	.05	.22	.33*	—	—	—
	58	.11	.32**	−.09	−.26**	−.44**	−.62**
Executive durability, 1967–1976	1	.13	.04	−.09	—	—	—
	44	.18	.03	.32*	.42**	.64**	.38**
Majority control, 1967–1976	12	.22	−.11	−.32	—	—	—
	41	.24	−.26	−.06	−.42**	.40**	.22
Low rioting,[d] 1958–1967	71	.87**	.06	−.11	—	—	—
	72	.90**	.05	−.03	.06	.10	.05
Low rioting,[d] 1967–1979	61	.80**	.12	−.12	—	—	—
	64	.80**	.09	−.13	−.17	−.02	−.03
Low deaths,[d] 1958–1967	76	.34**	.47**	.38**	—	—	—
	81	.28**	.45**	.32**	−.19*	−.11	.01
Low deaths,[d] 1967–1976	61	.27**	.64**	.10	—	—	—
	64	.24*	.62**	.01	−.13	−.20	−.04

a. Standardized regression coefficients are shown for two equations explaining each dependent variable. The first equation includes all environmental variables that were significant in the final analysis in Chapter 3. In the second equation, the constitutional variables are added. Comparing the first and second equations shows the additional explanatory power of the constitutional variables.

b. As in table 3.6. Population size and GNP/capita are logged.

c. From table 4.1 The majoritarian electoral laws variable is coded: single-member districts = 3; Germany, Ireland, Japan = 2; other = 1. Presidential executive variable coded: presidential system = 1; other = 0.

d. Again, extreme outliers on the riots and deaths variables have been truncated to the ninetieth percentile values to prevent bias. A log transformation yields similar results. For voting, 28 cases are used; all 1967–1976 analysis uses 27 cases; all 1958–1967 analysis uses 26 cases.

* = F level over 1.7 (significant at .10).

** F level over 3.0 (significant at .05).

This analysis emphasizes that the constitutional variables have a strong impact on voting and on the government performance measures but a limited impact on the measures of political order. When we enter the constitutional variables, the percentage of variance explained jumps very sharply for the measures of voting turnout, government stability, and majority control, but increases only slightly for the violence measures. Moreover, some of the coefficients for the environmental advantages change notably in the full explanation of voting and government performance but are hardly altered in the violence equations.

In explaining voting turnout, only the level of economic development remains significant as an environmental advantage: even with constitutional factors considered, the more economically developed countries have higher turnout. As expected from the theoretical discussion, both presidential executives and majoritarian election laws are sharply negatively related to turnout. The representational parliamentary systems manifest the highest voting participation, even with size, economic development, and ethnicity controlled. (As is discussed in Chapter 6, Switzerland has very low turnout.)

In explaining government stability and majority control, the constitutional variables dominate the equations, and act just as was predicted theoretically. Both presidential executives and majoritarian election laws are strong predictors of executive durability. The Swiss multiparty executive is also very durable. At the same time, the majoritarian election laws indeed promote majority governments, in which the same party or coalition of parties controls both the executive and the legislature. But the presidential executive arrangements are associated with substantial periods of minority government. The consideration of these relationships with controls does not change, then, the conclusion drawn from table 4.1.

In the analysis of violence, the constitutional differences do not add much to the environmental effects. The variance explained increases only slightly, and few of the coefficients for constitutional variables are significant. To put it another way, most of the advantages of the representational systems discussed early in this chapter, which appear very strong in table 4.1, seem to be artifacts of the location of these systems in more economically developed societies. However, we must not overstate this conclusion. In considering deaths by political violence, *all* the coefficients for presidential executives and majority legislative representation are associated with more deaths. Presidential executives are significantly associated with such violence in the first decade, even after the environmental controls are in the equation. Such executives are also associated with more riots in the second decade, although the relationships are not significant. There remains a tendency for the representational constitutions, with their parliamentary executives and multimember districts, to perform better in maintaining political order.

The patterns of government performance found in this chapter are highly consistent with theoretical expectations. Majoritarian legislative rules of representation are strongly related to more durable executive governments and to executive control of the legislature. Presidential executive arrangements are also strongly associated with more durable executives, but are linked to frequent minority governments. Representational parliamentary governments show both executive instability and frequent loss of majority control. Such constitutional features are much more important than any environmental advantages in explaining governmental performance.

The analysis of voting participation strongly favors one side of the debate about means of getting voters to the polls: the representational parliamentary systems are marked by high voting turnout, while both presidential executive arrangements and majoritarian election laws are strongly related to lower turnout. The analysis of political order yields much less conclusive results. The theoretical debate focuses on whether a strong executive or a representational system is a better way to inhibit disorder. In the data analysis, environmental advantages dominate the explanation of levels of violence. The representational approach does seem to have some net advantage in controlling violence, although few relationships are statistically significant.

Reconsideration of the effects of the environmental advantages that were discussed in Chapter 3 largely reconfirms the conclusions about violence drawn in that chapter, as population size remains the only major factor affecting rioting levels, while size, ethnic homogeneity, and especially level of economic development remain significant in their impact on deaths. However, the strong effects of constitutional arrangements on voting and government performance have some notable impacts on the environmental relationships. The impact of ethnic homogeneity on turnout becomes insignificant with the constitutional controls, but the effect of higher economic development on turnout becomes even clearer.

In the multivariate analysis of environmental relationships and government performance, the introduction of controls for constitutional factors increases the advantage of small population size, although not quite to a level of statistical significance. Still, the arguments of theorists who emphasize the usefulness of small population size for government performance do receive some support.[22] Moreover, an advantage of ethnic homogeneity for more durable executives now becomes apparent. The strong expectations about economic development and executive stability continue to be confounded. (We must keep in mind that we are talking about the durability of party governments and elected presidents, not about the survival of democracy, in most cases.)

The brief consideration of the cultural and geographic bases of constitutional arrangements in this chapter suggests a general problem for the analysis. Different constitutional patterns are quite strongly found in given geographic and cultural areas. It is difficult to be sure if a particular type of constitutional arrangement performs as it does because of the incentives and limitations on behavior that it encourages, or because a given cultural background shapes both constitutional choice and political performance. Insofar as we can solve the problem in this study, it is through tracing the intervening processes that link environment and constitutional setting, on one hand, and political performance on the other. In the chapters ahead I shall turn from testing expectations about relationships to tracing processes and testing hypotheses about linkages proposed in the theories.

Party Systems and Election Outcomes

5

In contemporary democracies political parties are the organizations designed to link citizens and leaders. They aggregate and bring to bear the electoral resources of citizens, individually weak and collectively powerful. Some of the most thoughtful and influential political theorists of our time have seen the system of parties in a society as the key to political performance.[1] Strong party systems, it is argued, both reflect and are indispensable prerequisites for good democratic performance. Weak party systems portend poor democratic performance.

Theorists disagree on how to recognize those "strong" party systems which contribute to positive democratic performance. The disagreements are based in part on different theorists' varying emphases on participation, government stability, and maintaining order as the goals of government performance, and in part on their differing theories about what leads to such performance. One line of thought emphasizes the value of a defractionalized, two-party, "centrist" party system that will aggregate citizens' resources behind governmental majorities responsive to citizen pressures.[2] Another approach emphasizes an expressive, mobilizing system of parties that will pull all major factions in the society into its representative, democratic decisionmaking institutions, co-opting dissent and accommodating demands that might otherwise turn to violence.[3]

The problem of formulating and testing propositions about parties and performance is compounded by the shifting, complex nature of parties and party systems themselves. At one level are the "parties in people's minds," the images citizens have about parties and what they represent.[4] At another level are the parties as sets of organizations, linking activists, members, and leaders through interwoven goals and incentives of various kinds.[5] The images and the organizations interact with each other, and both have, usually, staying power over the course of many elections. There are also party systems as configurations of citizen voting support, and as groupings of representatives in legislative and executive bodies.[6] All of these levels can be described and analyzed in various ways, static and dynamic.

The system of political parties in a society is in part a product of the choices of individual citizens as they work and vote for available parties. The party system is also in part the product of the organizational and strategic efforts of political leaders, as they build policy platforms, penetrate local organizations, enroll local leaders behind them, use patronage to mobilize workers, and the like. The choices of citizens and the efforts of leaders are themselves responses in large measure to the constitutional opportunities and the socioeconomic conditions in which they find themselves. In subsequent chapters I shall return repeatedly to the party system as I trace the linkages between environmental conditions and democratic outcomes. But the general shape of the existing party system at any given time is also a fact of the political environment. Indeed, established party systems are not easily changed, for they represent massive accumulations of organizational effort, political memory, and resource commitments.

This chapter prepares for the transition from a description of the levels of democratic performance associated with various environmental and constitutional variables across political systems, to an analysis of the processes generating these performance levels. The party system is a critical barometer of these processes. The images of "strong" and "weak" party systems constitute a shorthand summary of some of the process dynamics and their implications. Clear measures of the characteristics of party systems are needed that can be used in testing models of the processes of citizen choice and leadership strategy that link environmental conditions with democratic outcomes.

As many party systems have substantial continuity, particularly if their parties' electoral strength is founded on extensive organization, widespread and well reinforced images in citizens' minds,[7] or both, I shall begin by looking at the party systems of the early 1960s. Once established, as Seymour Martin Lipset and Stein Rokkan persuasively argue,[8] parties are not easily dislodged by changing conditions, or even new voting generations; thus we can expect the patterns of the early 1960s to have continuing influence on the politics of the following decade.

Attributes of Party Systems

Theorists conflict in their views on how party fractionalization and cleavage alignments affect the strength of a party system. According to advocates of what might be called "aggregative" party systems, a strong party system will contain a few strong parties, each capable of winning a clear electoral majority. Moreover, these parties should be all oriented toward the political center. Though perhaps representing different policy or group tendencies, they should each contain a variety of cross-cutting factions and work to reconcile or accommodate these.[9] If any party represents too clear-cut an alternative, the threat of dominance and majority control will be too great and the tensions may spill out into violent conflict. Under most conditions, so goes the argument, the limitation of alternatives to only a few options will encourage the parties in a two-party system to offer relatively similar choices, as each party jockeys for a potentially winning position.[10] From this point of view, therefore, we need a measure that will reflect dominance of the party system by a few strong, relatively equal, parties. Closely associated, as broadly aggregative parties are desired, should be an index reflecting the relative absence of close linkages between specific parties and distinct social groups in the society.

The other approaches emphasize the importance of parties in representing the interests of citizens and groups, mobilizing them into the political arena. These points of view reflect both the intrinsic value ascribed to citizen participation and a theoretical argument that it is more important to get groups and individuals involved in the democratic system than to promote the consolidation and aggregation of their resources at the election stage. It is not so important that parties cut across social groups in their electoral support; rather, coalitions across various cleavage lines can be worked out by accommodation-minded political leaders in the legislative arena. A strong party system, in these views, should present clear choices to citizens and groups and link them closely, in this way, to the political process.[11]

One line of thought about such representation calls for "responsible" party systems, which combine the stability of two-party systems with centralization, discipline, and reasonably strong party linkages to groups. Admirers of the British system have long stressed this combination.[12] Students of the smaller European democracies, meanwhile, have tended to emphasize the dangers of majorities, arguing that they threaten minority groups, especially in deeply divided societies. Where parties are strongly linked to social groups, it is important that majorities be avoided; a multiparty representational system offers the best prospects for stable democratic performance.[13]

It is worth noting that virtually no party theorists favor fractionalized parties not linked to social groups. Multiple parties that represent only elite factions and personal followings receive few favorable reviews from party theorists.[14] And in fact, among the 29 contemporary democracies, virtually all of the multiparty systems (except Venezuela in the 1960s) have clear linkages to social groups. Hence, for our purposes, the three major approaches to strong parties agree that party fractionalization and group alignment are relevant measures, but draw different conclusions about their desirability. The advocates of aggregative and responsible party systems favor low fractionalization but disagree about whether strong linkages between groups and parties are desirable. The representational theorists favor substantial fractionalization, as it prevents majority domination, and consider strong linkages essential. This confrontation follows much the same line of argument as the debate between majoritarian and representational constitutional theorists that was discussed in the last chapter. Indeed, the party systems associated with and shaped by the constitutional arrangements establish, in theory, the major processes linking constitutional settings and democratic performance.

All of the theorists favor parties that are committed to maintaining democracy itself, and committed to policy changes that can be bargained with or are not too divergent from the positions held by other parties. Even the representational approach recognizes the difficulty created by extremist parties with whom other parties cannot bargain or join in coalitions. However, the aggregative approach sees it as more desirable to submerge such factions within major parties, or deny them representation, while the representational approach argues that they should be given some direct stake in the constitutional process: that is, that they should be represented in the legislature.

There is, therefore, substantial convergence between party theorists on problems of extremism, hostility, and polarization. Party systems characterized by such properties are less likely to contribute to successful democratic performance. Similarly, most theorists believe that the parties themselves must agree to keep their competition within the constitutional arena and to control the amount of conflict among them. According to the representational view, however, simply submerging the attitudes that lead to support for extremist parties will not solve the problem they create for democratic politics, and an artificially defractionalized party system will not guarantee democratic performance unless it can positively mobilize group support. Majoritarian theorists, meanwhile, suggest that a multiplicity of parties in itself encourages extremism, as the parties lack the incentive to seek majority victories by converging on a median position. Hence, to argue that minority systems are desirable as long as they are not extremist is to miss a principal dynamic element in the majoritarian argument.

Finally, most lines of thought about parties agree that *volatility* in voting support for parties is a symptom of weak party systems. When voters continually support the same parties, with only relatively minor changes in balances of support, the parties evidently are satisfying important needs of the voters. Rapid and continuing shifts in support for parties are undesirable both as symptoms of citizen dissatisfaction and because they make it difficult to develop stable government policies.

Expectations about Party Systems and Performance   Attributes of party systems are explicitly linked to theoretical expectations about performance in table 5.1. I must reemphasize that the arguments in favor of multiparty systems assume that the parties are firmly linked to social groups, and are not merely personalistic leadership factions. Given such linkage, all sides of the theoretical controversy would probably expect substantial voting participation in multiparty systems. But the advocates of aggregative and responsible party systems expect multiple parties to be associated with unstable governments and with difficulties in maintaining the political order. Scholars such as Karl Bracher have attributed the overthrow of democracy in Weimar Germany and the upheavals that ended the French Fourth Republic in part to their multiparty systems.[15] The representational theorists, by contrast, think that multiparty systems can work out stable coalition governments as long as extremism is kept in check. They argue that the absence of single-party majorities will prevent abuse of political power by any one faction and will encourage involvement of all groups in the legitimate political process, thus inhibiting political disorder.

Strong alignments between groups and parties should encourage citizen involvement by making the electoral contest meaningful to many citizens. Such alignments are viewed with disfavor, however, by aggregative theorists. They are often skeptical of the desirability of citizen involvement, and they argue that parties drawing nearly equally on all social and political groups are needed to reconcile conflicting interests before these are mobilized to dangerous conflict. A party's internal diversity of interests, according to the aggregative argument, encourages it to be responsive to legitimate complaints from many sources while providing it with the strength to resist extremists. Both

Table 5.1 Theoretical expectations about party-system attributes and political performance.

	Performance Expectations		
Party-system attributes	Participation	Government stability	Maintaining political order
Fractionalization /multiparty systems[a]	High/moderate	Conflicting predictions	Conflicting predictions
Strong party linkages to social groups	High	Conflicting predictions	Conflicting predictions
Strong support for extremist parties	Moderate	Low	Low
Volatility of support for parties	Low	Low	Low

a. The arguments for multiparty systems assume that such systems reflect strong linkages between social groups and political parties and apply only with that condition.

responsible and representational theorists, meanwhile, doubt the ability of such diffuse, "catch-all" parties to govern effectively, because of their internal diversity, and suspect that the absence of strong ties between groups and individual parties will exclude important groups from the political process. Hence, such theorists favor strong linkages between groups and parties.

The table also indicates the largely negative implications of extremism and volatility as seen by most theorists. Extremism may either be associated with active mobilization of voters or their alienation in the face of unpalatable choices. But if extremist parties gain entry to the legislature, their presence will make governing more difficult. The constant presentation of demands for a reconstruction of the regime may make gradual accommodation of interests and the redress of injustice less likely. The prospect of major change in the regime is bound to threaten those advantaged by the present system, and thus to encourage violence and turmoil. Of course, the very real grievances that underlie extremist positions cannot be dismissed by observing that they make political performance more difficult. The point here is that support for parties calling for major changes in the boundaries of the nation, the regime's political structure, or the fundamental social and economic arrangements of the society reflects previous political failures *and* creates continuing performance problems. Strong party systems should be able to avoid the emergence of this kind of rejection of the present system. Similarly, strong party systems should be able to keep steady masses of supporters behind them. Where voting support does undergo volatile shifts, it is likely that voter mobilization will be uneven and uncertain, that governing will be made more difficult by uncertainties about future suppport, and that turmoil will be more frequent.

Fractionalization

The most widely discussed property of party systems is their fractionalization: the degree to which they are dominated by a few parties or divided among many parties. A great deal of time and energy have been devoted to analyzing the relative merits of two-party and multiparty systems. Various points of demarcation between the two have been suggested.[16] I have not found, empirically, that any particular dividing point is helpful; it seems most appropriate to use the simple, elegant measure of fractionalization suggested by Rae, which represents the probability that two legislators chosen at random will represent different parties.[17] Multiplying this probability by 100 yields the fractionalization index, which ranges between zero and 100: it is zero when one party is completely dominant and 100 when every legislator represents a different party.

Although the fractionalization index can be slightly misleading when there is one large party and a number of small ones, it is usually a good guide to party configuration. Fractionalization scores around 50 imply evenly balanced two-party systems. Scores below 55 suggest likely single-party majorities, while those over 60 are very seldom associated with single-party election victories. In the democracies, the smallest fractionalization indices are found in the two-party systems, such as the United States, Austria, Jamaica, New Zealand, the Philippines, Britain, and Costa Rica, all of whose fractionalization scores were around 50 in the 1960s. The highest fractionalization scores were found in Denmark, Switzerland, the Netherlands, and Finland, where the legislatures were divided among five or more small parties and scores ran around 80. These fractionalization measures are based simply on the party as a unit, and do not indicate either intraparty factions or interparty alliances and coalitions, some of which will be discussed in Chapters 7 and 8.

The fractionalization index can also be used to describe party voting configurations.[18] As different election laws convert voting patterns into legislative representation in different ways, there are some differences

Table 5.2 Party-system fractionalization in the early 1960s:[a] Bases in election laws and social heterogeneity.

Social heterogeneity	Country and basis of heterogeneity[b]	Party fractionalization		Average fractionalization	
		Votes	Seats	Votes	Seats
Majoritarian election laws					
Homogeneous	Jamaica	50	47		
	United Kingdom	59	50	60	53
	New Zealand	62	51		
	Australia	67	63		
Heterogeneous	India (E, R)	75	47		
	Ceylon (E, R)	75	73		
	Philippines (E)	51	48		
	Japan (A)	62	54	65	57
	Ireland (A)	63	62		
	France (A)	80	69		
	West Germany (R)	61	58		
	Canada (E, R)	67	62		
	U.S. (E, R)	49	44		
Representational election laws					
Homogeneous	Turkey	63	67		
	Costa Rica	58	54		
	Greece	65	59	63	60
	Austria	58	54		
	Sweden	71	69		
Heterogeneous	Chile (A)	76	65		
	Uruguay (A)	59	57		
	Venezuela (A)	79	76		
	Italy (A)	78	73		
	Finland (A)	82	80	75	71
	Norway (A)	72	69		
	Denmark (A)	74	72		
	Netherlands (R)	79	77		
	Belgium (E)	68	63		
	Switzerland (E, R)	82	79		

Sources: Computed from Mackie and Rose, *International Electoral Almanac; Keesing's Archives;* and various county sources.

a. From elections in 1960–1965 period.

b. Basis of heterogeneity: A = 20–45% employed in agriculture; E = ethnic fractionalization over 45; R = Catholic/Protestant or other religious division. Within each category, countries are listed in order of increasing GNP/capita in 1965.

between vote and representation, and the extent of these varies with constitutional and electoral arrangements. Table 5.2 shows both voting and legislative fractionalization of parties in the party systems of the early 1960s. These two measures are strongly related (r = .86), but each has more relevance for some purposes. As an indication of diversity in citizen choice, vote fractionalization is more important; in terms of the impact on government stability and ongoing party strategies, legislative fractionalization is more significant.

How is the fractionalization of the party system related to the social and constitutional environment? The most famous answer to this question was given by Maurice Duverger in his pathbreaking comparative study of political parties. Duverger wrote, *"the simple-majority single-ballot system favors the two-party system*...Of all the hypotheses that have been defined in this book, this approaches most nearly perhaps to a true sociological law."[19] His analysis leads to the expectation that majority-oriented electoral rules, above all the simple-plurity, single-ballot, single-member-district formulation of the Anglo-American type, encourage two-party systems, while proportional representation (PR) and multimember districts encourage multiparty systems.

There are a number of reasons why single-member districts discourage legislative fractionalization. Single-member-district systems shut out of the legislature any parties that do not carry pluralities in geographic districts. Thus, various minority groups offering their own parties are excluded unless they are highly geographically concentrated. Equally important, such groups are encouraged to form broader alliances in order to gain representation in the long run. Hence, many groups that might have sought direct representation under proportional representation do not even compete in a system of single-member districts. Or, if they do compete, voters do not waste votes supporting them.[20] It is also likely that the probability that some party will gain a national majority encourages opposing parties to coalesce into large parties, or at least pre-electoral coalitions.[21] Seeking legislative representation as a minority party may be highly useful in nonmajority systems; it is less so where one party is likely to win. In these ways, single-member districts (and various cut-off laws) shape long-term party strategies as well as the immediate translation of votes into seats.

Duverger was careful not to ascribe overwhelming power to such tendencies. He compared the influence of ballot systems to that of a brake or accelerator. The most decisive influences driving the multiplication of parties were to be found, he wrote, in "aspects of the life of the nation such as ideologies and particularly the socio-economic structure."[22]

Various scholars have quarreled with Duverger's emphasis on the electoral laws, pointing out that in a number of countries proportional representation was chosen as a compromise to save older parties threatened by new forces, and arguing that the electoral laws should be seen as consequences, not causes, of party division. While there is some truth in this argument in specific cases, we saw in the last chapter that cultural ideas about representation seem to dominate the broad differences in electoral systems, and overwhelm strategic party considerations. In his study of the origins of electoral systems, Stein Rokkan similarly concluded that proportional representation was eventually introduced in most European nations through interparty bargaining, but that "in the Anglo-Saxon countries this type of PR never caught on. There were strong party organizations, but there was also a strong tradition of direct territorial representation through individual representatives."[23]

In table 5.2 the countries are first grouped by electoral systems. It is primarily the Anglo-American countries and the constitutions developed under their tutelage that adopted the majority-oriented electoral systems. These electoral laws, in turn, encourage more consolidated, defractionalized party systems. The average fractionalization index of votes in these systems in the early 1960s was 63; the fractionalization index of seats in the legislature only 56. In contrast, the PR systems show a fractionalization index of 71 for votes, and 67 for seats.

The double effect of the majoritarian electoral laws in both encouraging consolidation of electoral parties and reducing legislative fractionalization is very evident. As Rae points out, all the electoral laws tend to reduce fractionalization of seats, in comparison to votes, and to reward the larger parties, but this is especially true of single-member-district plurality systems.[24] An example is the difficulty of small "third " parties in Britain, New Zealand, and Canada, where the electoral laws tend to shut them out of the legislature, as their votes are wasted unless concentrated in a few districts, and where seat fractionalization therefore is sharply reduced. In India, the vote fractionalization of opposition parties allowed the Congress party to capture 73 percent of the seats with only 45 percent of the votes and reduce legislative fractionalization accordingly.

However, Duverger, Anthony Downs,[25] and others are no doubt correct in thinking that the electoral laws operate *on* the clusters of opinion found in the society, as parties focus around these or ignore them. In a very homogeneous society, with few differences on issues, even a PR system probably wll not sustain many parties. In a sharply fragmented country, by contrast, parties will find various specialized lines of appeal, and multipartyism will be likely unless the electoral and constitutional system encourages consolidation. The problem here is to discern likely bases of party division, so as to contrast the societies with homogeneous and heterogeneous tendencies.

Table 5.2 does this in a very loose fashion, by contrasting societies having large ethnic, religious, and agricultural minorities with societies in which such subgroupings are less prominent. The measure of ethnic cleavage from Chapter 3 is useful again here. Countries in the top third of the ethnic division, or with a mixed Catholic-Protestant religious composition, or with an agricultural minority of 20–45 percent of the work force are indicated as heterogeneous. Other countries are designated as homogeneous. As the table shows, heterogeneity is associated with more fractionalized party systems, as are representational electoral laws. It is especially interesting that the degree of modernization does not have a simple linear effect. Both homogeneous traditional societies and homogeneous modern ones have less fractionalization. It is the middle levels, where large agricultural and modern sectors coexist, creating large social minorities that are divided in partisanship, that are most fractionalized. The particular difficulties experienced by societies at these middle levels of development, where agricultural interests and values are threatened by the dominating industrial sector, are often markedly reflected in their party systems.[26]

To observe these tendencies is not to deny the critical nature of historic party struggles and unique national events in shaping party outcomes. For example, the World War II experiences of foreign invasion and resistance clearly sharpened and altered the Communist-Socialist cleavage in the party systems of France, Italy, and Finland. In Uruguay a two-party system survived despite proportional representation and an agricultural minority, in part because of historical events in the 1930s, in part because the electoral law allowed a combination of personal contestation and intraparty coalition, in part because the collective executive encouraged parties to combine under a united electoral rubric. In Sweden the old Agrarian Center party lingers on in a very modernized nation, seeking a new role. But such historical events in individual countries create only partial exceptions within the pattern shaped by broad features of the constitutional and social structure.

Parties and Social Groups

While theorists disagree, as we have seen, on the significance of strong alignments between parties and social groups for democratic performance, few deny their importance in shaping the form and content of national political dialogue. the primary concern here is with measuring the strength of alignment. The nature of the groups—especially the predominance of class or religious groups—has major policy implications as well, as chapter 9 will show. It is worth taking a careful look at the bases and strength of party relationships with major social groups in the different party systems.

A decade ago in their influential essay on voter alignments and party systems in Western Europe, Lipset and Rokkan observed great continuity in the fundamental patterns of citizen support for the political parties in many nations. Historical events created enduring social and economic cleavages in each society. With the extension of the franchise and the mobilization of citizens into political participation, the organizational efforts and strategies of the political parties created alignments between the social and economic groups and the parties. These alignments, largely shaped in Western Europe between the late 1800s and 1920, could be used surprisingly effectively to explain voter support for parties in the 1960s.[27] Above all, the religious faith of the population was powerfully associated with the pattern of voter alignment. In countries where Catholicism had triumphed, as in Austria, France, Belgium, and Italy, citizens' religious involvement and attitudes toward the church were the most powerful predictor of party support. In countries where Protestantism was predominant, the role of religion in politics was largely unimportant by the early twentieth century. In Britain and the Scandinavian countries, for example, occupational divisions were much more important than religious ones. In the religiously divided countries—the Netherlands, Germany, and Switzerland—the religious factor was critical and included both a Protestant-Catholic division and a division between religious and nonreligious groups. These alignments could be inferred fairly directly from inspection of the party systems. Survey research analyses of the bases of party support in Western Europe supported these inferences.[28]

Many complexities of timing, historic conditions, organizational skills, and strategies create nuances in party formation and alignment. But the approach used by Lipset and Rokkan, identifying the major alignments of occupational, religious, and ethnic characteristics with party support, is a useful place from which to consider the mediating role of political parties between social environment and democratic outcome.

In considering the alignments of groups and parties across the full set of contemporary democracies, it is important to take into account the levels of modernization of the societies at the time of party development, as well as the differing religious and ethnic divisions of the societies. At the time when parties were formed in Western Europe, most of the nations were well into the industrial revolution. With the significant exceptions of Italy and Ireland, they had substantial industrial sectors. Except for Italy they were marked by relatively well-defined national structures of communication and interdependent national economies. In comparison with the nations of Asia, Africa, and Latin America today, they were quite modernized. Even Italy, less modernized and unified than most of Europe, had in the Catholic church a powerful national organization. In less modernized countries, it is difficult for party leaders to create national organizations. Illiteracy and weak mass media limit the development of distinctive awareness in citizens of their group identifications at the national level, as opposed to their local ties to village and patron.

The "traditional society" is characterized by an agriculturally based economic and social life, in which most citizens are illiterate peasants, living on the land and producing barely enough for their own families' sustenance. As a slightly more modern agricultural basis begins to create some surplus that can be sold to an outside market, various brokers appear to mediate between the traditional peasant society and the unfamiliar world beyond its borders. Commonly, these brokers are local elites, who agree to provide land, equipment, marketing services, loans, protection from bandits, negotiations with government officials and tax collectors, and even the arrangement of such general public works as roads and technical agricultural assistance stations. The clients provide labor for their patron's land, personal service for his family, and such political resources as are available—in a democracy this typically includes voting as directed by the patron. These patron-client relations are characterized by a highly personalistic pattern of exchange, and by a built-in advantage for the patron, who usually has many clients and hence needs each of them less than each of them needs him. Depending on traditional landholding patterns and cultural variations, as well as the degree of scarcity and isolation, the relationships may take on a more or less exploitative character.[29]

In a social structure in which most citizens are involved in personal patron-client relationships, the patrons will be the essential links between most citizens and the centers of political power. It will be difficult to mobilize citizens on the basis of national group appeals or organizations, because their orientations will be to the locality and the patron, and the critical exchanges of favors with the patron, rather than to the general interests of "peasants" or "poor people," or "rural people." Unless there is great inequality in ownership of land, it will be difficult for mass political conflict to emerge along occupational lines. Most citizens will share similar lifestyles; the most salient social links will tie them to patrons and others in their own village (or perhaps the new urban neighborhoods). Parties will have to create support by organizing local leaders.[30]

In modern, industrialized settings, the context of social life is vastly different from that in a traditional society. Modern economies rely on specialization. Individuals come to perform economically specialized tasks, and these occupational experiences create needs and interests that are similar among those with similar occupations, but differentiated from those in other occupations. Factory workers, white-collar office workers, small-business proprietors, professionals, managers, and farmers develop different interests and identifications, and become more dependent on national economic fortunes and policies rather than the immediate village setting. Unemployment, inflation, agricultural and industrial protection policies, marketing and production standards, and other matters of government policy have meaning for these occupational groups, even though a given group may be geographically diverse. The possibility of organizing parties through appealing to these occupational groups and organizations is promising, especially if the occupational differences go with systematic income and status inequality—as they usually do.

We would expect, then, all kinds of party alignments to be more blurred in the less modernized societies, and the importance of patronage and local leadership to be more pronounced. Above all, voting along occupational lines would be infrequent as a basis of party division in the less modernized societies. Where the majority of the population consists of peasants and agricultural workers, and the urban population is largely composed of migrants seeking temporary jobs, the creation of strong class-voting alignments will be difficult at best. Such strong alignments as are formed between parties and groups at the early stages of modernization will probably emphasize religious or ethnic attachments.

Strength and Types of Alignments   Available survey data from 23 of the democracies make it possible to test and compare these expectations about group and party alignments. The missing countries are among the less modernized, and the surveys in all such countries are less reliable, so the data must be viewed with care. But the general impressions are quite consistent with our expectations, and with other studies of the party systems in these nations. Table 5.3 shows the democracies, grouped by their levels of socioeconomic modernization and their major ethnic and religious cleavages. In the last column is a description of the major line-up of parties and groups in the party system, as characterized by informed observers' studies. The indices of alignment between parties and groups reflect the averages of all the available comparable surveys in the 1960–1976 period, not merely the early 1960s.[31]

The measures of alignment draw on the concept of "class voting" introduced by Robert Alford and explored further by Arend Lijphart.[32] In each country we divide the citizens into two major groups, each containing at least a third of the citizens. The groups are based on occupation of the head of the family. We can then compare the percentage of workers voting for "left" parties with the percentage of nonworkers voting for these parties. Thus, in Sweden in 1964, 84 percent of the manual workers voted for the Social Democrats or the Communists, while only 32 percent of those in other occupations did so. The difference between these two percentages is 52, which is the "index of class voting" in Sweden in that year. In the United States, in contrast, in 1964, 78 percent of the manual workers favored the Democrats over the Republicans, while 61 percent of those in other occupations did so— yielding a "class support index" of only 17 for that year. Religion is treated similarly: in Italy in 1968 some 77 percent of the churchgoers voted for the Christian Democrats, while only 34 percent of the nonchurchgoers did so. The difference of 43 is the religious voting index for Italy for that year. The data in table 5.3 are based where possible on the party preferences of all citizens having a preference, rather than on voters alone. In subsequent discussions I shall refer to the stronger index score (whether of class or religion) as the party-group alignment index.

The data on such alignments generally support the expectations from modernization theory. The less modernized countries in general had lower levels of either class or religious-ethnic distinctiveness in their alignments. The average alignment score for the stronger cleavage was 19 in the less modern countries, and 41 in the more modern ones. Of the countries on which data are lacking, secondary studies suggest only Ceylon as a case where parties have effectively organized support along national cleavage lines: the Sri Lanka Freedom Party's mobilization of Sinhalese nationalism and Buddhist religiosity. Indeed, some of these numbers probably overstate the case somewhat: the Philippines' score comes from summing up various ethnic-religious factions who favored or opposed Marcos in 1965. As various scholars have pointed out, these alignments of ethnicity in the Philippines tended to shift with realignment of local groups and leaders into the parties, rather than represent stable citizen support.[33] Only in the somewhat more modernized systems of Chile and Japan are citizens more stably aligned behind parties or blocs of parties along social-class lines. Even in these two nations, patronage and blurring alignments and realignments of specific leaders have great influence on the relationship between class and party support.

In the more modernized nations of Western Europe, Canada, New Zealand, and Australia, the voting alignments of citizens are more clearly linked to demographic groups. As we expect from the Lipset and Rokkan analysis and the work of Richard Rose and Lijphart, religion is an important factor.[34] In the Catholic countries and those with substantial Catholic populations, religion is usually a major predictor of party support. Typically, the Catholics or frequent church attenders are less likely to vote for the parties of the left. The United States and Canada are the exceptions here, with in general quite weak alignments of demography and party, and with the Catholic populations inclining to the more leftist of the rather centrist major parties in both countries. In ethnically and religiously homogeneous nations—Scandinavia, Britain, New Zealand, and Australia—class voting is pronounced. It is quite clear that the presence of substantial Catholic populations tends to limit class voting in the nations with Catholic subcultures, as Catholic parties often pull substantial working-class support across the lines of class to support rightist or centrist parties. There is some suggestion that ethnicity may also tend to weaken class voting, and perhaps even religious voting, for similar reasons.

In addition to a society's historical cleavages and its level of modernization, its constitutional arrangements affect the alignments between parties and groups, just as they do the fractionalization of parties. The single-member-district electoral laws and other majority-oriented rules seem to weaken or discourage strong linkages between groups and parties. Representation-oriented rules are strongly as-

Table 5.3 Social structure and party-group alignments.

Modernization 1965[a]	Cultural cleavage 1960s[b]	Country	Indices of party-group alignments		General description of alignments
			Class	Religion/ ethnicity	
Predominantly traditional	Ethnic fragmentation	India	13	9	National patron-client
		Ceylon	low	moderate	Religious/ethnic client
		Philippines	4	20	Local patron-client
	Catholic subculture only	Costa Rica	low	low	National patron-client
	Homogeneous	Turkey	low	low/ moderate	National patron-client
		Jamaica	18	low	National patron-client
Mixed traditional and modern	Ethnic fragmentation	—	—	—	—
	Catholic subculture only	Chile	24	26	Religion, class, client
		Uruguay	low	low	National patron-client
		Venezuela	8	13	National patron-client
		Ireland	21	5	National patron-client
	Homogeneous	Greece	low/ moderate	low	Mixed patron-client, class
		Japan	24	low	Class, national patron-client

Modern with traditional sector	Ethnic fragmentation	—	—	—	—
	Catholic subculture only	Italy	17	40	Religion
		Austria	36	49	Religion, class
		France	20	34	Religion
	Homogeneous	Finland	55	low	Class
		Norway	40	17	Class
		Denmark	47	low	Class
Predominantly modern	Ethnic fragmentation (also Catholic)	Belgium	24	50	Religion, class
		Switzerland	22	45	Religion, localized
		Canada	6	28	Heterogeneous, religion
		U.S.	18	20	Heterogeneous
	Catholic subculture only	Netherlands	17	64	Religion (class)
		West Germany	20	36	Religion
	Homogeneous	U.K.	38	13	Class
		New Zealand	42	low	Class
		Australia	33	16	Class
		Sweden	46	23	Class

a. See table 3.2

b. See table 3.3.

c. The index of class alignment is the percentage of voters in working-class occupations who supported left parties minus the percentage of voters in other occupations who did so. Religious and ethnic alignments are similarly calculated.

sociated with stronger linkages between groups and parties. Two theoretical reasons for this pattern may be offered. First, in the proportional systems parties can win seats by appealing to small, geographically dispersed groups, such as small businessmen, whose distinctive importance and support are blurred in the broader coalitions needed to win whole districts. Second, where the rules make pure majorities likely, strong pressure exists to move to a "centrist" median position to try to win the election. As the work of Downs and other formal theorists suggests, parties can indulge in noncentrist appeals in majoritarian systems only at the risk of permanent minority status.[35] This pressure to move to the center will make parties more alike and blur the clarity of ties between parties and groups. The more difficult the entry of new parties, the more compelling the logic of moving toward the center of the national spectrum, although centralization and district differences, nominations, and the role of activists will countervail.[36] Differences are quite sharp: the average party-group alignment index score is 33 in the modernized societies with majority-oriented arrangements and 49 in the modern societies with representation-oriented ones. In the traditional societies, the electoral effects are not pronounced, but there are few cases with data, and the apparently cleavage-weakening effects of presidential systems are hard to disentangle.

It is worth emphasizing the similarities and differences between the basis of party fractionalization and the strength of national alignments between parties and groups. Proportional representation and other representation-oriented election laws contribute sharply to both. Presidential systems tend to diminish both, but their effect is weaker and less certain. Social heterogeneity encourages party fractionalization but has no effect on strength of alignments. If anything, some aspects of heterogeneity, such as ethnic divisions, may weaken the class and religious alignments upon which most of these party systems are founded. Modernization has no apparent effects on fractionalization of party systems, but is strongly related to strength of party-group alignments, at least through the industrialization phase.

Extremist Parties

Extremism, the promise of radical change in the social, economic, and political fabric, is threatening to democratic stability.[37] It may imply a commitment to alter the democratic rules. Or it may lead other groups to abandon their support of democracy in fear of the extremist policies. In the case of an extremist contender like the Nazi party in Weimar

Germany, the party promised to do away with the democratic regime—and kept its promise. In Greece in 1967 the army's fear of what the leftists might do if they came to power precipitated a military coup. In Chile in the early 1970s the extremist nature of the government's promises and policies encouraged violent conflict from the threatened middle- and upper-class groups, even though the government professed its commitment to democratic rules. Even where extremist parties do not come to power, they often make stable and effective government more difficult or complicate the introduction of gradual, acceptable social change, as we shall see in Chapters 6 to 8.

Table 5.4 shows the support for extremist parties in the democracies in the early 1960s.[38] Following a convention long used in comparative analysis, I distinguish here between two types of extremist parties, "contenders" and "protest parties." Although occasionally arbitrary, the distinction is informative. Extremist contenders are parties that promise radical changes, gain sufficient voting support to be perceived as serious contenders for political power, and hold a relatively stable base of organization and citizen commitment. The most clear-cut cases of extremist contenders in the democracies in the early 1960s are the Communist parties of Italy, France, and Finland. Holding about a quarter of the citizen voting support, linked to an external power, calling for fundamental economic and political change, demonstrating solid support over time, these three parties meet every criterion of extremist contenders, and they had a major impact on politics in these nations. The combined Communist and Socialist parties in Chile fall into a similar category, as the Socialist party was long further to the left than European Socialist parties, although in Chile the organization and bases of support were less firmly established.

The other important extremist contenders in the early 1960s might include the Socialist People's party in Denmark, which carried about only 6 percent of the vote but was strong enough to be potentially critical in a party system as fractionalized as that of Denmark. In India and Ceylon the Communist or Trotskyite parties had small but notable footholds on the far left. In India the anti-Moslem Jan Sangh was appealing on a different dimension. And although it is not shown in the table, a case could be made for considering the SLFP in Ceylon, with a strongly anti-Tamil, anti-Hindu set of appeals to Sinhalese ethnic nationalism, as an extremist party also. However, the SLFP had come to power in 1960, and its changes proved less radical than initial promises had suggested.

It is probably dangerous to attempt too broad an explanation of the existence of these stable extremist contenders in the early 1960s. Unique historical events in each country consolidated extremist potential. In Italy and France the role of the Communists in the Resistance during World War II gave them a critical advantage over more moderate Socialist parties. In Finland, the Civil War of the 1920s and Finland's proximity to Russia are important influences on the strength of the Communist party. The absence of a strong Communist party in Germany is partly a result of the division of the country after World War II and of the virtual extermination of the Communists under Nazi rule.

John Kautsky traced the mobilization and then decline of Communist party membership crossnationally in terms of the level of modernization.[39] All the strong Communist contenders (over 10 percent of the electorate) are found in countries where between a quarter and a half of the work force is employed in agriculture. The largely agricultural countries give the next most support to the Communists or the far left, and the nonagricultural, modern nations the least. This fact is consistent with Barrington Moore's argument that societies entering their modernized period with large traditional sectors intact face serious internal conflicts.[40] However, the marked changes in size of the agricultural sector that took place in some countries during the 1960s did not do much to weaken the Communist parties once they were established.

Another way of considering Kautsky's point is to think of agricultural minorities as an example of social heterogeneity, arguing that social minorities of all kinds are potential foci of extremist appeals if they are excluded from power. Although, as already noted, ethnicity is not a major source of cleavage in most societies, it obviously is a focus of extremist party activity in a few, as in India and Belgium. The data do suggest that social heterogeneity is associated with voting support for extremist parties. Of course, it is not necessarily the minority that votes for the extremist party. Minorities may also be a focus of majority-group fears, prompting members of the majority to support extremist parties.

A protest party is a party representing relatively diffuse protest against the present society, either from the right or from the left. The classic example is the "Poujadist" party of France of the mid-1950s, which came from nowhere, behind the antitax movement led by Pierre Poujade, to capture over 11 percent of the vote. Often such parties, unlike contenders, have no real expectation of taking or sharing power. Often they are parties of "surge and decline" whose support rests on sudden, intense citizen dissatisfaction, but which fall apart in subsequent campaigns, as they have no sustaining base of support.

Table 5.4 suggests that citizen support for extremist parties, especially

Table 5.4 Support for extremist parties in the 1960s, by election laws and social heterogeneity.

Social heterogeneity	Country and basis of heterogeneity[a]	Vote support[b] for		Average total extremist vote
		Extremist contenders	Protest parties	
	Majoritarian election laws			
Homogeneous	Jamaica	0	0	
	U.K.	0	0	
	New Zealand	0	0	0
	Australia	0	0	
Heterogeneous	India (E, R)	16	2	
	Ceylon (E, R)	10	0	
	Philippines (E)	0	0	
	Japan (A)	0	4	
	Ireland (A)	0	2	7%
	France (A)	22	3	
	West Germany (R)	0	2	
	Canada (E, R)	0	0	
	U.S. (E, R)	0	0	
	Representational election laws			
Homogeneous	Turkey	0	9	
	Costa Rica	0	0	
	Greece	15	0	6%
	Austria	0	0	
	Sweden	0	5	
Heterogeneous	Chile (A)	22	0	
	Uruguay (A)	0	5	
	Venezuela (A)	0	5	
	Italy (A)	25	6	
	Finland (A)	22	2	
	Norway (A)	0	5	11%
	Denmark (A)	6	3	
	Netherlands (R)	0	0	
	Belgium (E)	0	7	
	Switzerland (E, R)	0	2	

a. Basis of heterogeneity: A = 20–45% employed in agriculture; E = ethnic fractionalization over .45; R = Catholic/Protestant or other religious division.

b. See Appendix for specific parties classified as extremist. Most elections are from about 1965, with Belgium, Denmark, France, India, and Norway earlier in the 1960s. In some countries, small parties with 3% or less may not have been identified.

protest parties, is encouraged by representation-oriented constitutional arrangements. These present few barriers to small parties, and the proportional representation approach, especially with large districts, can gain representation for a party that appeals to the grievances of a rather small group. The table indicates that both social heterogeneity and proportional representation are associated with party extremism, as they were with fractionalization in table 5.2, although unique historical events are especially important in extremism.

Volatility of Party Strength

Most observers view rapid changes in the pattern of support for parties as evidence of weakness in party systems. Both aggregational and representational theorists expect strong party systems to exhibit relatively stable patterns of party support. Of course, the electoral laws in a given country may act to exaggerate swings in voting support into much wider swings in party representation. This typical property of single-member-district systems contributes to their ability to elect party majorities. The volatility of the underlying pattern of citizen support for parties, therefore, is presumably a more important indication of party-system weakness than the legislative outcomes.

Table 5.5 presents a measure of voting volatility for the different types of party systems. The measure was proposed by Adam Przeworski and John Sprague as an indication of failure in party institutionalization.[41] It can be thought of as representing the net transfer of votes from each party to others: take the percentage of votes added *or* lost by each party in the present election, as compared to the previous election, sum up the absolute values of these numbers, and divide by two. A new party adds all its new votes; a party that no longer exists adds all of its previous votes.

In Britain in the 1966 election, for example, the Labour party gained 4 percent; the Liberals lost about 2.5 percent; and the Conservatives lost 1.5 pecent. These total to about 8 percent; dividing by two leaves a net vote volatility score of about 4 percent for the 1966 election. This figure is rather low compared to the average volatility score of around 10 percent for all the party systems in these elections of the early 1960s. The volatility in number of legislative representatives was somewhat greater: Labour picked up 9 percent in 1966, the Liberals gained a small fraction, and the Conservatives lost 10 percent, for a total legislative volatility score of about 9.5 percent.

Table 5.5 Volatility in party voting support and legislative representation in the early 1960s, by modernization level and constitutional type.

Type of constitution	Country	Voting volatility	Legislative volatility	Averages of volatility	
				Votes	Seats
Traditional or transitional					
Presidential	Philippines	15	15		
	Costa Rica	7	4	23	24
	Chile	29	44		
	Venezuela	39	33		
Majoritarian	India	14	6		
	Ceylon	6	26		
	Jamaica	1	5	7	9
	Japan	5	3		
	Ireland	10	6		
Representational	Greece	20	22		
	Turkey	13	13	13	14
	Uruguay	7	7		
Modernized					
Presidential	France	19	11		
	U.S.	5	8	12	10
Majoritarian	U.K.	4	10		
	New Zealand	6	1		
	West Germany	5	4	6	6
	Canada	10	7		
	Australia	5	9		
Representational	Italy	7	8		
	Austria	6	3		
	Finland	5	7		
	Norway	7	4		
	Belgium	5	4	5	5
	Denmark	2	2		
	Netherlands	5	6		
	Sweden	3	4		
	Switzerland	5	5		

Sources: Computed from data in Mackie and Rose, *International Electoral Almanac; Keesing's Archives.* The volatility measure is the sum of the percentage of votes (or seats) gained or lost by each party (taken as an absolute value) divided by two.

Table 5.5 shows how volatility relates to constitutional arrangements and to general level of modernization. Not very surprisingly, the more modern societies manifest more stable party systems, at least in terms of voting volatility in the early 1960s. The modern systems are only about half as volatile as their transitional or traditional counterparts. This no doubt reflects in large part their longer periods of stable constitutional arrangements and sustained citizen involvement. (France, with its numerous constitutional changes, was highly volatile.) Social heterogeneity does not have any significant impact on volatility.

Interestingly enough, electoral laws do not seem to have much net effect on voting volatility. The typically few, large parties in single-member-district systems experience the same amount of net vote transfers as the more numerous, smaller parties in the proportional representative systems. Nor does net volatility in number of legislative seats differ much between the two systems; exaggeration of major-party swings in the majority-oriented systems is often canceled by their elimination of small-party efforts, which are excluded from the legislature entirely. However, as might be expected, the range of volatility is greater as are differences between vote and seat volatility, within the majority-oriented type.

What stands out in the table is the greater volatility of voting in the presidential systems, regardless of their election laws. It should be emphasized that these figures are for voting in *legislative* elections. In presidential elections, the swings in party voting are greater still, as in the United States. Although the presidential election figures shift with coalitions and specific candidates far more than do the corresponding legislative votes, it seems clear that presidential systems are usually associated with more fluid patterns of voting for political parties.

Party-System Dynamics

Thus far I have considered each of the properties of party systems as a dependent variable, shaped independently by social conditions, electoral setting, and historic accident. Theoretically, however, some of these properties should interact. In a two-party system the parties are likely to offer fairly similar policies in order to attract the median voter. Although this centripetal tendency may be restrained by the need to mobilize activists, the degree of polarization of opinion, the level of decentralization in organization and campaigns, and so forth, it is likely to have some centralizing effect on party strategies.[42] In multiparty systems it often happens that no party has a chance of wining a majority. If any party moves to the median in an effort to gain a majority, its more extreme position will be taken over by new parties. Hence, in theory, parties in such systems should appeal to rather narrow constituencies, and interparty competition should take place only between adjacent parties of the many on the spectrum.[43] Such a strategic logic will encourage strong linkages between parties and social groups. Moreover, if clusters of extremist dissatisfaction of even moderate size exist, it will be rewarding to some party leader or innovator to appeal to them directly. For these reasons, party fractionalization should encourage stronger linkages between parties and groups and representation of extremist parties, while two-party systems should discourage both. Indeed, proportional representation is expected to encourage linkages and extremism partly because it affects parties' choices of majoritarian or representational strategies, as well as because it facilitates appeals to geographically dispersed groups.

Data are not available on campaign appeals that would make possible direct tests of theories about party strategy. But it is possible to examine relationships between the properties of party systems in a cross-sectional comparison, and to look at changes in the party systems over several elections. Multivariate analysis reveals whether the party-system properties show continuity over time and whether their interrelationships are stronger than might be caused by election laws and social heterogeneity alone.

Cross-Sectional Comparison Party-group linkages, fractionalization, and extremist representation are all facilitated by proportional representation; thus they should be related to one another. And in fact they are correlated, whether we look at the systems of the early 1960s or the mid 1970s, or at average election outcomes. Fractionalization and extremism are especially strongly related ($r = .65$). Although part of the strong correlation between fractionalization and extremist representation comes from their common antecedents in electoral laws and social heterogeneity, multivariate regression also indicates that each adds some additional explanatory power to the other. In a cross-sectional correlation we cannot tell which, if either, is the primary independent variable, but they are definitely associated.

The case of party-group alignment is less clear-cut. It is strongly associated with fractionalization ($r = .44$), but less so with extremism. In regression analysis with the party systems of the 1960s, fractionalization seems to have little net impact on strength of linkages, once we control for the powerful effect of electoral laws on both. Some effect of linkages between groups and parties on fractionalization does appear, especially toward the end of the time period. It may be that systems with stronger alignments were less open to new interests. Hence, in such systems the new groups and interests had to find expression through new (fractionalizing) small parties. Systems with weaker alignments were more easily able to incorporate new interests within the old parties.[44] The evidence is only indirect, however, and the absence of reliable series of surveys for measuring linkages between parties and groups means that changes in them are difficult to ascertain.

Over-Time Comparison   Except for the party-group-linkage variable, on which I have had to use a single average estimate, it is possible to trace changes in the properties of party systems over the time of this analysis. The data for the early 1960s presented in earlier tables can be compared to data from elections in the mid-1970s.

The party-system properties are, as expected, quite stable over this time period. The correlations between extremist vote in the early 1960s and in the mid-1970s is .81; between the legislative fractionalization measures it is .83. Moreover, in a regression analysis, the earlier property of a party system is always the strongest predictor of its later counterpart, even when the measures of heterogeneity and election laws are included in the equation. It seems likely that these patterns of continuity reflect the importance of citizen's party perceptions and identities, on the one hand, and the continuity of party organization and strategic decisions, on the other. These high correlations make it difficult to say very much about special factors leading to change, or about dynamic tendencies. Majoritarian electoral laws (B = $-.26$) and extremist voting in the early 1960s (B = $+.73$) alone explain 80 percent of the variance in extremist vote in the mid-1970s (R = .88). And majoritarian electoral laws (B = $-.36$) and the legislative fractionalization of the early 1960s (B = $+.62$) explain a similar amount of variation in the legislative fractionalization of the mid-1970s.

However, several minor points about the changes over time are worthy of note. First, a look at increases in extremist vote and fractionalization (and both did increase somewhat during this period) reveals no strong centrifugal dynamic. That is, extremist voting did not predict increases in extremist voting; nor did fractionalization predict increased fractionalization. The relationships were positive, but not significant, originally; they vanished when the electoral laws were controlled. Second, there was a tendency for majoritarian electoral laws to inhibit both increases in extremist representation (B = -.50) and increases in fractionalization (B = -.48). Heterogeneity and inflation seemed to have some impact on extremist-party growth, which, in turn, seemed to increase fractionalization.[45] Slow economic growth was not related to increased support for extremist parties.

In general the increases in extremism and fractionalization seemed to reflect party and, especially, constitutional arrangements in which previously unrepresented cleavage groups (Uruguay, Belgium) or dissatisfied subgroups (the right in Denmark and the left in Japan) can fairly easily gain entry into the political system. Increased dissatisfaction about social conditions will be reflected in increased and usually fractionalizing support for extremist parties, which often will decline again in better times. The interplay of the combination of party system and constitutional rules is exemplified by the Danish case: the failure of the rightist coalition of 1968 to repeal the leftist initiatives of its predecessor led directly to an extremist challenge from its own side of the spectrum.[46] However, in most of the working democracies at this time, conditions were relatively stable, as the high over-time correlations suggest.[47]

Overview   Table 5.6 presents a regression analysis that summarizes the relationships among environmental conditions and party-system characteristics. A somewhat more elaborate and contemporary test of the earlier observations is provided by basing the regression on 84 elections between 1967 and 1976, rather than on averages. (Coefficients using averages are, however, very similar.)

This regression analysis reconfirms most of the earlier inferences drawn from our examination of the party systems in the early 1960s. Strong party-group linkages (for which the analysis rests on averages, as individual election data were not available) are associated with higher levels of development and with less majoritarian electoral laws. No other variables are significant, but presidential executives and large minority groups seem to blur these linkages, perhaps because of the consolidating tendencies encouraged by the former and the "cross-cutting" pressures created by the latter. Fractionalization is encouraged above all by the nonmajoritarian electoral laws, but also by all of the heterogeneity measures, and discouraged by presidential executives. Extremist support, too, is encouraged by nonmajoritarian electoral laws, and it is related powerfully to agricultural minorities and less

Table 5.6 Bases of party systems: Correlation and regression analysis of effects of social environment and constitutional setting, 1965–1976.[a]

Party-system attributes 1965–1976	Social environment, mid-1960s					Constitutional arrangements	
	Small population	Economic development	Heterogeneity[b]			Presidential executive	Majoritarian electoral laws[c]
			Ethnic	Agricultural	Catholic		
Multi-party: legislative fractionalization[d]							
Correlation	.15	.24	−.17	.26	.07	−.14	−.60
Regression	−.02	.33**	.45**	.59**	.22**	−.32**	−.67**
R² = 61%							
Strong party-group linkages							
Correlation	.35	.55	−.27	−.26	.02	−.48	−.54
Regression	.03	.37**	.08	−.27	−.13	−.22	−.52**
R² = 66%							

Extremist-party voting support[d]						
Correlation	−.11	−.12	−.13	.51	−.16	.04
Regression	−.29**	.10	.27**	.62**	.04	−.14*
R^2 = 50%						
Volatility of party representation[d]						
Correlation	−.05	−.51	.13	.17	−.23	.27
Regression	.06	−.33**	.14	.22*	−.08	.16*
R^2 = 32%						

Sources: Election data from Mackie and Rose, *International Electoral Almanac; European Journal of Political Research; Keesing's Archives;* country studies.

a. Regression entries are standardized regression coefficients.

b. Coding for heterogeneity variables: Ethnic is directly from table 3.4 and is a continuous measure. Agricultural minorities coded 20–49% = 3; 50–80% = 2; 5–19% = 1, from table 3.2. Catholic minorities coded similarly, using percentage Catholic from Taylor and Hudson, *World Handbook.*

c. Electoral laws coded single-member district = 3; Germany, Japan, and Ireland = 2; other = 1, from table 4.1. Presidential executive coded: presidential system = 1; other = 0.

d. Analyses of fractionalization, extremist voting support, and volatility based on 84 elections in 27 countries. Each country was weighted equally to prevent bias; 81 weighted cases. See Appendix for fractionalization measure and parties classified extremist.

e. Party-group linkage analysis based on 23 countries. See table 5.3.

* = F level over 1.7 (significant at .10).

** = F level over 3.0 (significant at .05).

strongly to ethnic minorities. Legislative volatility is associated with less modernized societies and with presidential constitutions.[48]

Several points do appear in the multivariate analysis that were not obvious earlier. First, population size is related to extremism. Support for extremist parties is more common in the larger countries. Careful examination shows that the large extremist contenders of the 1950s and 1960s were disproportionately found in the larger nations. In fact, effects of both population size and heterogeneity on support for extremist parties in the 1970s seem to reflect primarily continuations of the associations present earlier when the extremist contenders were established. If support for extremist contenders in the early 1960s (from table 5.3) is entered as a predictive variable in the analysis of extremist support in the elections of 1966–1976, only the electoral laws remain significant (at .05) as an additional variable.

A second point is that the more modernized nations manifest significantly more legislative fractionalization, an effect that is notably sharper in the multivariate analysis than it was in simple comparisons. It seems likely that the greater mobilization of citizens in modernized societies creates a substantial potential for electoral expression of diverse interests. Insofar as such fractionalization makes governing difficult—a point of dispute to be explored later in this chapter and in Chapter 7—the higher levels of modernization will be somewhat destabilizing. This aspect of more modernized societies, the greater group pressures under which they may operate, has been suggested by recent work on difficulties of governing modern democracies,[49] and could in theory account for the failure to find modernized societies more governmentally stable.

A final point must be stressed. The environmental measures in table 5.6 are all taken from the mid-1960s. As few net changes occurred in size, level of development, ethnicity, or Catholic-Protestant balance (although this last factor may have become less salient in some countries), the equivalent measures from the early 1970s yield virtually identical coefficients. One exception is very revealing, however. The percentage of the population employed in agriculture declined rapidly in most of the European nations in the 1960s and 1970s, but extremist voting support did not decline in most of these countries. France, for example, was as modern in the 1970s, and had as small an agricultural sector, as most of the "agriculturally homogeneous" nations in 1960. Yet support for the Communist party remained strong throughout the period and did not decline until the elections of 1978 and 1981. In fact, rerunning the regressions in table 5.6 using the agricultural minorities of 1970 as the measure of agricultural heterogeneity, makes the agricultural variable's explanatory power decline sharply.[50] This decline is notable for both extremism and fractionalization. The occupational structure may have become more homogeneous, but the patterns of voting support did not.

This is a sharp reminder that party systems often change only gradually, more slowly than the conditions that helped shape them. The accumulations of memory, organization, and issues that accompany the formation of a major contending party resist dissolution. The period of this study is too short to grapple adequately with party change. The continuities in support for the extremist contender parties also emphasize that "heterogeneity" is a shorthand expression for a complex interaction of environmental conditions and unique historical events which bequeathed the extremist contenders to some party systems.

Party Systems and Democratic Performance

The first step in examining the key role parties play in the democratic process is to see how well the theoretical expectations about parties and performance, founded on a very large political science literature, succeed in predicting relationships between the attributes of party systems and political outcomes in the democracies. Systematic comparison of tables 5.1 and 5.7 allows us to see which of the plausible arguments about party systems and political performance are supported by the data. Table 5.7 shows how each performance measure was related to the attributes of party systems. First, for each performance measure, the simple (Pearson) correlations between that measure and the party-system attributes are given. These are followed by the regression results, looking at all three party-system attributes simultaneously and adding controls for some important environmental conditions. These relationships are not substantially altered when all the other environmental and constitutional variables suggested by Chapters 3 and 4 are also introduced. The controls that are shown clarify the party-system effects without creating an impossibly complex table.[51] For simplicity, volatility, which is weakly and inconsistently linked to the dependent variables, is omitted here, although we shall see later that it does have a minor role to play.

Examination of the table shows that the expectations about political participation are well realized. All three party-system attributes—

Table 5.7 Party-system attributes, environmental characteristics, and political performance: correlation and regression analysis.[a]

Performance Dimension	Party-system attributes[b]			Major environmental advantages[c]			
	Multi-party Fraction-alization	Strong party-group linkages	Extremist-party voting	Small popul-ation	Economic develop-ment	Compulsory voting laws	Ethnic homogeneity
Voting turnout, 1958–1976							
Correlation	.30	.58	.21	.27	.26	.42	
Regression	−.35	.68**	.12	.11	.03	.43**	
R² = 52%							
Executive durability, 1967–1976							
Correlation	−.71	−.48	−.82	.08	−.07	—	
Regression	−.13	−.19	−.70**	−.08	.02	—	
R² = 74%							
Majority control, 1967–1976							
Correlation	−.37	−.17	−.11	−.15	−.24	—	
Regression	−.62*	.34	.14	−.10	−.19	—	
R² = 22%							
Low rioting, 1958–1967[d]							
Correlation	.48	−.46	−.27	.86	.25	—	.23
Regression	.36*	.00	−.35**	.72**	−.21*	—	−.06
R² = 81%							

Low rioting, 1967–1976						
Correlation	.28	.43	−.18	.80	.29	—	.30
Regressions	.24	.15	−.27*	.67**	−.06	—	−.02
$R^2 = 69\%$						
Low deaths, 1958–1967						
Correlation	.57	.62	−.06	.65	.67	—	.67
Regression	.13	.07	−.07	.26*	.32**	—	.37**
$R^2 = 76\%$						
Low deaths, 1967–1976						
Correlation	.40	.53	−.03	.46	.72	—	.41
Regression	.29	.01	−.17	.18	.53**	—	.09
$R^2 = 62\%$						

a. Regression entries are standardized regression coefficients. For consistency, only the cases with all party variables measured are used. Including the missing countries (Ceylon, Costa Rica, Greece, Turkey, and Uruguay) does not substantially change results. Voting turnout and riots and deaths for 1967–1976 based on 23 cases; riots and deaths for 1958–1967 based on 21 cases. Executive durability and control equations based on 17 parliamentary systems (see table 4.1). Fractionalization and extremist voting measures are the averages from all elections in the 1965–1976 period. See Sources as in table 5.6.

Appendix for party-system averages.

b. Sources as in table 5.6.

c. Population size and GNP/capita are logged. Compulsory voting measure described in Chapter 6, table 6.1. Ethnicity from table 3.4.

d. Extreme outliers on riots and deaths have been truncated to the ninetieth percentile values to prevent bias. A log transformation yields similar results.

* F level over 1.7 (significant at .10).

** F level over 3.0 (significant at .05).

fractionalization, party-group linkages, and extremist support—are associated with higher voting turnout. The regression analysis adds a measure of laws requiring citizens to vote (discussed in detail in the next chapter), and considers all three party variables simultaneously. The strength of linkages between groups and parties is by far the dominant factor in getting citizens to the polls. This result, to be discussed at more length in Chapter 6, is consistent with the theoretical expectations.

In the dimension of government performance, there is some controversy about theoretical expectations. As expected, more support for extremist parties is powerfully related to less durable executives. The simple correlation is quite strong, and the standardized regression coefficient is very large and dominates the equation. In the simple correlations, fractionalization and strong linkages are both associated with less stability, as predicted by the aggregative theorists. But in the regression analysis, neither party variable is significant, once account is taken of the impact of extremist-party representation. The implication is clear. Multi-party (fractionalized) systems do tend to have less stable governments, but it is their association with extremism, not fractionalization as such, that leads to lack of executive stability. As the theorists of aggregative and responsible party systems argue, multiparty systems are often unstable. As the theorists of representational party systems argue, fractionalization need not lead to instability, as long as extremism is inhibited. (A dummy variable analysis of system types reaches the same conclusion, as does running the regressions within only the parliamentary systems.)[52] However, multiparty systems are more likely to experience an absence of majority control, and extremism is unrelated to such control.

These results raise two questions. First, how can it be possible for (nonextremist) fractionalized party systems to be as stable as those with party majorities? Chapter 7 will address this puzzle by looking at the pattern of formation and durability of coalitions in different party settings.

Second, do fractionalized party systems that are not extremist tend to become so over time, hence favoring, in the long run, the argument that nonrepresentational systems are preferable? This puzzle is not easily solved with the available data, because the relative durability of the party systems themselves makes it difficult to investigate. As pointed out in the previous section, fractionalization and extremist support are associated with each other, primarily because certain environmental and constitutional factors encourage both of them. But the association continues, weakly, when these environmental variables are controlled, and it is hard to pin down the direction of causality, if any. In the limited over-time analysis that was possible, fractionalization in 1965 did not seem to be a significant cause of increases in extremism in the subsequent decade. At most, effects of fractionalization in encouraging extremism seem to be slight. But we cannot draw conclusions with great confidence until the processes of change are studied in more detail than is possible here.

Three important points emerge from the analysis of violence. First, it is striking that none of the party attributes is very strongly related to deaths by violence, once we take account of levels of modernity. In simple correlations the multiparty and strong linkage variables are related to less deadly violence. But with the environmental controls, the party effects become mostly insignificant, although the fractionalized systems have an advantage in the second decade. Probably the most surprising point here is the lack of association between extremism and deadly violence. Despite all of the theorists' concerns, extremist support is not significantly related to this serious form of the breakdown of order.

Second, as most of the party theorists would expect, extremist support is related to more rioting in both decades. Strong extremist parties are associated with mass turmoil even more clearly after population size is taken into account. Although support for extremist parties is not linked to deadly violence, its association with both low executive durability and more rioting justifies to some extent the unanimous concern of theorists about party systems manifesting such support.

Finally, the evidence clearly favors the advocates of representational systems in the dispute over multiparty systems and rioting. Fractionalization is associated with less rioting, and the association continues after other variables are controlled. The standardized regression coefficient is significant at the .05 level in the first decade, and falls just below .10 in the second. (With the better data later available for the second decade, it becomes clearly significant; see table 10.1 and the Appendix.

The results of this initial comparison of party system and performance are interesting and provocative. For one trained to admire the Anglo-American two-party type of system, the good performance of the multiparty systems with strong linkages is impressive and somewhat surprising. Multiparty fractionalization is associated with higher voting turnout (because of strong linkages), with less rioting, and with only slightly more unstable executives, as long as extremism is avoided. The failure of any of these party variables to have much effect on deadly violence is also notable. It is, however, dangerous to proceed further without more complete and complex modeling. Party systems are not simply another independent variable or environmental condition. They have independent existence and continuity, but they are also affected by the constitutional and social environments and serve to link these to performance outcomes. It is time to turn to more complex models of the processes that shape political performance.

Citizen Involvement /
Participation or Turmoil

6

Thus far I have been looking at the beginning and end of the democratic process, so to speak, in considering relatively stable environmental and constitutional conditions on one side, and aspects of performance on the other. Now it is time to focus on the processes that link the environmental and constitutional elements to democratic performance. This change in focus requires some changes in organization and analysis. First, I shall consider the different elements in the process separately, dealing with citizen involvement in this chapter, legislative processes in the next, and so on. Second, I shall turn from the presentation of average scores or simple correlations and regressions to more complex forms of analysis. I shall generate predictions about causal sequences and then see whether statistically based causal models seem in fact to approximate these across the democratic countries.

Getting Citizens to the Polls

Although it is only one of the forms of citizen involvement in politics, voting occupies the central place in democratic politics and in contemporary political science. A vast number of studies have analyzed the sources of partisan support and voting participation within nations, particularly in the United States. Other studies have touched on the consequences of voting: the way election results are determined by which citizens choose to stay home and which ones go to the polls. Students of elite responsiveness, moreover, stress that voting is the major instrument, albeit a clumsy one, through which leaders can be compelled to be attentive to citizens.

At the individual level, voting is a distinctive form of political involvement. Various students of individual behavior, stimulated by the crossnational studies of Sidney Verba, Norman Nie, and Jae-On Kim, have explored citizen participation in politics. In virtually all of these

studies voting participation emerges as a unique dimension of involvement, more frequently performed, less related to other forms of
political activity, than most of the other types of citizen action. Voting is
distinctive for two reasons: the relative ease of performing it and its
virtually total dependence on citizens' relationships to the party
institutions that set the alternatives in the election. In their seven-nation
study, Verba, Nie, and Kim found that the individual social and
economic resources possessed by citizens were powerful facilitators to
political activities of most kinds. The better-off citizens were consistently, in nation after nation, more likely to be informed about politics,
to form local organizations, to work with others on community
problems, to contribute time and money to political parties, to persuade
others how to vote, and so forth. But voting depended on the
individual's attachment to the institutions of the society, especially the
parties, not on personal social or economic resources.[1]

Despite the many studies of individual voting decisions, there have
been few attempts to compare and explain the large and rather stable
differences in voting turnout across the democratic nations. As we saw
in table 2.1, average turnout levels in recent decades ranged from 60
percent or less in India, Switzerland, and the United States to around 90
percent in Italy, the Netherlands, and Austria. Moreover, those
crossnational differences are quite consistent from election to election.
An increase or decrease in turnout of 5 percent is a large shift. Of
course, dramatic contests do occasionally affect turnout. A good
example is the surge in turnout in India in 1967, when the opposition
parties first united to challenge seriously the Congress party's dominance: turnout increased from 55 to 61 percent of the registered
electorate. This level was reached again in the dramatic election that
ousted Mrs. Gandhi and her party in 1977. Nonetheless, the 61 percent
level of India's highest turnout remains extremely low by crossnational
standards. The relative consistency of turnout levels from election to
election within nations indicates that stable features of the political
situation are having powerful aggregate effects on the outcomes of
millions of individual citizens' voting decisions.

The average levels of voting participation in a society are likely to be
shaped by a variety of factors, including the values and skills of citizens,
the issues and problems of the society, the legal and constitutional rules,
and the political structure. Comparative data are not available on
citizens' normative beliefs about the importance of participation,
although some studies of voting participation within individual countries
have demonstrated the importance of such attitudes.[2] However, as we

shall see, the broad environmental setting in which citizens make their choices does explain a great deal of the crossnational variation. The two aspects of the environment most immediately proximate to the citizen seem to be the national party system, which presents the voting alternatives, and the incentives to vote created by the legal system.

Compulsory Voting and Registration Laws   In about a quarter of the democracies substantial penalties for not voting exist, or did exist during several elections between 1958 and 1976. As Herbert Tingsten demonstrated quite clearly forty years ago, the imposition of relatively small fines or other penalties can have a major impact on voting turnout.[3]

In Australia, Belgium, and Venezuela a citizen who does not vote is in violation of the law and subject to fines and other penalties unless excused by illness. The potential sanctions in Venezuela are particularly harsh. Such penalties have also existed in Costa Rica since 1960 and were in effect in the Netherlands until the 1971 election. Similar penalties and requirements also existed in Chile before its democracy was overthrown, and apparently in Greece before the 1967 military coup as well as at present. Italy does not have legally designated compulsory voting, but nonvoters are stamped as such on their official work and identification papers, and it is widely believed that they are discriminated against in employment and other benefits.[4]

The impact of these sanctions can be seen in summary in table 6.1 or for individual countries in table 2.1. None of the countries with penalties

Table 6.1   Voting laws and turnout.[a]

Voting law provisions		Average turnout					
Penalties for not voting	Automatic registration	50–65%	66–75%	76–85%	86–95%	Total	N
No	No	40%	40%	20%	0	100%	5
No	Yes	19	31	31	19	100	16
Yes	No	0	50	25	25	100	4
Yes	Yes	0	0	25	75	100	4

a. Turnout is percentage of the population of eligible voting age. Turnout data are from table 2.1. Countries with penalties for failure to vote are Australia, Belgium, Chile, Costa Rica, Greece, Italy, the Netherlands, and Venezuela. Countries in which registration is by application of citizens, rather than automatic, are Australia, Chile, Costa Rica, France, Jamaica, New Zealand, United States, Uruguay, and Venezuela. New Zealand and Uruguay, as well as the compulsory voting countries, provide some penalties for failure to make registration application.

for not voting had average turnout levels under 70 percent of the eligible electorate, or under 80 percent of the registered electorate. The average turnout, by any measure, was about 10 percent higher in the countries with such penalties. The relationship is strong and statistically significant at the .01 level. Further evidence comes from three nations that changed their laws on penalties for not voting: Costa Rica, the Netherlands, and Uruguay. The introduction of penalties in Costa Rica increased turnout by about 15 percent. Elimination of penalties in the Netherlands led to an initial decrease of 16 percent, although turnout has leveled off at less than 10 percent below earlier levels. Uruguay enforced constitutional provisions for compulsory voting for the first time in the 1971 election; turnout increased sharply in that election, from 67 percent to 84 percent.[5] Moreover, Tingsten reports that the introduction of compulsory voting in Australia in 1924 led to an average increase in turnout of around 18 percent for men, 30 percent for women.

Thus we have both cross-sectional and longitudinal evidence that penalties for not voting have a significant impact on turnout across the contemporary democracies. Establishing such penalties, however, does not guarantee turnout. The extent of enforcement and the magnitude of penalties vary greatly. Moreover, different penalties affect different parts of the population. The aged and unemployed, those in remote villages, those outside the cash economy are often untouched by various penalties for failing to vote; they may even be unnoticed by registration officials.

A second way in which the legal setting may affect voting turnout is through variations in registration laws and bureaucratic machinery. In two-thirds of the democracies, the government assumes the responsibility for voter registration, either through maintaining continually updated lists of registered citizens compiled from census and other official materials, or through periodic canvasses of all citizens to update registration rolls. In the other countries it is up to the potential voter to apply to the proper authorities to be registered. In most of the latter countries, there is some legal requirement for citizens to register, either in conjunction with compulsory voting, or as a duty of citizenship where voting itself is voluntary (New Zealand). Only the United States, France and post-1962 Jamaica rely totally on the initiative of citizens, perhaps encouraged by their political parties, to get on the electoral rolls.[6] Clearly, when citizens must make the double effort to register and to vote, voting becomes a significantly more difficult act, and turnout is likely to be lower.

These differences in registration procedures often confound efforts to make crossnational comparisons. The calculation of the percentage of voter participation depends on one's definition of the universe of potential voters. Examining reports of voting participation from different nations makes it clear that governments and reporters vary substantially in their assumptions. In discussing European nations scholars and journalists invariably use percentage of the registered electorate as their measure of turnout. In discussing the United States, election observers usually report voting participation as a percentage of the population of voting age. (National registration figures were not available until recently.) In Third World nations, especially in Latin America, the practices vary sharply from one individual or government to another. Throughout this work I use percentage of the population of voting age (except excluding illiterates in pre-1970 Chile and the Philippines), both because this measure makes comparison more meaningful and because only in this fashion can we see the importance of the registration laws themselves.

Table 6.1 shows that the presence of automatic registration procedures facilitates citizen turnout, even in countries with penalties for not voting. These effects appear also in multivariate analysis, and Ann Spackman has described the drop in registration in Jamaica in areas where "enumerated" citizens were additionally required to take their enumeration certificates and a photograph to a registration center to be enrolled.[7] Studies in the United States have demonstrated that the registration laws in some states are much more facilitating than in others, although these differences have probably declined.[8]

Other legal arrangements for voting seem much less significant than the various experiments with compulsory voting and the automatic registration of eligible citizens. Different arrangements for absentee voting, for example, do not seem to be associated with major differences in turnout, although data are incomplete and these may be important in a few specific areas.

Party System Mobilization   The political parties are the institutions that link the voting choices of individual citizens with aggregate electoral outcomes in the competitive democracies. The parties set the alternatives offered to the citizens in elections, and their organized activities can encourage both registration and election-day turnout. The relationships between party systems and national cleavage structures should play a major role in shaping voting participation levels. In some countries the national parties have close and enduring ties to particular demographic groups. A survey of Austrian voters in 1969 showed, for example, that those who thought that one party or another was a better outcome for various groups considered a People's party government better for farmers and "believing Catholics" by a ten-to-one margin, while nearly as high a proportion thought that a Socialist government would be better for "workers."[9] Similar results would probably emerge in many of the other Western European party systems. In other countries, however, the parties have relied on more diffuse, less differentiated support, as in the United States, or upon varying alliances with local organizations and factions, as in many developing nations.

Theoretically, strong linkages between national parties or blocs of parties and demographic groups should encourage voting participation. Robert Alford suggested in his original analysis of class voting that where workers have a party that clearly appeals to their interests, their participation and sense of political efficacy are as great as those of middle-class persons.[10] Thus, where the national parties represent different, meaningful religious or occupational groups, the electoral outcomes take on an easily identifiable significance. Where these linkages are relatively stable, they give even poorly informed and uninterested voters cues as to how to interpret the issue and candidate choices in given elections. That such linkages can be highly durable has been demonstrated by Lipset and Rokkan, who point out that the efforts of particular Western European parties to organize and mobilize particular demographic groups—workers, farmers, believing Catholics, businessmen—in the period between 1880 and 1920 had continuing effects on voting alignments through the 1960s.[11] Moreover, the presence of strong, continuing expectations about parties and the interests of social groups not only creates easily identifiable choices for citizens, it also makes it easier for parties to seek out their probable supporters and mobilize them at election time. The creation of enduring relationships between parties and organized social and economic organizations, such as trade unions and religious associations, is no doubt also encouraged by such identification of party and group interests. These relationships contribute further to expectations about linkages, and such organizations themselves can play an important role in mobilizing citizens.[12]

For mutually reinforcing reasons, then, we expect national voting participation to be higher where political parties establish attitudinal and organizational linkages to nationally identifiable groups. The critical empirical question here is not one of party labels and aspirations, but of the *de facto* success of the parties in creating these linkages. We are not concerned with the presence of "Socialist" or "Catholic" parties as such, but with differential success achieved by such parties in building linkages to workers, believing Catholics, and so on.

A simple and straightforward measure of the strength of the alignment between parties and groups is the degree to which individuals' partisan preferences can be predicted from knowledge of their demographic characteristics. Where such predictive capacity is high, party-group alignments are strong and we expect rather high levels of voting participation. Where knowledge of individuals' group memberships is of little help in predicting their partisanship, party-group alignments are weak, and, other things being equal, we expect lower levels of voting participation. I presented some measures of these alignments in table 5.3, where I showed the effects of occupation and religion on party preference for the 23 democracies for which survey data are available. Although these measures are not ideal, as the quality of the surveys varies and citizens without a preference are usually excluded, they do offer a good basic assessment of the strength of the alignments between groups and parties. They contrast quite clearly the weak alignments in such nations as the United States, where manual workers favored the Democrats by only 18 percent more than did those in other occupations, with the strong alignments in nations such as Sweden, where the manual workers were 46 percent more likely to favor the leftist parties than were those in other occupations. (Although I have been using occupational examples here, recall from Chapter 5 that religious practice is the more powerful discriminator of party preference in many countries.)

Table 6.2 shows the relationship between the strength of party-group linkages and voting turnout in the nations for which surveys showing bases of partisan support were available. The nations with compulsory voting are shown separately. It is very clear from the table that the relationship between participation and strength of alignment is a powerful one. Analyses using other measures of alignment, available for fewer countries, support this very strong relationship (the simple Pearson correlation is .58, as seen in Table 5.7), as does multivariate analysis.[13] Because the survey evidence is available over time in very few countries, we cannot trace the effects of changes in the strength of alignment on changes in turnout. Indeed, the available evidence suggests that the party-group alignments do not change very rapidly; the complex ties of organization and historical identification, perhaps reinforced by repeated voter actions, are not easily eroded. For example, although class voting was declining in Britain from the 1950s to the mid-1970s, as was voting turnout,[14] the size of the shifts was such that Britain's comparative rank in alignment and turnout did not change much. Similar comments would apply to the United States. In the long run we might expect, however, that such large-scale social effects as the apparent decline in the salience of religious practices, as suggested by the decline in church attendance throughout Western Europe in the 1960s and 1970s, would weaken the association between religion and party, and hence cause turnout to decline, unless a new cleavage was found to organize party life.

The major exception to the powerful relationship between the strength of party-group alignments and voting participation is Switzerland. Party support in Switzerland can be predicted quite well from knowledge of the citizen's religion and occupation. Moreover, Switzerland has automatic registration of eligible voters, and is a highly modernized nation. Four cantons even have compulsory voting. These features would lead us to expect very high voting participation in national elections. But in fact Swiss voting participation is very low, and was among the lowest in any democracy even before the enfranchisement of inexperienced female voters in the early 1970s. Turnout has been steadily declining, moreover, several percent in each election,

Table 6.2   Linkages between groups and parties and average voting turnout.[a]

National party-group linkage index	Average turnout					
	50–65%	66–75%	76–85%	86–95%	Total	N
Countries without compulsory voting						
0–30	43%	43%	14%	0	100%	7
31–45	17	33	50	0	100	6
46–70	0	0	25	75	100	4
Countries with compulsory voting						
0–30	0	50	50	0	100	2
31–45	0	0	0	100	100	2
46–70	0	0	0	100	100	2

a. Twenty-three countries are included here. Average turnout data from table 2.1 National party-group linkage index scores from table 5.3. Tau-C for 17 nations without compulsory voting penalties is .69, significant at the .01 level. Tau-C for all 23 nations combined is .68, also significant at .01. Relationships are also significant using turnout as percentage of registered electorate.

since World War II. The Swiss case is interesting for a variety of reasons. One is that it directs our attention to a characteristic of the party system which has interested many political scientists, particularly Americans: the degree of competition.

The most likely explanation of Switzerland's low turnout has been offered by Adam Przeworski: the deliberate demobilization of party competition by the major national parties themselves.[15] Since 1943 the four major parties, each linked to particular social groups, have guaranteed themselves a place in the collective national executive(which has a rotating chairmanship). Unless a new party should suddenly break into the big four, the party electoral outcomes at the national level are virtually meaningless. There is not the intense juggling of ministries and party balances that marked the responsiveness of the German and Austrian "grand coalitions" to electoral outcomes. Moreover, most important policy decisions in Switzerland are made at the cantonal level.[16] There is little incentive for voters to go to the polls, or for the major parties to try to mobilize them. Competition among the major parties is deliberately suspended.

The suggestion that intensity of party competition should affect levels of voting participation seems plausible, both from the point of view of citizen interest and from the point of view of party incentives to mobilize supporters. Several studies of voting turnout across the various American states and cities have lent support to such a theory. Moreover, a close look at the individual democracies reveals examples where changes in the level of competition between parties seem to have the expected effect on voting turnout. The 5 percent increase in turnout in India in the elections of 1967 and 1977, where the Congress party, long predominant, was first challenged and then defeated by a more united opposition, is one example. Similarly, turnout in Norway and Denmark rose in the late 1960s and the 1970s along with serious challenges to the Social Democratic parties. Turnout fell in Canada in the periods when the Liberals seemed to be in more or less permanent command of the national government

Nonetheless, it proves surprisingly difficult to demonstrate crossnational effects of competitiveness, at least after we take account of a few extreme cases. Table 2.1 showed one measure of competitiveness— changes in control of the chief executive in response to voting outcomes in the previous decade. The results of rather elaborate analysis can be quite easily summarized: the three countries that, during the time period in question, had seen no responses of executive control to election outcomes clearly had lower than average levels of turnout.[17] Switzerland had the lowest levels of all; India was nearly as low; Japan had turnout slightly below average. But the other degrees of competitiveness have no significant effects on average voting turnout. Other measures of competitiveness, such as the difference in size between the largest party and its closest challenger, also fail to yield consistent or significant results. (The existence of party coalitions, formal and informal, may, of course, be responsible for the failure of these measures to generate clear results. But efforts to take account of such coalitions do not seem to help in explaining turnout.) In short, the moderately varying degrees of party competition found in most of the democracies are not very powerful shapers of the level of turnout, at least not in comparison to such factors as registration laws, compulsory voting, and the strength of party-group alignments. Only where a very marked failure of the electoral process to bring about any alterations in power is present is citizen participation seriously reduced.

A Causal Model of Voting Participation

Having explored the legal and party environments that encourage or inhibit the citizen's participation in the electoral arena, I can now present an overview of the process of mobilizing citizens to vote. As seen earlier, participation in national elections is higher in the more modernized nations, and in those nations with representational constitutions. Figure 6.1 shows a regression model of the causal political process that links the socioeconomic and constitutional setting to varying average participation in the competitive democracies. This model assumes the causal directions between variables to be as shown in the figure, and does not allow for reciprocal or feedback effects. The analysis then shows that neither modernization nor the constitutional structure directly mobilizes the citizenry. Rather, they lead to or help sustain the development of party systems and the choice of voting laws, which do get voters to the polls.[18]

The role of modernization is especially interesting here. The studies of individual participation have suggested that such personal characteristics as education, income, and higher-status occupations, which facilitate most forms of political participation, are rather unrelated to voting participation. Thus, as modernization leads to more widespread distribution of these characteristics, such socioeconomic development should encourage the formation of political organizations, campaign

Figure 6.1   Mobilization of the electorate in competitive democracies: Path coefficients.[a]

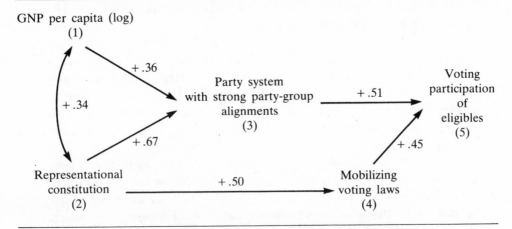

a. The arrows and path coefficients represent the standardized regression coefficients significant at the .10 level in a set of recursive regression equations. As indicated by the direction of the arrows, the model assumes that all variables with smaller identifying numbers are causally prior to variables with larger identifying numbers. Specific equations, variables, and sources are described in the Appendix.

involvement, persuading others, and so forth, but not necessarily encourage greater voting turnout. Despite such theoretical doubts, however, the more modernized countries do in fact have higher turnout. The reason seems to lie in the structure of the party system. As figure 6.1 shows (and as was pointed out in Chapter 5), the party systems in the more modernized nations are more likely to be firmly linked to citizens' social characteristics, such as religion, ethnicity, and class. The party systems in the less modernized nations are usually little more than electoral coalitions of local notables; individual parties draw on different social groups in different areas, or rely on personal appeals across a variety of groups. These differences in the type of party systems make all the difference in voting participation.

Party systems with strong ties between parties and groups are even more closely linked to representational constitutions than to modernization. As discussed in the last chapter, the presidential systems in particular, as well as the majoritarian parliamentary systems, tend to blur the party-group ties. Where the majoritarian systems do develop strong ties between parties and social groups, as in New Zealand or in Britain in the 1950s, they also tend to mobilize quite high levels of electoral turnout.

The representational constitutions are also strongly associated with the provision of voting laws designed to facilitate citizen activity. This association is particularly linked to the registration laws. Compulsory voting has been introduced in a number of countries, especially less modernized ones, in order to get citizens to the polls in the absence of encouraging party systems and good communications. Registration laws also seem to reflect the same values embodied in a nation's constitutional arrangements. Countries with representational constitutions are also highly likely to have automatic citizen registration. Countries favoring executive stability (or at least legislative majorities) tend to place more of the burden of involvement upon the individual citizen.

Figure 6.1 does not include Switzerland or the nations for which we have no survey data. The secondary studies that are available suggest that the addition of more survey data would support the pattern revealed in the figure. All the missing countries are poor nations, and the fragmentary surveys that do exist, as well as accounts by country experts, emphasize that in most of those nations the party systems are localized, personalistic electoral coalitions. (Ceylon, as noted in the last chapter, is a likely exception here and has relatively high turnout for a less economically developed country.) The omission of Switzerland is deliberate and important. The process simply does not work the same way in that nation. The party-group linkages are not important there in mobilizing citizens. As we shall see in discussing other aspects of the political process, the Swiss have developed a unique approach to democratic performance. I do not wish to imply that Switzerland is not democratic, that its citizens could not, if they wished, repudiate the elite demobilization of competition. The Swiss system is relatively open to the formation of new parties and their entry into the legislature. If they became strong enough there, they could demand entry into the executive council. Moreover, the Swiss system relies heavily on national referenda, which pose important questions directly to the citizens. Although turnout here, too, is not terribly impressive (around 50 percent), there are plenty of opportunities for citizens to demand greater elite responsiveness through the electoral mechanism. But thus far in the postwar period they have not done so. Citizens have allowed the parties to demobilize the competitive process; their low levels of voting participation respond to and reflect that demobilization. The unique nature of the Swiss solution is reflected in another fact as well— Switzerland manages to avoid turmoil, even without high levels of citizen participation at the polls.

Turmoil and Its Containment

The containment of violence is one of the goals of any democratic regime. Most crossnational studies of political violence have concluded that there are several distinctively different types of political violence. These have been given different names in different studies; but the major distinction usually sets apart activities that involve large numbers of citizens expressing discontent in a loosely organized or disorganized fashion, from activities in which smaller groups of well-organized and trained individuals systematically attack their adversaries. Douglas Hibbs refers to the first dimension of violence as "collective protest" and to the second as "internal war." Both riots and demonstrations are included in the former, while armed attacks and deaths due to political violence are included in the latter.[19] I find a similar distinction within the democracies, as discussed in Chapters 2 and 3.

I also find, as did Hibbs, that the size of the population is strongly related to the first dimension's activities, while it is only weakly related to the second. (See Chapters 3 and 4, especially table 4.4). Riots and protest demonstrations are particularly frequent in the larger countries; population size is the most powerful single predictor of their occurrence. In this sense, larger countries are more difficult to govern than smaller ones. This fact also suggests that riots and protests have their bases in mass discontent, while organized violence may often be the expression of smaller, elite groups.

Democracy is a political system that gambles that mass discontent can be channeled through the electoral system. Thus it is likely that a nation's party and electoral system plays a significant role in containing mass-based violence. Indeed, a first glance at the relationships among various aspects of democratic performance suggested that citizen turmoil and legitimate participation might be alternative forms of citizen involvement in politics. This suggestion is, we shall see, only partially true, but it contains some significant elements. Having traced the major sources of citizen mobilization into electoral politics, we can now see whether those same processes help to contain mass violence.

Rioting   Riots are defined as illegal, largely unorganized actions by a substantial number of individuals which result in property destruction or assaults. A riot may grow out of an organized protest or strike, but if it involves a planned, organized attack on people or property it falls into the category of elite-directed activity, to be discussed in a later chapter.

The specific goals and causes of riots vary greatly. David Bayley, for example, discussing public conflict in India, distinguishes between riots growing out of clashes with the authorities, usually based in antigovernment grievances ("remonstrance"); riots growing out of intergroup antagonisms ("confrontation"); and riots lashing out against impersonal, frustrating circumstances, such as commuter train delays or food shortages ("frustration").[20] Such types of riots vary substantially in their root causes, the danger to life and property they generate, and the ways anger is expressed.

The participants in riots have a shared sense of frustration, directed or not at specific targets, and some shared sense of appropriate riot behavior. The latter is frequently grounded in cultural norms and values, although it may also be shaped by the outcomes of other, recent riots participated in or heard about or seen on television. Various studies have shown that the behavior of rioting crowds in different cultures tends to be relatively predictable in terms of the forms of action taken, although the actions may vary sharply across cultures.

The riots that have taken place in the democracies in the last few decades encompass a great range of types and circumstances: riots by urban blacks and university students in the United States; riots growing out of clashes between Protestants and Catholics (and both with police) in Northern Ireland; political protests that became riots in Italy, France, Venezuela, Chile, and the Philippines; strikes and protests that became riots in Turkey, Uruguay, Japan, Lebanon, and Germany; outbursts in response to bread prices in India and Italy; tumultuous reactions to government language policies in India and Switzerland; student riots and demonstrations that became riots over a host of grievances, domestic, national, and international, in a dozen countries. Moreover, riots are quite clearly episodic. A country will often have a burst of riots, some clearly stimulating others, as well as responding to the same causes, then have several years of relative quiescence.

It is possible to identify some consistent properties that affect the propensities of some countries to have riots while others are much less likely to experience them. Somewhat surprisingly, as seen in Chapter 3, poverty, inequality, and even ethnicity, although often involved with the causes of the frustrations that can spark rioting, are all rather poor predictors of whether or not a nation will experience substantial rioting in some given time period. In part these uncertainties no doubt reflect variations in the concentration of grievances, in police control and tactics, and in cultural values. But they also reflect sharply varying political situations.

A key element in these political situations is the system of political parties. As we saw in Chapter 5, the strength of linkages between groups and parties, so important in mobilizing citizens to vote, has little effect on rioting. Much more important in affecting rioting are two other characteristics of party systems: support for extremist parties and fractionalization. Support for extremist parties is positively associated with rioting. I cannot demonstrate conclusively why these are associated, but studies of individual countries and riots suggest not only that support for extremist parties is an indicator of citizen discontent, but that election rallies and demonstrations staged by such parties frequently escalate into rioting. Sometimes the riots stem from attacks on the extremists by other groups; on other occasions the extremist leaders encourage their followers' frustration and outrage, or even provide a core of leadership for attacks that become disorganized rioting.

The more fractionalized, multiparty systems tend to have fewer riots, especially once we take account of the direct effects of the extremist parties. We saw this riot-dampening effect of multipartyism in table 5.7; it appears again in the summary path analysis of rioting in figure 6.2. Moreover, a dummy variable analysis of party-system types, based on the same data, shows that the representational type of party system— combining an absence of party majorities with strong linkages to groups and low extremist support—is especially able to prevent large-scale rioting. The results on fractionalization are supportive of the argument that citizen turmoil can best be contained by providing all groups with direct representation in the legitimate political structures and avoiding simple, broadly encompassing majorities directly chosen by the electorate.[21]

However, figure 6.2 also shows the limitation in the representational argument. Even if I am correct in drawing the arrow from extremist support to fractionalization (and, as discussed in Chapter 5, there are reasons to think that fractionalization has some encouraging effects on extremism itself), the electoral laws and social conditions that encourage fractionalization are also those which, for the most part, encourage extremist-party support. Thus, while multiparty systems may dampen citizen turmoil as long as they are not extremist, the proportional representation constitutions that help sustain multiparty systems also make it easy for extremist parties to gain support and entry.

Figure 6.2 also helps show why the environmental and constitutional conditions discussed in Chapter 4 have little net effect on the likelihood of rioting: they are mediated through divergent party systems.[22]

Figure 6.2   Riots: A path model of environmental effects mediated through the party system. Reduced standardized regression coefficients, 1958–1976.[a]

Environmental conditions	Party-system measures	Riots

Population size (log) (1) ——————————— +.66 [+.68]

Majoritarian election laws (3) + −

Extremist-party voting support (8)   +.30   [+.27]

Social heterogeneity
Ethnic fractionalization (5) +
Agricultural minority (6) +
Catholic minority (7) +

Riots 1967–1976 [1958–1967] (10)

−.36   [−.25]

Majoritarian election laws (3) + + −

Legislative fractionalization (9)

Presidential executive (4) −

GNP per capita (log) (2) +

a. The arrows and path coefficients represent the standardized regression coefficients significant at the .10 level in a set of recursive regression equations. As indicated by the direction of the arrows, the model assumes that all variables with smaller identifying numbers are causally prior to variables with larger identifying numbers. Arrows leading to party-system variables represent coefficients significant at .05 in table 5.6. Coefficients shown are based on equations recalculated with insignificant variables deleted. Specific equations, variables, and sources are described in the Appendix.

Population size has a major direct effect on rioting as well as a minor positive relationship with extremist vote. But most of the relevant constitutional and environmental variables tend to be associated with both propensities toward extremist-party support and propensities toward party fractionalization. The former encourages rioting, while the latter discourages it; the net effect varies in individual situations. The figure also is consistent, however, with the point, made by Maurice Duverger and Giovanni Sartori, that even if extremist-party strength becomes substantial, its disruptive effects may be somewhat mitigated in the multiparty situation.[23]

The complex relationship between support for extremist parties, multiparty systems, and rioting can also be illuminated by looking directly at the types of rioting. In collecting the data for 1967–1976 I recorded whether or not party activity seemed to be involved in the origins of the riots. The confusion of riot events, as well as my limited sources, keep these characterizations from being very reliable, but they are suggestive.

Table 6.3 classifies the party systems by whether or not elections in the 1967–1976 period resulted in a single-party majority at least half of the time.[24] The 15 countries with such majority tendencies are referred to in line 1. In 20 percent of those countries rioting was related to both party and nonparty activity, while in 40 percent the rioting did not seem to have any connections with political parties. In total, 60 percent of these majority-dominated countries experienced serious levels of rioting. (Here "serious" is defined as above the median level of one riot per 2 million citizens in a decade of democracy.)

Table 6.3 Serious rioting and party activity in majoritarian and multiparty systems, 1967–1976.[a]

Type of party system	Percentage of countries with					
	Riots both party and nonparty related[b]	Riots not party related[c]	Serious rioting of any type[d]	Rioting below serious level	Total	N
Majority-producing in most elections	20%	40%	60%	40%	100%	15
Multiparty: produced a majority in fewer than half of elections	33	8	42	58	100	12
All systems	26	26	52	48	100	27

Sources: For rioting and association with party activity: *Keesing's Archives* and *Facts on File.* For election outcome data: Mackie and Rose, *International Electoral Almanac; European Journal of Political Research; Keesing's Archives.*

a. "Serious" rioting defined as at least one riot per 2 million citizens, during a decade of democracy.

b. In Jamaica, all rioting seemed to be party-related. In Belgium, Chile, India, Italy, Turkey, and Venezuela both party-related riots and non-party riots were reported. As noted in the text, data on links between rioting and party activity are not too reliable and should be considered suggestive.

c. Costa Rica, France, Ireland, Philippines, U.S., U.K., Uruguay.

d. This column is, except for rounding error, the sum of the two previous columns.

The countries in which elections seldom or ever produced majorities (the fractionalized, multiparty systems), shown in line 2, had about the same amount of party-related and mixed rioting. But the multiparty countries seldom experienced only rioting that was not linked to political party action. Only one of these 12 countries (8 percent) had serious rioting only of this type. Consequently, the total probability of experiencing serious rioting was notably less in the multiparty countries than in the majoritarian ones—42 percent versus 60 percent.

The party-related rioting in all the countries usually appeared in conjunction with substantial support for extremist parties, and reports suggested that extremist-party activity was involved in stimulating at least some of the riots. (Jamaica, where the rioting involved supporters of the two major parties, neither of which had usually been considered extremist, is the major exception.) Moreover, the multiparty systems tended to be systems with substantial extremist-party support. In half of the multiparty systems, as compared to only one-eighth of the majoritarian systems, at least an average of 15 percent of the vote went to extremist parties. Extremist support of this magnitude made party-related or mixed rioting three times as likely as it was in countries with less extremist voting.

Yet, this apparent disadvantage of the multiparty systems—that they often included strong extremist parties and that these often were associated with rioting—was more than offset by two facts: (1) not all extremist-party activity was associated with notable rioting (Denmark, Finland); (2) diffuse, nonparty rioting was much more frequent in the majority-dominated systems than in the multiparty ones. As shown in table 6.3, 40 percent of the majority systems, as compared to 8 percent of the multiparty ones, had solely nonparty riots. These results help support and clarify the countervailing tendencies of extremism and fractionalization seen in table 5.7 and figure 6.2.

Another point is also suggestive. Given some arbitrariness in classifying parties as extremist, there is even less certainty about subclassification. But some of the "extremist" parties in the 1960s and 1970s, especially, seemed much more clearly to represent diffuse protest, rather than explicit ideologies or programs to change the national boundaries or political and social structure. Such parties as Values in New Zealand, Democrats 66 in the Netherlands, the Rural party in Finland, Progress in Denmark, and the Komeito in Japan seemed to be purely "protest" parties, rather than ideological or communal contenders.[25] If we subtract support for such parties from the measures of extremist voting support, the coefficients actually improve slightly, and in neither cross-sectional nor over-time comparisons does support for such parties seem related to rioting. Given the small number of such parties, and the limited time span, I do not want to make too much of these findings, but they point again to the importance of political decisions in a political setting in encouraging or restraining citizen turmoil, and they reemphasize the critical role of the historical events that gave rise to the major extremist contenders.

Finally, if we examine changes over time in the party systems and rioting, we do find some of the expected changes. The new issues raised by extremist parties in Belgium and Uruguay seemed to be associated with turmoil (but not with increased rioting as measured here). The growth of the neofascists in Italy and the far left in Chile were accompanied by increased levels of rioting. In Japan, however, rioting declined at the same time that the Komeito and Communists were gaining strength, perhaps due to the simultaneous moderation in the position of the Socialists. Growth in support for "protest" extremist parties in Denmark and Norway was also not accompanied by increased levels of rioting. Thus, although the stability of most party systems prevents the over-time comparisons from being very helpful, there seems to be a weak association between extremist-party support and riots, especially if the parties are ideological or communal. In any case, party-related rioting in the multiparty systems is often outweighed by the other types of rioting in the majoritarian systems.

Peaceful Protests   This picture of rioting from a political perspective is reinforced by recent data on political protests. The new *World Handbook of Political and Social Indicators* makes available statistics on political protests for both decades of concern here.[26] Various crossnational analyses have found rioting and peaceful protests associated. Peaceful protests are organized events in which substantial numbers of citizens participate in an endeavor to win the support of others or of the authorities for a political cause. Protests are strongly associated with population size. As in the case of riots, large nations are more likely to experience such protests, no doubt because of the greater number of possible causes. And protests are more likely in nations that experience rioting; discontent is involved in both cases, and some protests do become riots.

But protests differ somewhat from riots in their nature and in the countries in which they appear. They differ from riots in always requiring a substantial amount of citizen organization and coordination. The larger the protest, of course, the greater the organization and coordination required. The huge civil rights and antiwar demonstrations in the United States in the 1960s and 1970s, for example, were impressive organizational feats. For this reason, peaceful protests should be more likely to occur in more modernized countries, with their greater density of organizations, superior communication networks, and more widespread individual social resources such as education. At the individual level, studies have suggested that while rioting and voting are acts rather unrelated to the social resources of participants, protest participation is much more frequently an activity of the socially and economically advantaged citizens.[27] Peter Eisinger's study of protests in Milwaukee showed that among the better-off citizens protests could be organized from scratch fairly easily; among those who were less well-off, protests were more likely to be built from existing organizations, drawing on their ready-made skills and communication networks.[28] Crossnationally, the multivariate analysis summarized in figure 6.3 finds that protests are more common in the economically developed and modernized nations, other things being equal.

After taking population size into account, however, the most important direct effect on the degree of peaceful protest seems to be, again, the party system. Figure 6.3 looks very much like figure 6.2, except that the direct effects of level of economic development in encouraging protest activity appear in the protest path model. As in the case of riots, strong support for extremist political parties is associated with higher levels of protests. The effects are, perhaps surprisingly, not as strong as in the case of rioting, but the differences are probably not significant. Multiparty systems, measured by legislative fractionalization, are even more inhibiting to protests than they are to rioting. Given the potential that these multiparty systems, almost all with strong linkages to social groups, offer for the organization of protests, their inhibiting effect across party systems is remarkable. It is hard to resist the inference that protest activity is very frequently an organized mass alternative to the electoral system, when the latter seems unresponsive or inaccessible. In countries where multiple political parties organize many interests, and access to legitimate political channels is easy to achieve through the electoral process by direct sponsorship of a political party representing specific interests, potential discontent turns into regular political campaign activities.[29] In countries where the party systems do not effectively organize the various social groups, yet which are modernized and possess large numbers of citizens with the personal

Figure 6.3 Peaceful protests: A path model of environmental effects mediated through the party system. Reduced standardized regression coefficients, 1958–1976.[a]

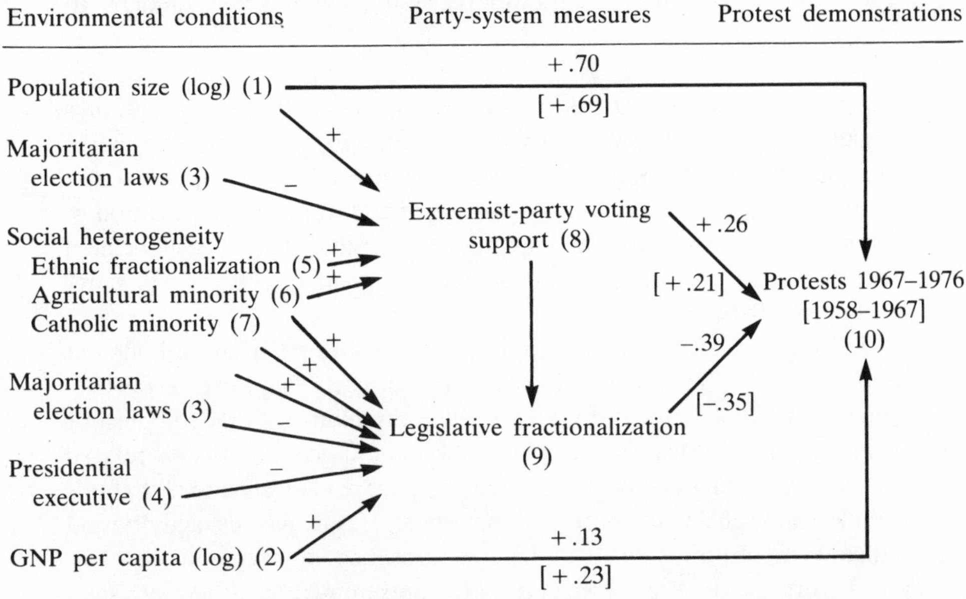

a. The arrows and path coefficients represent the standardized regression coefficients significant at the .10 level in a set of recursive regression equations. As indicated by the direction of the arrows, the model assumes that all variables with smaller identifying numbers are causally prior to variables with larger identifying numbers. Arrows leading to party-system variables represent coefficients significant at .05 in table 5.6. Coefficients shown are based on equations recalculated with insignificant variables deleted. Specific equations, variables, and sources are described in the Appendix.

skills and organizational connections to make protest organization feasible, protest activities are highly likely. The United States is the prototype of such a country. Here again, then, seems to be strong evidence in favor of representational party systems.

Figure 6.3 traces the way in which the constitutional and environmental factors shape protest outcomes. Level of economic development, for example, has in general only a weak relationship to protest activity. This weak association seems to reflect contradictory forces: on the one hand, citizens in the more modern societies have skills for easy protest mobilization; on the other hand, the more modern societies are more likely to have party systems that channel discontent through multiple, organized political parties. Representational constitutions, however, have a fairly strongly negative relationship to protest activity. Although such constitutional arrangements are associated with both extremist representation and fractionalization, the inhibiting effect of the latter on protests is stronger than the encouraging effect of the former. The net balance, even more sharply than for rioting, favors the representational constitutional type and the multiparty systems with strong linkages to groups.

Citizen voting participation is mobilized by the party system's organization of political cleavages, constrained by extreme forms of elite limitation of competition, and encouraged by automatic voter registration and penalties for not voting. The level of modernization of the society and the national constitutional arrangements are associated with levels of voting participation through their effects on the party system and voting laws.

The party system also has important effects on citizen turmoil, violent and peaceful. The strength of extremist-party support, especially support for parties offering explicitly antidemocratic ideologies or promising radical transformation of the national community, is related to levels of rioting and protests. There is good reason to believe that this relationship reflects the precipitating effects of such parties' activities on citizens' frustrations, as well as the presence of severe discontent. However, a more fractionalized and representative multiparty system also serves to dampen and inhibit rioting and protests. Not all the multiparty systems experience extremist-party support, which is related to unique historical upheavals and grievances in countries with strong extremist contenders. Not all extremist parties are found together with rioting and protest. And the more representative systems seem especially unlikely to suffer from rioting unrelated to party actions, which is common in the majority systems.

Voting and rioting levels are negatively related to each other, as we saw in the factor analyses in Chapters 2 and 4. These nations with higher voting turnout have, on average, less rioting, less turmoil of all kinds. In part this relationship is due to a persistent negative relationship that suggests a trade-off between legitimate and illegitimate participation (see table 10.1). But much of the relationship is due to the contrast between constitutional structures and, most powerfully, party systems that emphasize either the quiescence of citizens and the concentration of political resources, or the mobilization of citizens and direct representation of their views through electoral and legislative processes. Despite the turmoil-inducing role of extremist parties, which are encouraged somewhat by representational constitutions, the net effects of the mobilizing and representative strategy seems to be to involve citizens legitimately and to lessen their riot and protest activity.

Government Performance /
Executive Stability

7

The stability and effectiveness of the chief executive have long been major criteria of democratic performance for political theorists. The interest in executive performance has stimulated substantial speculative analysis and some rigorous theory construction and testing.[1] In Chapters 2–4 I found that constitutional factors dominate explanations of executive performance, while the environmental setting has relatively little impact. The presidential systems are relatively durable, but likely to produce minority governments. The majoritarian parliamentary constitutions are likely to produce both durability and executive control. The representational parliamentary constitutions tend to be weak in both respects.

The brief look at party systems in Chapter 5 provided a surprising addition to this picture: in the regression analysis, it was primarily the presence of extremist parties, not party fractionalization, that predicted low executive durability. Analysis of party-system types yields similar results: once extremist party systems are excluded, majoritarian party systems are no more likely than minority ones to have durable executives.[2] The task of this chapter is to explain such results by looking at the full chain of effects: from social and constitutional environment, through election outcomes, to executive durability and control. I shall make use of coalition theory in this analysis of processes shaping government performance. The presidential systems and the parliamentary ones must be treated separately, as the logic that shapes relationships among the electorate, the parties, and the government is quite different in the two constitutional settings.

Parliamentary Systems: Government Formation

Despite important differences from constitution to constitution, the parliamentary systems considered here share a common feature: after an election a prime minister must be chosen who will be acceptable to the legislature. Moreover, the government can at any time be replaced by action of the legislative majority.[3] The critical and perpetual question is: Which parties will agree to form or support a given government, and for how long?

Parties and Coalition Preferences   In analyzing parliamentary governments I shall treat the party as the basic unit of analysis in the theory—disregarding the potentially fruitful, but complex, problem of intraparty factions[4]—and I shall think of parties as having a dual set of objectives. On the one hand, parties struggle for participation in and control of the policymaking process, through which leaders can realize their office-holding aspirations and policy objectives and can fulfill their commitments to their followers.

On the other hand, even while parties engage in short-term bargaining about policy and participation, they must look ahead to the opportunities and dangers of the next election.

Each party and group of parties in the legislature can be considered a possible coalition that might form a government. Assuming that each party wishes as much as possible to enjoy cabinet membership, shape policies, and maintain or increase its future electoral position, what kinds of coalitions will each party prefer? Without developing detailed formal analysis of coalition theory, we can say that the following expectations are reasonable: *(a)* A party will prefer coalitions with as few other parties as possible, so as to share fewer cabinet positions and other benefits of government and to maximize its influence in policy-making within the coalition. That is, parties prefer coalitions of minimum size, all else equal.[5] *(b)* A party will prefer coalitions in which the "average" policy preferences of other members are as close to its own policy preferences as possible.[6] Such coalitions will enhance the probability that the policies approximate the party's preferences, and they will reassure supporters and potential voters that the party is not straying too far from their wishes. *(c)* A party will prefer coalitions that are large enough to secure formation of a government and to carry the policy initiatives it desires—that is, it will prefer winning coalitions. The necessary size depends, of course, on the legislature's rules and the policies in question.

It is easy to see intuitively that these preferences will often conflict with each other. The minimum coalition would be a coalition of just one party by itself. The most secure winning coalition would include all possible parties and hence be as far as possible from minimum.

However, in comparing the specific coalitions available in a given situation, it will often be clear that some coalitions are going to be preferred by all of their potential members. From such an analysis, it is possible to predict what coalitions are likely to form and how stable they will be.[7]

Which Governments Form   The most clear-cut expectation about coalitions following from the discussion of preferences is that if a party can win alone, it will prefer to govern alone. In practical terms, this means that if a single party wins an absolute majority of legislative seats, it will form a single-party government and force the other parties into opposition. A single-party government will not have to share the benefits of office. If it has legislative strength to sustain its government and to carry its policies, it will prefer to govern alone. In fact, this has generally been the case. Table 7.1 shows the election outcomes and the types of governments formed in the 19 parliamentary countries of the 1967–1976 period. In 12 countries, at least one election resulted in a clear majority for a single party. Of the 25 elections in these 12 countries, a single-party government was formed after the election in all but 2 cases. In none of those countries was the government later expanded to include an additional party. This is not to say such expansions never take place. The experience of Britain and other countries during the crisis of World War II provide examples, but such cases are rare.

Two exceptions, where parties did after the election join with another party despite having a majority of their own, illustrate that the rule is not inexorable and reveal the logic of the exceptions. In Ceylon in 1970 and in Australia in 1975 the governments were built upon very strong pre-election agreements between the parties. These agreements in both cases included supporting the other's candidates in some geographic areas. Attainment of a pure majority by one party was unexpected, and because of the particular strategic situation—the multiparty fragmentation in Ceylon; the preferential ballot in Australia—would probably not have been achieved without the alliance. These alliances were then honored when it came time to form a government. The need to build and sustain electoral alliances is a condition outside the legislative arena that nonetheless can and does shape conflict within its boundaries. It remains true that single-party majority government is the rule where possible.

In 15 countries, however, and after 60 percent of all the elections in

Table 7.1 Type and durability of party governments in parliamentary systems, 1967–1976.[a]

Election outcomes	Single-party majority	Minority	Minimum winning coalition		Oversize coalition	
			Connected	Not connected	Connected	Not connected
Single-member-district system						
Single-party majority						
Australia	x					
Canada	x					
Ceylon					x	
India	x	x				
Jamaica	x					
New Zealand	x					
U.K.	x					
No single-party majority						
Australia		x				
Canada		x				
Ceylon					x	
U.K.		x				
Multimember-district PR system						
Single-party majority						
Austria	x					
Ireland	x					
Japan	x					
Sweden	x					
Turkey	x	x				
No single-party majority						
Austria		x				
West Germany			x			
Ireland			x			
Netherlands		x	x		x	
Norway		x	x			
Sweden		x	x			
Turkey		x		x		
Belgium		x	x		x	
Denmark		x	x			
Finland		x	x		x	
Italy		x		x	x	(x)
Median cabinet durability (months)[c]	36	18	31	(10)	15	(9)

Sources: Keesing's Archives. Classification of types of party government made by the author.

a. In Australia the Labour party government had a majority in the lower house only. Here it is counted as a minority government. The permanent coalition of National and Country parties is counted as one party. Minority governments after majority elections appear in India and Turkey because of the defections of factions of the majority party.

b. Parties are considered to be in the government only if they share in cabinet seats. A government is minimum winning if the deletion of one party will leave the government without majority control. A government is oversize if the deletion of one party will still leave the government with a majority.

c. Thirty-six months is used as the maximum durability for purposes of analysis.

the parliamentary systems during this time, no single party commanded a majority. Here, the conflicting pressures of the different coalition preferences are apparent. In 15 of the 36 cases, in 10 different countries, the solution was to form a minority government. These governments, usually of a single party, did not include in the cabinet enough parties to control a clear legislative majority. For the party forming the government, this situation meant that the rewards of office-holding were unshared, certainly an important prize. However, it meant also dependence on the tolerance of parties outside the government for the continued maintenance of that government, and an apparent absence of executive control over policy. I shall look more closely at minority governments later.

Pure coalition theory predicts that when coalitions do form they should be minimum winning coalitions. Because I am using the parties as the units of analysis, I shall consider "minimum winning" to mean that the coalition will lose its majority if any one party leaves it.[8] A coalition in which one party could leave and the remaining coalition partners would still have enough seats to command a majority is *oversize*. As parties should want to share their prize as little as possible, we expect oversize coalitions to be unusual. We have already seen this to be true in the majority legislatures. It is also true among the nonmajority legislatures. Of the 21 coalitions initially formed in the nonmajority legislatures, 16 were minimal winning, and only 5 were oversize. However, in some countries—Italy, Finland and Ceylon—oversize coalitions were very common. As these coalitions are not very durable, a large number of oversize coalitions did form during the decade. Because of this fact, there are about as many oversize coalitions as minimum winning ones among the nonmajority legislatures in the decade.

To see why this may be so, we need to look beyond the mere size of the coalitions and consider their policy content as well. We postulated that parties had three goals in joining coalitions: to limit the size, to get enough strength to win, and to keep the average distance between their policies and those of the coalition as a whole as low as possible. This minimization of the internal dissonance of the coalition will depend on the issues salient to the different parties and other complex considerations. But we can gain a fairly simple approximation of it if we range the parties—as they see each other—on a composite single dimension of some kind. If the parties are arrayed on such a "right to left" dimension, the consideration of minimizing internal dissonance leads us to expect

Figure 7.1   Single-dimensional view of parties in Finland and Italy: Bases of connected coalitions, 1967–1976.[a]

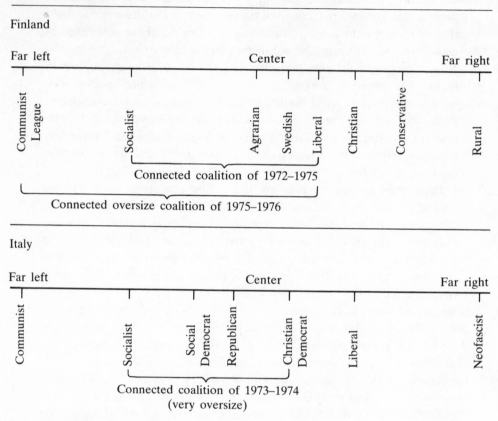

a. Only the relative right-to-left placing is determined, not exact positions on the continuum.

the formation of connected coalitions.[9] That is, the coalitions will be formed from parties that are adjacent to each other on the continuum.

Figure 7.1 shows the continuum that most parties and observers assign to the party systems in Italy and Finland. The Communist parties are on the far left; extreme right-wing parties are found on the other side—the neofascist MSI in Italy and the populist Rural party in Finland. Other parties occupy fairly clearly defined gradations in between. The expectation that coalitions will form among adjacent parties fits the coalitions shown in the diagram. "Connectivity" of coalitions fits both common sense and more systematic technical considerations. We would not expect, for example, a coalition between the Communists and a "rightist" party in general, and certainly not unless middle parties connected them. The addition of a connecting party to a potentially separated coalition will lower the average distance between parties in the coalition.[10] If the average distance is lowered, internal bargaining should be easier. Perhaps more important, the degree to which the party seems to be moving away from its initial supporters' preferences by joining a coalition will be lessened. Thus, the party that considers forming a coalition with a party some distance away on the continuum can serve its policy and, probably, its reelection goals better by including a connecting party. However, it will have to give up some cabinet ministries to the additional party. If the parties are very similar to one another, or if the parties represent several different dimensions on political issues and cannot easily be placed on a single "right-to-left" continuum, these considerations are less important.

We expect from this discussion to find few, if any, coalitions that are neither connected nor of minimum winning size. The oversize, nonconnected coalition is, indeed, virtually absent in the democracies. Only four countries had oversize coalitions formed as a result of legislative bargaining:[11] Finland, Italy, the Netherlands, and Belgium. The coalition in Belgium was connected, as were all five in Finland during this period, and so probably was the one in the Netherlands, although the complexity of the religious and socioeconomic issue dimensions makes the connectivity criterion less clear. In any case, it is just where the parties fail to form a coherent issue or ideological continuum that connectivity becomes less important for policy and electoral standing. In Italy there were six oversize coalitions: all included the Socialists and the Christian Democrats and all included the Social Democrats as connectors (see Figure 7.1). Four also included the Republicans as connectors, but two did not. These last two cases are the closest to oversize nonconnected coalitions. Even in them, however, some connecting is clearly present, and the Republicans did give outside support to the government.

Where parties can form minimum winning connected coalitions, we expect them to do so, rather than forming either oversize or nonconnected ones. In general, this expectation is realized. In Italy and Turkey, the minimum winning connected combinations were just not available: given the configurations of parties, coalitions could be minimum winning or connected, but not both. In Belgium, the oversize coalition was needed to make key constitutional changes in dealing with the language crisis. From that point of view, the coalition was not oversize. All other Belgian coalitions were minimum winning and connected. In Australia, Norway, Sweden, Germany, Denmark, and probably Ireland,[12] all coalitions were minority or minimum winning connected. However, once in the Netherlands and several times in Finland, connected oversize coalitions were chosen over available connected minimum winning ones. Both these countries were in volatile electoral periods, and in Finland it was argued that broad support for emergency measures to cope with economic crises was necessary. The "unnecessarily" large Finnish coalitions also involve Communist participation in the government and reflect both the Socialists' desire for a more leftward coalition balance and the center-right parties' desire for control over the Communists' role in government.

The experience of the 1965–1975 decade in general supports the conclusion of Abram DeSwaan, based on six of these countries plus Weimar Germany and Fourth Republic France, that "parliamentary majority coalitions...[tend] to form from actors that are adjacent on the policy scale, and these closed coalitions are of minimal range in times of normalcy."[13]

The factors leading to the formation of minority and oversize coalitions are further explicated in table 7.2. The countries are broken down here by the "usual" party outcomes of elections, as well as by the election laws. As in Chapter 6, I use the propensity to create single-party majorities in elections to classify the party systems as majoritarian or minority in type. Among the 7 countries with single-member districts, the "expected" outcome was a majority-party victory.[14] In 15 of the 21 elections, such victories did occur and the party formed a government, as we see in the top block of table 7.2. Usually, that government had a single party. But in Ceylon the preelectoral coalitions led to a series of oversize government coalitions. In India the Congress party split in 1967, leading to a minority government. Nonetheless, single-party-majority cabinets, (which are minimum winning), were the rule in these countries following majority elections. But in 5 of the 6 cases where no party won a clear victory, a minority government was formed, rather than a coalition. (In Ceylon the 1965 preelectoral coalition stayed together and formed a government.) The expectation seemed to be that soon new elections would be held and that these would result in an elected majority government.

The results were rather similar in the multimember-district countries in which single parties usually won majorities. These four countries are shown in the second block in table 7.2. Whether because of special

Table 7.2 Impact of party-system type on cabinet formation and durability, 1967–1976.

Usual election outcome	Outcome of specific elections for largest party	Durability of cabinets by type (months) Minimum winning[a]	Other	All	(N)[b]	% of cabinets that are minimum winning
	Single-member-district systems					
Majoritarian	Majority 15	36	20	32	(19)	74%
Australia[c]	Minority 6	—	21	21	(7)	0
Canada						
Ceylon	All 21	36	21	29	(26)	54
India						
Jamaica						
New Zealand						
U.K.						
	Multimember district PR systems					
Majoritarian	Majority 8	32	12	30	(10)	90
Austria	Minority 3	36	15	20	(4)	25
Ireland						
Japan	All 11	32	14	27	(14)	71
Turkey						
Minority: nonextremist	Majority 1	36[d]	—	36	(1)	100
West Germany	Minority 12	30	27	28	(15)	47
Netherlands						
Norway	All 13	31	27[e]	29	(16)	50
Sweden						
Minority: extremist	Majority 0	—	—	—	(0)	—
Belgium	Minority 15	26	11	15	(29)	25
Denmark						
Finland	All 15	26	11[f]	15	(29)	25
Italy						

Sources: Calculated using data from *Keesing's Archives.*

a. Cabinets are minimum winning if the deletion of one party would leave the government without majority control.

b. There are more cabinets than election outcomes because in some countries several governments may be formed (and fall) between elections.

c. Australia: the two governments with Labour majority in the lower house only are counted as majority; the permanent pre-election alliance of National and Country parties is counted as one party.

d. The Swedish majority government lasted only 24 months, but that was the maximum, as the constitution was being changed.

e. These contain 7 minority governments and 1 oversize government.

f. These contain 10 minority governments and 11 oversize governments.

nuances of the election laws, voting volatility, or the historical configuration of parties, elections in these countries produced single-party majorities more than half of the time. Again, if the election failed to produce a majority, the largest party usually governed alone as a minority government. Coalitions were not negotiated after the election. Only a pre-election coalition in Ireland formed a government coalition.

The two bottom blocks of countries in the table—the minority party systems—showed quite different patterns. In countries with low extremist strength, minimum winning coalitions formed in about half of the cabinets. The alternative was usually a minority government. By contrast, in countries where extremist-party representation averaged over 15 percent or so, the formation of minimum winning coalitions was less likely, and oversize coalitions were a frequent alternative. Examination of over-time results in those countries in which extremist support changed during the decade also suggests that minimum winning coalitions were more likely when extremist representation was lower.

Minority Governments and Executive Control   Minority governments are worth a special look for two reasons. First, they are surprisingly common occurrences in parliamentary systems and represent the major source of the absence of executive control. (However, the time spent without any government, while party bargaining goes on and the civil service runs the nation, has been considerable in some countries, such as the Netherlands.) Second, the minority governments represent in practice several different situations in legislative-executive relations.[15]

In some cases the formation of a minority government represents intense legislative conflict. The parties are too deeply divided to agree on a stable coalition capable of positive action, so they accept a minority "caretaker." The government is kept in office as long as it remains passive in policy formation. Its retention depends on outside parties who prefer it to other governments as a temporary measure and prefer it to an absence of government, but will not join it in positive policies. The minority Liberal party government in Denmark, following the 1973 election, a government commanding only 13 percent of the legislative seats, is a good example of a deadlock caretaker of this kind. The 1972 Labour party government in Finland and a number of Christian Democratic governments in Italy provide other examples. The minority governments in the countries in the bottom block of countries in table 7.2 were usually of this type.

Similarly limited in policy capacity is perhaps the largest group of minority governments, the "pre-election caretakers." In the systems in which the elections usually produce single-party parliamentary majorities, the failure to get a majority in a given election may be viewed as an aberration. The party leaders often feel it is easier, or customary, to let the largest party govern alone as a minority until the next election. Typically, these systems provide for an early election in case of such an outcome. If the regular election does not generate a majority, the single-party minority administers the government, but does not attempt major policy initiatives. Britain and Canada follow this custom.

As noted, if in table 7.2 we contrast the eleven countries in which elections created majorities half of the time with the eight countries in which elections rarely produce single-party majorities, the treatment of nonmajority situations looks quite different. In the single-party-majoritarian systems, in those elections when no party won a victory, the formation of a coalition government was extremely unusual. Only pre-election agreements in Ceylon and Ireland were springboards to government coalitions. In the minority systems, by contrast, two-thirds of the governments formed after elections were coalition governments with majorities. In the nonextremist situations, these coalitions were usually minimum winning. Many of these coalitions were the result of postelection negotiation. In short, where the party and electoral system typically produces majorities, the elites tend to rely on direct election outcomes and orient themselves to the forthcoming election, rather than to legislative bargaining for a coalition. Where the electoral system does not usually produce majorities, the parties respond to the need for coalition-building.

A third kind of minority government is one in which the governing party has consistent support from one or more parties outside the government, parties that support at least some of its policy initiatives. Arrangements between parties range from informal understandings to written agreements for full consultations and policy vetoes (as in the long-lived Communist- and Socialist-supported Christian Democratic governments in Italy in the late 1970s). The clearest cases are the support given to Social Democratic (Labour) governments by parties to their extreme left in Denmark, Sweden, and Norway in the 1960s. Although, for electoral reasons, and perhaps because of distrust of the extremists in some policy areas, the large parties did not permit the small extremists to join the government, these informal alliances often allowed the minority governments to move important policy initiatives through the legislature. I have not counted these alliances as coalitions unless the parties shared cabinet seats, but they did act virtually as minimum winning coalitions on domestic welfare policies. Such policy-oriented minority coalitions seemed especially likely in the countries where extremist parties were quite weak, the next-to-last block in table 7.2.

It is clear that the presence of strong extremist parties is associated with less durable types of minority government and with the choice of minority or oversize governments over majority minimum winning coalitions. But in some countries—especially Finland, Belgium, and the Netherlands—the parties virtually never chose minority governments. Rather than a minority deadlock, they preferred long bargaining or bringing extremist parties into minimal or oversize coalitions. In conditions that seemed quite similar in, say, Denmark, a caretaker minority was preferred. Matters of custom and leadership must be invoked to account for such differences (see Chapter 10 for a discussion of leadership).

Parliamentary Systems: Durability of Governments

There is substantial predictability in the formation of cabinet governments and even more in their durability. For, although the decision of a set of parties to choose a minority government rather than an oversize coalition may involve a complex balancing of policy objectives, perceived voter reactions, and personal goals—all shaped by imperfect information—the probable conflicts resulting from such choices are more easily seen. We expect party governments to be less durable when they do not command a majority of legislative seats; when they are oversize in that a party can be forced out, while still keeping the coalition strong enough to rule; and when the coalitions are not connected, suggesting higher internal division and a highly suitable replacement, in policy terms, for a coalition member.

Tables 7.1 and 7.2 present material on the durability of cabinet governments, by type of coalition and country. Durability is counted from the forming of a government until either it is dissolved or new elections are held, whichever comes first. If the parties in the government change, or when a party split changes the coalition from majority to minority (as in India and Turkey), a new government is held to have begun. As in earlier chapters, governments lasting over three years are counted as enduring 36 months for comparative purposes.

It is quite apparent, from analysis both within and across countries,

that the most durable governments are single-party-majority governments. This outcome is consistent with both conventional wisdom and
coalition analysis. The single-party-majority government has control of
the legislature for policy purposes, yet does not have to share its offices
or seats with any party. Unless the party splits, or is in command of such
a narrow margin that death or illness of a few members jeopardizes its
control, there is every reason for such a government to endure.
Opposition challenges to such parties are largely formal and designed to
raise issues for the next election. The opposition can use a variety of
tactics to bring pressure on the government,[16] but it is unlikely to
displace it from power. (As studies of policymaking in Britain have
suggested, however, much consultation and accommodation with opposition parties on many issues can lie behind the apparent facade of one-
party absolutism in countries with stable majority government.)[17]

One point about such majority governments is of special interest. In
India, Turkey, Ireland, and apparently Japan, the government did lose
control of the legislature due to splits within its party. In India and
Turkey, at least, major splits cost the government its identity; new
parties formed and soon forced the minority government to call an early
election. No such failure of control seems to have appeared in the
majority-party governments in Austria, Britain, Ceylon, Canada,
Sweden, or New Zealand. (Information is lacking in the case of
Jamaica.) Although various factors are responsible, no doubt, it is clear
that strong cleavage alignments between parties and groups are
associated with coherence and durability of these majority parties.
Although parties choosing a narrower, mobilizational strategy seem to
be less likely to attain legislative majorities, their coherence gives them
a powerful and durable position once they do so. For the 8 of these
nations on which data are available, the average cleavage alignment
index is 17 for the 3 nations with governmental splits; it is 41 for the 5
nations whose parties remained durable. The well-known internal
fracturing of American parties in the legislature, although not strictly
comparable, given the presidential system, is also consistent with such
effects.

The next most durable form of government, as theory predicts,[18] is
the minimum winning connected coalition. Although not quite as
durable as single-party-majority governments, we see here, as Dodd
demonstrated with a somewhat different set of countries and time
periods, that the minimum winning coalitions are quite durable, at least
if they are reasonably connected.[19] The single-party-majority govern-

ments lasted, on average, for 34 months. The minimum winning connected coalitions lasted for 29 months. Some coalitions, like those in Ireland (FinGael/Labour), Denmark (Conservative/Liberal/Radical), West Germany (both SPD/CDU and SPD/FDP), and Norway (Conservative/Liberal/Christian/Agrarian) up to the EEC crisis, were very long-lived. Even in Finland and Belgium there were some very durable minimum winning connected coalitions, and these were more durable than the minority and oversize coalitions in these countries. Indeed, the early collapse of such coalitions seems to be caused as often by a party break-up (Belgium in 1971 over the language cleavage) as by a party defection from the coalition (the Netherlands in 1971 by DS-70). Appearance of a new issue, such as the dispute over entering the common market in Norway in 1971, can break up a coalition for both reasons. However, despite the advantages of such minimum winning connected coalitions, they work no magic in the presence of strong internal polarization and conflict. Extremist party seats are related to the durability of such coalitions—negatively—as well as to their formation.[20]

Clearly nonconnected coalitions are so rare that statistical analysis is hazardous. The only two clear cases are found in Italy and Turkey. In Turkey following the 1973 election, the Republican party and the new Moslem-extremist, traditionalist National Salvation party formed a minimum winning coalition that was clearly not connected. It joined the right and left ends of the Turkish spectrum. The coalition aroused shocked comment all around, proved totally unworkable on the first serious issues it confronted, and collapsed in 8 months. In Italy, by contrast, the minimum winning, but not connected coalition of Liberals, Christian Democrats, and Social Democrats—leaving out the tiny Republican party—was Italy's most durable coalition in the decade. This durability, however, lasted exactly a year. It is worth reemphasizing that in countries such as Ireland and the Netherlands where the parties fail to form a single continuum and/or differences between parties are slight, the nonconnectivity criterion is both more difficult to apply to analysis and less likely to be determining.

The minority governments were on average not nearly as durable as the minimum winning connected coalitions, but they did survive an average of about 18 months. Some of these, drawing on consistent support from an outsider party, were quite durable, as in Sweden. As shown in table 7.2, minority governments in the nonextremist situations were quite often long-lived. The crisis minority governments in Belgium, Italy, Denmark (Liberals in 1973), and Finland were, however, very short-lived. The pre-election caretaker governments fell in between these extremes. It is perhaps worth noting that in the countries with a majority tradition, where the largest party took over as a minority, then called for early elections—India after the break-up of Congress in 1969, Austria, Britain, and Canada—it was in each case rewarded with a majority by the electorate.

The oversize coalition governments, despite usually being connected, tended to fall apart far more quickly than the minimum winning connected coalitions. None of the 6 oversize Italian coalitions lasted a year—the average was 7 months. The oversize Belgian coalition formed to affect constitutional change lasted only about a year. Two of the Finnish oversize coalition governments lasted about 9 months; however, in the late 1960s 2 oversize governments, which included the Communists, lasted nearly 2 years each. In Ceylon, the oversize coalitions created by pre-election imperatives lasted a bit under 2 years on average; eventually some of the "extra" parties left in frustration at their weak bargaining role. The only extremely durable oversize coalition was that in the Netherlands, built after a long crisis and lasting from 1972 to the 1977 election. One factor here may have been the negotiations, temporarily successful in 1977, to unify the religious parties into a single party. Across the full set of countries, the median life of such coalitions was about 15 months.

Figure 7.2 summarizes the analysis of cabinet durability in the parliamentary systems. The left of the figure reworks the analysis of the bases of party fractionalization, extremist representation, and party volatility initially developed in Chapter 5. The right-hand part of the figure shows the results of the regression analysis of the durability of the 85 cabinet governments formed and ended during this period (using 36 months as the maximum duration possible). As the figure shows, majorities and volatility—the measure of change in party strength from the last election—affect the probability that a minimum winning connected coalition will be formed, as does the amount of extremist-party representation in the legislature. Single-party majorities almost always lead to single-party-majority government, unless there was a pre-electoral coalition. More volatile patterns of representation lead to fewer minimum winning coalitions, other things being equal. The negative effect of volatility apparently reflects in part the greater reliance on the purely electoral outcomes in countries with volatile representation. Volatility also increases the likelihood that an appar-

Figure 7.2 Cabinet durability: A path model of environmental effects mediated through election outcomes and legislative coalition formation. Reduced standardized regression coefficients, 1967–1976.[a]

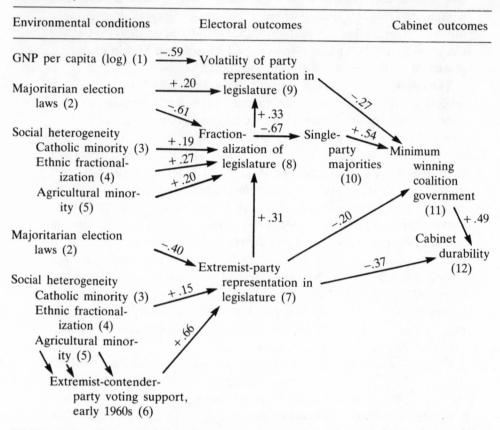

a. The arrows and path coefficients represent the standardized regression coefficients significant at the .10 level in a set of recursive regression equations. As indicated by the direction of the arrows, the model assumes that all variables with smaller identifying numbers are causally prior to variables with larger identifying numbers. Election outcome equations are computed on 60 elections, each country weighted equally. Cabinet outcome equations are computed on 84 cabinets, each country weighted equally. Specific equations, variables, and sources are described in the Appendix.

ently minimum winning pre-election coalition will turn out to be oversize after the election. As Lawrence Dodd suggests, the problem of getting good information for bargaining may also impede the formation of minimum winning coalitions, and this problem is increased by shifting party representation.[21] Such volatility is especially common in developing countries. As was clear in table 7.2, the presence of extremist parties makes minimum winning coalitions less likely, both directly and because of its fractionalizing tendency, and makes all kinds of coalitions less durable.

Only the type of coalition and extremist-party representation directly affect cabinet durability. In large simultaneous regressions, all the variables on the left of the figure are insignificant after coalition type and extremist representation are entered. These two variables explain 50 percent of the variance in durability of the 85 cabinets. (The coefficients in figure 7.2 are computed weighting each country equally, so as not to be biased by the frequent cabinet changes in Italy.)

If we divide the cabinets into those in which there was originally a legislative majority for one party and those in which there was not, we get, naturally, somewhat different regression estimates for the two situations. For the majority legislatures, extremist representation and volatility still do affect the type of cabinet. Most cabinets were single-party majorities, but the breakup of majority governments and the initial formation of oversize coalitions were more likely under conditions of volatility and extremism. Strong cleavage alignments between parties and groups are positively related to durability in majority situations, due to their association, apparently, with coherence of the majority party.

In the minority legislatures only, considering a weighted 33 cabinets, extremist-party representation is the strongest direct preditor of durability (B = −.50), with minimum winning connected coalitions also clearly significant (B = + .38). These two variables explain about 45 percent of the variance in durability.

In predicting the formation of minimum winning connected coalitions, extremist representation (B = −.25) and party volatility (B = −.20) are both still relevant. These subanalyses certainly suggest that the general summary provided by figure 7.2 is well grounded in theory and the underlying processes.

Figure 7.2 and table 7.2 also show why simple consideration of such environmental conditions as homogeneity and modernity do not go very far in explaining government performance. They are strongly moderated through and by such factors as party strategies, electoral laws, and elite bargaining. The more modernized systems, for example, are less volatile, which is stabilizing in cabinet formation. But the modern systems are also more likely to have proportional representation; and somewhat less extreme. Volatility is far less important than extremist representation. Agricultural and ethnic heterogeneity fractionalize the legislature and encourage extremism. Hence they are associated with less durable governments. But the effects were operative only in the ministerial systems, and they are powerfully mediated through the party system, especially the originally developed extremist divisions. Even the electoral laws have a somewhat mixed effect, as the majority-oriented laws do encourage more volatility in party representation, and make minimum winning coalitions less likely even as they often create party majorities.

The table and the figure provide a clear resolution of the apparent paradox of the greater explanatory power of extremism over fractionalization. While less fractionalization does encourage more frequent appearance of electoral majorities, and while simple majorities are very durable, the conditions that lead to majorities also discourage bargaining in those not infrequent elections without majorities. They also sometimes lead to oversize governments based on pre-election coalitions. The top blocks of countries in table 7.2 show this tendency quite clearly. Simple majorities were the most common outcome in these countries and were very durable. But the much lower durability of the minority governments that were almost invariably formed when elections did not lead to a majority brought down the average cabinet duration from 36 months to 29 months. In the nonextremist minority countries, minimum winning coalitions were formed half the time, and were quite durable, and their minority governments (frequently enjoying support from small parties outside the government) were also much longer-lived than the election caretaker minorities in the first blocks of countries. Hence, average cabinet durability was about as great in the nonextremist minority party systems as in the majority systems. Extremist representation, by contrast, was associated with more frequent minority and oversize coalitions.[22] Although the minimum winning coalitions were fairly durable, even here, they were formed only a quarter of the time, and the minority governments were usually of the very fragile "crisis deadlock" type, lasting only 11 months on average. Extremism was also associated, of course, with the failure of simple majority governments to appear in the first place.

While this analysis is favorable to the argument that majoritarianism as a constitutional and party-system strategy does not, as such, create greater executive stability, we must not overlook the party and electoral dynamics discussed in Chapter 5. The conditions that generate multiparty systems—heterogeneity and proportional representation—also make the appearance of extremist parties likely if general conditions deteriorate or special discontents emerge. Where such parties gain substantial legislative representation, they tend to impede the formation of durable cabinet governments. Such tendencies are overwhelming in the cross-sectional comparison, and apparent in the examination of individual countries over time. Thus, the good short-run performance of nonextremist minority systems in creating stable executives must be weighed against the fact that representational constitutional arrangements seem to encourage destabilizing representation of extremist parties. It is upon this basis, above all, that the superior governmental performance of the majority strategy rests.

Presidential Government

While some 21 countries (including Greece and Israel) operated under parliamentary constitutions of the sort I have been analyzing, another 8 made the executive relatively independent of legislative majorities. In seven of these countries, citizens selected the chief executive through elections, while in Switzerland the legislature chose the collective executive council. Even among the systems with popularly elected presidents, constitutional arrangements vary substantially. In France the requirement that the president appoint a prime minister who is responsible to the legislature creates more interdependence than in most presidential systems. Executive durability was quite high under all these constitutional variations, regardless of party system and environmental conditions. The median executive durability was 36 months; in most cases the executive served at least one complete term of four to seven years.

All of the 7 presidential systems, however, faced the frequent experience of presidents being elected whose party did not command a legislative majority. In these countries, such minority executives were in power about 44 percent of the time between 1967 and 1976. Political leaders dealt with the failure of the electorate to create executive control in a variety of ways. In the United States and Costa Rica the presidents accepted legislative obstacles to the formation of policy, and attempted to take policy initiatives from a minority position by dealing with leaders of both parties in the legislature.[23] In Uruguay and generally in France, the president attempted to bring opposition-party factions into the cabinet and create clear executive control as in a parliamentary situation. In Venezuela the minority presidents of the early 1960s also attempted to build majority coalitions, but the Caldera government of 1969–1973 operated as a minority presidency in the American and Costa Rican fashion, negotiating relatively harmoniously with opposition parties, but not bringing them into the government.[24] In Chile the Allende government functioned as a minority coalition of the parties that supported the Allende electoral coalition. Not all Allende policies were unpopular; and his nationalization of the copper companies, for example, had broad legislative support. But as the government attempted to initiate a more thoroughgoing "transition to socialism," the conflict between the government minority and the opposition legislative parties became more intense, compounded by growing economic crises. Government ministers were impeached by Congress; the president attempted to bypass congressional authority by ruling by decree; budgets were blocked. In the Philippines, by contrast, the immense powers of the presidency and the personalistic party system created great temptations for legislators to defect to the president's party. Presidents elected as minority governments in 1961 and 1965 eventually became leaders of majority parties through such defections.[25]

Thus, the handicaps in legislative relations faced by minority presidents were as varied as those faced by minority parliamentary governments. Obviously, the presidential governments were much more durable than prime ministerial governments in minority situations. Most minority presidents served out their full term of office, which was rare for minority governments. (Sweden in 1973–1976 does provide an example.) Minority presidential governments were, in fact, about as durable as majority parliamentary ones. However, the only examples of lessened presidential durability were all under minority governments: Nixon in the United States in 1974, Allende in Chile in 1973, the curbing of presidential power in Uruguay by the military in 1973. Examples of presidential cabinet reshuffles and interparty negotiations under minority governments also testify to difficulties, although the meaning of such examples varies greatly with the country.

Except in Chile (and potentially in France), the very weak party systems in most presidential countries, as measured by low party-group linkages and high volatility, made it easier for minority presidents to deal with their legislatures. As Duverger suggests, weak parties increase presidential authority.[26] As we saw in Chapter 5, presidential systems seem to encourage party weaknesses. At the same time, the low levels of party organization and centralized policy coherence in presidential systems, as well as the lowered costs of deviant legislative voting when a defeat for the government does not mean a new election, make it hard for most majority presidents to enjoy the degree of legislative control held by prime ministers of majority parties or firm coalition governments. The American situation, in which majority presidents have only rarely been able to get their programs easily adopted by Congresses controlled by their own party, is in fact typical of presidential systems. The separation of powers indeed operates to require more complex negotiations between presidents and their legislative parties, whose different electoral base often creates substantially different political interests. To a large extent, then, whether the government has a majority or a minority, although it is still relevant to governmental performance, is less critical to legislative-executive relations in presidential systems than in parliamentary ones.

By assuming simple party goals of governmental participation and electoral advantage, and combining these with coalition theory, we can explain a good deal about the type and durability of party governments. Many important considerations, however, such as intraparty divisions and the role of creative leadership, have been set aside. I shall discuss some of these more generally in Chapter 10. But the importance of the general party configurations, especially the role of extremist-party strength in making stable government difficult to achieve, has been clarified. Majoritarian constitutions are more stable than representational ones for several reasons, but their tendency to limit the legislative strength of extremist parties is the primary factor in their greater durability. Nations with representational constitutions are capable of enjoying stable and effective governments, but to do so their party leaders must be able to negotiate minimum winning coalitions, or at least policy-supported minority governments. The presence of extremist parties is the major impediment to such stable coalition-building, given willingness of leaders to attempt it. The presidential constitutions, by contrast, virtually guarantee executive durability, but force continual policy negotiation among leaders whose political interests diverge, even if their party label is the same.

Managing Violence
and Sustaining Democracy

8

Democracy is a strategy of government based on the gamble that the potential for participation and responsiveness that it offers will make possible a resolution of conflict without violence. Where large-scale violence or coercion does appear, democracy is fundamentally threatened. Not only does the influence of coercion on decisionmaking weaken the importance of democratic resources, but the failure of government to maintain order and security leads citizens to look more positively on authoritarian alternatives. In this chapter I shall examine the origins of violence and the successes and failures of contemporary democratic regimes in dealing with it.

Elite Bases of Deadly Violence

Most comparative studies of violence have distinguished between the rather disorganized, mass-involving, diffuse activities of rioting and related turmoil, on the one hand, and organized attacks by purposive and armed insurgents, on the other.[1] Although there is some tendency for riots and armed attacks to appear in the same countries, the differences far outweigh the similarities. The only general environmental variable that consistently and directly predicts frequency of rioting is population size. By contrast, the degree of modernization, the extent of ethnic fractionalization, and the constitutional arrangements, as well as population size, are systematic predictors of deaths by political violence. In examining the process of citizen involvement in politics in Chapter 6, I noted the role of the party system in constraining or encouraging riots. Where a number of parties attained political representation and directly linked social and political groups to the legislative setting in nonmajoritarian circumstances, riot propensities were dampened and discontent channeled into legitimate forms of participation. Where citizens voted in substantial numbers for extremist parties, rioting was more probable. These party-system outcomes mediated and diffused the potential impact of the environmental and constitutional variables on riot activity.

But, as indicated in figure 8.1, the patterns of party support do not seem to mediate the impact of the environmental factors on deaths by political violence. It is especially interesting that the extent of support for extremist parties has little systematic relationship to deaths; it neither increases nor reduces them. The simple correlations between voting for extremist parties and deaths are insignificant and in the regression analyses the relationship is weakly negative (B = −.07) in the first decade and weakly positive (B = +.16) in the second, both statistically insignificant. The relationship between fractionalization and deadly violence is similarly weak and inconsistent.

High levels of voting turnout are quite strongly associated with lower levels of deaths by violence, as seen in Chapter 2. The simple correlation is around −.50 in both decades. But in the regression analysis the relationship is greatly reduced. Whereas the party and electoral patterns mediated the impact of modernization on rioting, helping to explain the nature of the relationships, the reverse seems to be true for modernization and deaths by violence. The poorer, less modernized countries are much more likely to have more deadly violence, regardless of their voting turnout; controlling for modernization level, the relationship between voting turnout and deadly violence, although negative, becomes virtually insignificant. (See table 10.1 and the accompanying text discussion for further analysis of the relationship between voting turnout and political order.) Introducing the variable for the representativeness of the constitutional structure further reduces the weight of the voting turnout variable, while constitutional structure continues to have some direct, unmediated impact. The countries with more representational constitutions tend to have slightly fewer deaths by political violence, and this tendency, unlike the relationships with rioting and voting activity, does not seem to be mediated through the party system and citizen action.

In short, the attempt to model the bases of deadly violence brings out once again the conclusion that deadly violence is not, systematically and crossnationally, a product of patterns of citizen involvement and support, but of the strategic efforts of small groups of political elites.[2] These elites respond rather directly to the strains and limitations of ethnicity and lower modernization, to the checks of constitutional structure, to the policies of political opponents. Factors of citizen

Figure 8.1 The role of party-system variables in paths to riots and deaths by political violence. Reduced standardized regression coefficients, 1958–1976.[a]

Environmental conditions	Party system	Violence

Riots

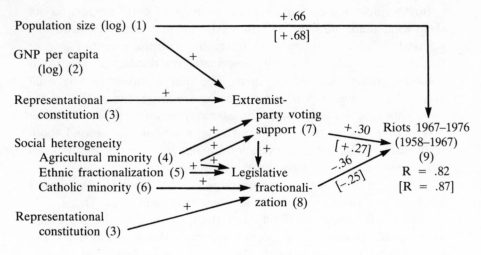

Deaths by political violence

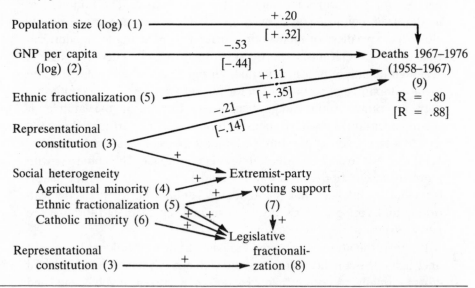

a. The arrows and path coefficients represent the standardized regression coefficients significant at the .10 level in a set of recursive regression equations. As indicated by the direction of the arrows, the model assumes that all variables with smaller identifying numbers are causally prior to variables with larger identifying numbers. Arrows leading to party-system variables represent coefficients significant at .05 in table 5.6. Coefficients shown are based on equations recalculated with insignificant variables deleted. Specific equations, variables and sources are described in the Appendix.

support and involvement can be critical to the impact of elite-based violence on the maintenance of the democratic system. I shall argue that the reactions to deadly violence by leaders of the major contending political parties are extremely important to the ability of democracy to survive violent shocks. The interaction between these party leaders and their supporters is both directly and indirectly a weighty factor in the strategies adopted by the leaders. But efforts to understand the origins and impacts of deadly violence must include, at least, consideration of the goals and strategies of the armed activists and their leaders who organize it.

A partial exception to these observations about deadly violence appears in the countries with serious ethnic rioting. I pointed out in Chapter 3 that the association between rioting and deaths by violence was notably higher in ethnically fractionalized countries. Examination of specific riots shows that large numbers of deadly attacks committed by riot crowds seem exclusively a property of clashes between ethnic communities. In the democracies, the major examples were found in the Hindu-Moslem riots in India. Moreover, a reading of riot accounts seems to suggest that governments are more likely to use deadly force in suppressing ethnically based riots. Whether they do so out of greater personal fear or a greater sense of estrangement from the rioters, or in response to greater violence from the rioters, is unclear. Ethnic conflicts that intensify can also spark simultaneously the deadly violence of the lynch mob or the armed assault of small groups of retaliators or aggressors on members of the other faction. The attacks by American whites on civil rights workers in the early 1960s provide a number of examples, as do clashes in India, the Philippines, and Northern Ireland. Only in the United States and pre-1970 Ceylon, however, were the majority of deaths related to unorganized or small-scale ethnic clashes.

Organized Violence: Strategic Objectives and Consequences

Most of the deaths from political violence in the democracies resulted from organized armed attacks by political groups—attacks on their opponents, on the symbols of government, or on unprotected citizens. In each case, doubtless, a number of personal and political motives were involved. But because the actions were organized, planned behavior, typically carried out by highly committed political actors, it is useful to look at the general objectives of organized violence. These objectives have important implications for the impact of the violence on the survival of the democratic regime.

Anger and Strategy   From a strategic point of view organized political violence has three very general objectives: to change the bargaining rules of the democratic game, to undermine the support enjoyed by the regime or its major parties, or to intimidate the opposition while mobilizing support.[3] Under certain conditions any political group may be tempted to use violence for one of these purposes. No group gets its way all the time; even those which had hold power may be threatened with its loss; violence may seem to be one way of changing a losing position. By the same token, each of these temptations can under some conditions generate responses that can lead to the overthrow of democratic government.

To emphasize the strategic bases of organized violence is not to deny the importance of other motivations for the individuals involved. Studies of terrorism often suggest that some terrorists are pathological personalities, cloaking in political purpose deep-seated rages and distortions that are personal in origin.[4] Moreover, anger and frustration at injustices suffered by self, family, and friends are often critical factors in turning the sympathizing dissident into the active terrorist. It is, after all, a highly dangerous business to use organized violence, and the normative and legal barriers that most societies erect against unsanctioned assaults on others must be hurdled. Democracies in particular claim to offer nonviolent political resources to the dissatisfied, and the terrorist in a democratic society must reject that claim. Given the dangers and inhibitions involved, it is not surprising that often those recruited to the use of violence are driven by angers that make that use personally satisfying.

It is likely that in every society individuals can be found for whom the use of violence would provide some internal satisfactions. Assassinations by pathologically disturbed persons, for example, are a hazard of political prominence everywhere, although availability of weapons and cultural channeling of violence have some effect on the frequency of attempts.[5] But anger and frustration become especially important in political violence where political events generate intense grievances. Such grievances can create cycles of violence that are especially difficult to curb once they are under way. By the mid-1970s most families in Northern Ireland could personally claim a casualty of the violence and identify the "other side" as the cause of that tragic loss. Under such conditions the desire for peace may be more than counterbalanced by the ease of recruiting more angry terrorists, eager to revenge their personal, but also political, grievances.

Nonetheless, the strategic bases of political violence, I think, hold the key to its relationship to the broader political systems of the democratic nations. Isolated outbreaks of terrorism have, as we shall see, rather little impact on democratic politics. It is when violence demonstrates some success in mobilizing broader support, undermining support for democratic government, or intimidating political opposition that it must be taken most seriously by those concerned with democratic political performance. Let us look more carefully, then, at the major strategic types of organized violence in the contemporary democracies.

Separatist Violence   Democratic regimes offer political resources to all citizens. Citizens who are dissatisfied with political outcomes can form new groups and parties and attempt to change those outcomes. But for this bargain of democratic resources and support for democratic regimes to work, it must be possible for losers on one issue to become winners on other issues. And there must be some agreement that the boundaries of the community from which the participants are drawn are reasonable ones. Democracy can be cruel to minorities, particularly groups whose interests and identities are so distinctive as to single them out permanently—at least to themselves—as delineated minority groups. As I have already observed, ethnic and religious divisions can be particularly difficult to deal with for that reason. The use of systematic violence by minority groups attempting to gain consideration for their minority views is not uncommon. It gains special impact and difficulty, however, where the minority group desires to change the boundaries of the political community and set up its own regime or join another one.[6]

If leaders of minority organizations can convince substantial parts of the minority community that separatism is a desirable goal, then bases for serious use of organized violence are at hand. Because the present democratic regime is not legitimate—imposing, as it does, a majority rule which would be eliminated in a new set of national arrangements— members of the oppressed minority owe no obedience to its laws. The minority leaders may even attempt to set up a countergovernment and impose their own rules and demands on the citizens of the disputed areas. If they have substantial citizen support, they can gain the cover and information needed for sustained terrorist activity or, eventually, guerrilla warfare. Attacks on government forces and symbols take on the dual purpose of making the costs of forcing the minority area to remain in the nation too high to be worthwhile and of provoking the government to create victims and martyrs through retaliatory action.

Hibbs's crossnational analysis found separatist movements the critical link between ethnolinguistic fractionalization and serious political violence.[7] It would be going too far to advance that argument generally in the democracies. We have already seen that ethnic riots, for instance, even if without a separatist basis, are likely to be more costly in human lives than riots in nonethnic nations. The urban riots in the United States in the late 1960s and early 1970s were ethnic, costly in lives, and nonseparatist. But there is little question that some of the most serious democratic conflicts in the period under study did involve separatist efforts to redraw the political boundaries, and that these separatist efforts usually built from a base of both geographic concentration and ethnic distinctiveness. In three democracies separatist violence took on very serious proportions: India, the Philippines, and Northern Ireland in the United Kingdom.

The specific forms of organized violence in these nations varied substantially. One factor was the presence or absence of dual ethnic communities in the separatist areas. In India the separatist violence, carried out by separatist rebels in the Eastern Hill territories in the late 1960s and early 1970s, took the form of assaults on government troops and symbols and clashes between rebels and government forces. In the Philippines the Moro Homeland movement grew into a major guerrilla war, but it involved violent armed clashes between Christian and Moslem communities, as well as fighting between the Moro guerrillas and government troops. The government estimated that a thousand persons died between July 1970 and March 1971 alone. In Northern Ireland the Catholic civil rights movement, pressuring the local, and largely autonomous, Protestant-dominated government for equal rights of various kinds, was met with violent Protestant resistance. In response, the separatist IRA organizations, which had languished for lack of support in the Catholic community for over a decade, found new backing and eager recruits, and led terrorist assaults on Protestant groups, then later on British occupying forces.

Once these separatist movements got under way, each was costly in terms of human lives, and difficult to suppress. Each received outside aid in the form of weapons and other support. The Indian Hill tribe rebellion was suppressed most successfully, perhaps in part because events in Pakistan robbed the rebels of a major base of support. In the Philippines the guerrilla war continued long after the overthrow of democratic government there, to which it in part contributed by general weakening of the government's legitimacy.[8] Despite repeated efforts of many kinds the local government in Northern Ireland was made untenable by the continuing violent conflict, and no solution to armed occupation had been found after a decade of strife. Of course, in the three cases involving direct confrontations between local groups, the accumulated grievances and hatred caused by so many deaths and attacks made development of cooperative democratic action that much more difficult. Moreover, as long as fundamental change in the political community was demanded, violently, by one side, and violently opposed by the other, there was simply no room for democratic compromise.

That separatism, even ethnic separatism, is not necessarily an intractable problem for democratic government was illustrated by the handling of separatist conflicts in Belgium, Canada, and Switzerland during the same period. The accommodative efforts and constitutional and political arrangements made by both national and local leaders to keep separatist demands within democratic boundaries are discussed in Chapter 10. But it is important to note here that in each case tremendous efforts were made to recognize the seriousness of potential separatist violence, and to get the situation under control by forces oriented to regular democratic processes before escalating terrorism could create the deadly cycle of mutual grievance and anger. The conditions of geographically concentrated ethnic minorities are made to order for strategic terrorism to turn discrimination and smoldering frustration into full-scale violent resistance.

Violence against United Democratic Contenders   In the case of ethnic separatism we have seen the deliberate efforts of leaders "outside" the political system to change their minority status by forcing the formation of new boundaries for the political community. (The Catholic minority in Northern Ireland would be part of a Catholic majority in the Irish Republic.) Where leaders of minority factions have no prospect of forcing a new political community, one alternative is to change the type of regime and its rules for making decisions instead. Two routes are possible. First, by bombing, assassinations, and terrorism the dissidents can harass government officials, and perhaps persuade them to yield on key issues of concern to the minority. The rules of the democratic game are thus being altered to count more heavily those willing to use violence on behalf of their preferences. Or, violence may be used to frighten the average citizen so that he will withdraw his support from a government unable to protect his security. The weakened government will be easy prey to direct violent attack or to intervention by military forces or others willing to use violence.

Direct use of armed violence as blackmail along these lines was attempted in a number of the democratic regimes.[9] The most spectacular examples are the raids, kidnappings, and hijackings by international organizations, especially the Palestinian organizations, against Israel or various governments involved with Israel in the conflict in the Middle East. But some important examples can also be found in domestic politics. The most obvious and perhaps most interesting example was the terrorist campaign waged by the French Secret Army Organization, OAS, against the DeGaulle government in the early 1960s, when DeGaulle announced his intention of granting Algeria independence. In 1963, at the height of the campaign, over 80 people were killed, and 7 assassination attempts were made against DeGaulle himself. Nonetheless, although the DeGaulle government yielded to other domestic pressures, some backed by civil disobedience, by farmers and other groups, it refused to bow to OAS pressure, and eventually it was able to destroy the organization.

More diffuse terrorist campaigns, evidently designed to undermine backing for the regime itself rather than to get specific policies adopted, were mounted in Venezuela, Ceylon, and West Germany, and more sporadic instances appeared in the United States and Japan. In Venezuela the terrorists received substantial Cuban support and financing, but the failure to gain citizen support or to force government concessions led to declining activity by the 1970s and the abandonment of violent strategies, at least ostensibly, by most local leftist leaders. In Ceylon a massive attack on police stations and other government posts in 1971 met firm resistance from Mrs. Bandaranaike's leftist government, elected a year earlier. Although some 1200 persons were reported killed, and the shocks of these assaults by leftist guerrillas were felt throughout the next half-decade, with various forms of censorship and curtailing of political freedoms (although not elections), the terrorists failed to gain their objectives. The more varied assaults and assassinations by the leftist Bader-Meinhoff group in West Germany in the mid-1970s led to some government suspensions of citizens' personal rights, but had little effect, it would seem, on policy or regime. Nor did terrorist efforts in Japan or the United States.

The common theme that runs through these cases is that terror tactics and armed violence were used against regimes whose governments were able to draw upon united resistance to terror by all major political factions. In France, Ceylon, and West Germany this unity in resistance was facilitated by the fact that the political incumbents came from the same general side of the spectrum as the terrorists. There was little danger that the leftist parties would come to support the OAS in France, or that rightist parties would support Maoist guerrillas in Ceylon or far-left terrorists in Germany. Much the same point might be made about the resistance of Mrs. Gandhi's Indian government, in which her leftist faction of the Congress party could count on the backing of rightist parties, as well as the regular Communist groups, against the revolutionary far-leftist Naxhalite Revolutionary groups, which launched a campaign of terror in several states in the early 1970s. Faced by a unified government with parties of all political shades backing it, the terrorist campaigns designed to undermine the government never accomplished more than temporary disruption and discomfort of the democratic processes.

Violence against Divided Democratic Contenders   The prospects for pressuring the government, or at least undermining its support sufficiently to render it vulnerable to armed intervention, are greatly facilitated where the democratic contenders, the political parties dominating the regular political processes, are themselves divided in their views of the terrorists and their demands. Such divisions greatly hamper the development of clear policies for dealing with terrorist pressures. Moreover, they typically reflect the same kinds of deep social divisions from which the terrorists themselves draw support. In this kind of situation, the terrorist groups can be catalysts for exacerbated conflict between the major parties themselves. Or they can, with some sympathy and support from regular parties, as well as substantial reservoirs of support among citizens at large, prove extremely difficult to suppress without a major retrenchment of democratic freedoms and processes. Such a retrenchment may either itself prove fatal to the democratic regime, or stimulate further resistance and violence. At the same time, failure to control really widespread and spectacular terrorism and turmoil will certainly undermine support for the regime and make military intervention a serious possibility.[10] The terrorists or insurgents intend precisely to bring about such a breakdown of normal democratic processes, although they can only hope that the subsequent authoritarian government will belong to them rather than to their opponents.

That the operation can succeed while the patient fails to survive is tragically illustrated by the events in Uruguay in the late 1960s and early 1970s.[11] One of Latin America's oldest and most stable democracies, Uruguay had been facing serious economic crises throughout the 1960s.

With a declining demand for Uruguay's international exports, and a rather unproductive transitional economy, the Uruguayan standard of living faced a steady decline, and the nation's welfare programs proved expensive to sustain. High inflation and negative economic "growth" created serious strains. The two traditional Uruguayan political parties, the Colorados and the Blancos, were little more than very loose electoral coalitions of personalistic factions. In the late 1960s an urban guerrilla movement, calling itself the Tupamaros, mounted a spectacular, even theatrical, campaign of kidnapping, bank robberies, prison breaks, and publicity stunts, calling for revolutionary redistribution of income to eliminate poverty, and for the destruction of economic capitalism. Sympathy for the movement was evident, both in its notable successes and in the appearance of a political party coalition articulating leftist-redistributive demands which won about 20 percent of the vote in the 1971 election. The late 1960s had also seen notable labor agitation and strikes over wages and inflation (160 percent in 1968) and several impositions of martial law and national emergency.

In 1970 and 1971 the clashes between the Tupamaros and government police forces became more violent, and conflicts within the Chamber of Deputies and between the Chamber and the government intensified. In 1972 the Tuparmaros turned more explicitly to terrorist tactics, and the government's response included suspension of internal liberties, prohibition of antigovernment criticism, and calling the military in to deal with the Tupamaros. Despite efforts by the president to build a multiparty coalition to support his State of Seige policy, disputes appeared between parties and between the government and the army. On one side, arrests of antigovernment critics led to direct congressional pressure on the government; on the other side, by late 1972 a number of civilian leaders were calling for a direct military takeover to meet the crisis.

Under such circumstances of divided authority and continued clashes between guerrillas and the military, the overthrow of the constitutional processes by direct military pressure could come as no surprise. In February 1973 the military took a predominant role, seizing radio and television centers, sealing off Montevideo with naval units, moving tanks into key positions, demanding that civilian politicians be made subject to prosecution for various offenses, and issuing its own national program. The president agreed to set up a National Security Council dominated by the military. The military increased its hold in the subsequent six months, took various actions to break strikes and demonstrations by organized labor, and eventually had the president dissolve Congress and break all links with the democratic processes. The Tupamaros, with assistance from the incumbent groups, had managed indeed to bring about fundamental change in the political regime in Uruguay. But as of this writing, the military government remains in power, and the political and social reforms sought by the Tupamaros were not, of course, attempted.

Four other assaults on regimes with weak or divided political parties are worth noting. In the Philippines the once defeated Huk leftist guerrilla movement appeared again in strength in the late 1960s, and dozens of persons were killed in raids and clashes between government forces and the Huk insurgents. Lack of government success in finding and destroying the Huks, together with resentment at various suppressive measures, and some sympathy with insurgent demands for redistribution and responsiveness, all undermined support for the government and the regime. Growing conflict over these issues, manifested in large numbers of demonstrations and riots in the urban areas, mounted within the democratic forces in 1971 and 1972. These events, together with the ethnic separatist violence involving the Moro independence movement, as well as intense partisan and factional conflict, provided the occasion for President Marcos's suspension of democratic processes in 1972.

In Turkey the highly politicized student movements in the 1960s took on more violent form, and the older organizations were in part superseded by armed paramilitary groups on both the far right and the far left.[12] Although disavowed by the major parties, these groups in part expressed bitter tensions and antagonisms between major party groups, a fact that greatly inhibited government efforts to deal with them. These efforts were also hindered by weak, shifting government legislative control and the inability of the parties to agree on how to control student terrorist violence. In 1971 the military stepped in to restore order and to preserve, in its view, the democratic regime in the face of civilian inability to do so. The intervention suspended democratic government for about a year.

Although on a somewhat lesser scale, the Marxist government of Salvador Allende in Chile also experienced terrorist attacks, from both far right and far left, that were part of the growing turmoil of the early 1970s. The government's hesitation in dealing with violent attacks and illegal land-seizures engineered by the far left cost it substantial public support. The rightist bombings, along with the numerous major strikes and demonstrations, helped convey the impression that the government had lost control of the society in the period shortly before the military coup of August 1973.

Italy's experience has some important similarities with, and one critical difference from, the terrorist assaults in these countries. The late 1960s and 1970s saw two major terrorist campaigns in Italy. The first was apparently undertaken largely by neofascist groups, who set off bombs and engaged in other armed attacks on leftist rallies and organizational headquarters. There is some evidence that these efforts were encouraged by rightist government officials seeking to promote a "strategy of tension" that would justify a conservative dictatorship.[13] General Vito Miceli, former head of the Italian Secret Service, was convicted of involvement in such a conspiracy. The Secret Service was believed involved in a Milan political bombing in which 16 persons were killed. Despite encouragement from some officials, and despite the very serious conflicts among major parties of right, left, and center over both religious and class issues, the weak Christian Democratic–based governments were able to resist the attacks from the right. The leftist parties, which were the objects of many of the terrorist attacks, gave the government support here.

The second major terrorist assault came after the 1976 election. It was organized by the so-called Red Brigades, who were violently critical of the Communists' indirect support of Christian Democratic governments, which the Communists exchanged for consultation and key legislative posts, but not direct cabinet participation, following the national election. With the economy in trouble after the 1973 oil price increases, and with a tense political atmosphere and numerous strikes, clashes, and demonstrations involving many groups, as well as the major parties, the situation seemed ripe for terrorist assaults upon the regime, to complete the process of undermining its legitimacy. However, all the major parties, including the Communists, united to resist the Red Brigade terrorist campaign. Major interparty agreements, signed pledges to cooperate in the "national interest," despite continuing policy disagreements, emphasized united antiterrorist actions. The explicit commitment of the parties to work to sustain the democratic regime was probably essential to the survival of Italian democracy in the face of continuing Red Brigade pressure, including the kidnapping and murder of Christian Democratic leader Aldo Moro.[14]

Violence to Intimidate Opponents and Mobilize Support   In this examination of the various cases of terrorist efforts to bargain with or undermine the democratic regimes, it is hard to escape the conclusion that the reactions of the democratic parties are at least as important as the terrorist strategies or military sympathies. This point is underlined when we consider another form of the use of violence: its employment by electoral parties or their supporters to intimidate opponents and mobilize backing. Such violence appeared in a number of the contemporary democracies in the period studied, and was invariably associated with a serious threat to the democratic regime. In Turkey, the Philippines, and Chile elections in the late 1960s and early 1970s found serious clashes breaking out among party groups, with substantial numbers of deaths, as well as many injuries, resulting. Electoral violence with serious consequences was also reported on a rather widespread basis in India, and to a lesser degree in Lebanon and Italy. In Jamaica violence between organized gangs of party followers led to perhaps 200 deaths in the period leading up to the 1976 election, and the imposition of a national state of emergency and many arrests, including some of important opposition party leaders.[15] These clashes partly reflected the hostility and bitterness that divided the political parties, a gulf that would be difficult to bridge to defend the regime when it was seriously threatened. Such electoral violence also undermined the claim of democracy to be able to manage conflict through peaceful electoral processes, justifying the use of various coercive resources by any groups possessing them.

It is worth noting, moreover, that the two most famous historical cases of the overthrow of democratic regimes, the Nazi destruction of the Weimar Republic in Germany in the early 1930s and the suppression of the First Austrian Republic in 1934, were also accompanied by violent interparty strife, as well as terrorist activity by other groups. The Nazis used systematic violence and intimidation, admittedly usually short of deadly violence, to generate the impression that the government could not maintain internal order; to intimidate their major opponents, the Socialists; and to present themselves as the only hope for restoring internal harmony. It proved largely impossible for the mildly prodemocratic parties of the right and center to join forces with the prodemocratic Socialists across the deep gulf of class distrust and revolutionary rhetoric. The Nazis were successful in creating contempt for the democratic regime, and in replacing the weak middle-class Protestant parties as the only defenders of anti-Marxist values. Although the Socialists were not really intimidated, and remained ready to resist an armed "putsch" by Nazis against the government, they failed to check the growing violence and polarization that led to Nazi victory at the polls.[16] And in Austria the development of large paramilitary organizations by both Socialists and Christian Social forces culminated in a brief civil war when the Christian Social government attempted to seize Socialist weapons caches in 1934. After using troops to suppress Socialist resistance in Vienna and other strongholds, the Christian Social government established an authoritarian "corporatist" government.

This brief examination of the use of violence by electorally oriented major parties sheds light on the differences noted earlier in the relationships between extremist-party support and rioting, on the one hand, and deadly violence, on the other. We saw in Chapter 6 that rioting occurred more frequently in the large nations. But beyond the size of the country, the prevalence of rioting was related to lower levels of party fractionalization and to more support for extremist political parties. But support for extremist parties is largely unrelated to deadly violence. Parties may offer extreme policy alternatives, but not engage in armed attacks on other political groups, even while they may organize demonstrations or stimulate rioting. And parties that are in principle committed to the democratic system and to moderate or widely acceptable policies may become locked in violent strife with their political opponents, succumbing to the temptation to attack and harass them, to arouse the violent passions of supporters, or at least to meet violence with violence.

Parties, Violence, and Sustaining Democracy   I have suggested that party involvement in violence is particularly dangerous to the survival of the democratic regime. Table 8.1 summarizes the evidence that supports this proposition, for the 1967–1976 decade, when most of the suspensions or overthrows of democratic regimes occurred. In this decade, at least, deadly violence was virtually a precondition for the suspension of democratic politics. And, as noted in Chapter 3, except for the regional termination of democracy in Northern Ireland, the failure of democracy to sustain itself continuously was exclusively found in the less modernized countries. But the special role of party involvement in violence is also evident. In countries where the major parties presented a united front against the use of violence and kept themselves and their supporters from engaging in it, the democratic processes continued unchecked. Where violence involved the parties themselves, even in a limited way, it was much more difficult—for a variety of reasons, including the weakening of the regime's legitimacy and the inability of

Table 8.1 Party involvement in violence and the failure to sustain democratic regimes; 1967–1976.

Party involvement in deaths by political violence	Continuity of democratic regime		
	Regime largely unaffected	Major suspension of democracy	Regime overthrown
Fewer than 1 death per year	Australia, Austria, Belgium, Canada, Costa Rica, Denmark, Finland, France, Netherlands, Norway, New Zealand, Sweden, Switzerland, (England)		
No party involvement	West Germany, Japan, U.S., Ireland		
Limited party support, sympathy, or involvement	Italy, Venezuela	Ceylon	Uruguay
Violent clashes between major-party supporters, leading to deaths		India Jamaica Turkey	Chile Philippines (Northern Ireland)

Sources: Keesing's Archives, Facts on File, and individual country studies.

the democratic forces to join forces in defense of the regime—to sustain democracy.

In a regression analysis of the suspension of democratic processes, the number of deaths ($+.29$) and the involvement of the parties in deadly violence ($+.62$) are significant at least the .05 level.[17] The level of modernization is strongly associated with suspension of democracy in the simple correlations, but is insignificant in the regression analysis, once account is taken of the amount of deadly violence and party involvement in such activities. This conclusion holds as well if the analysis considers only those countries which did experience at least one death per year. As noted above, the historical overthrows of democracy in Weimer Germany and Austria certainly fit the pattern of party involvement in deadly violence, as does the survival of French democracy given the resistance of all parties to OAS terrorism in the 1960s. Italian party resistance to Red Brigade terrorism has also helped sustain democracy. A number of students of democratic stability, most notably

Juan Linz, have suggested that the willingness of legitimate, elected political parties to work to sustain the regime is essential for its survival in the face of various crises.[18] My own evidence on the role of political parties in deadly violence certainly seems to support this contention.

In tense political situations, the leaders of political parties may face a terribly difficult task, given deep antagonisms among their followers, and often quite real doubts and grievances on both sides. Not only must they control their own frustrations, and resist the temptation to use interparty hostility as a mobilizing device, but they must persuade their political opponents in the democratic process to take a similar attitude. And they must accomplish this while maintaining the support of their party and of the voters.[19] These last elements are especially difficult if the party is itself a loose coalition, or if the creation of challenging factions within the party is likely. It is precisely in those Third World countries where limited resources and severe differences of class and culture make tensions high and violence likely, that, as we saw in Chapter 5, party organizations are likely to be weak and localized and their support volatile.

How Democracies Are Replaced: Military and Executive Coups

Table 8.2 lists the twentieth-century examples of prolonged or permanent suspension of working democratic regimes because of internal conflict, grouped according to the final process by which democracy was halted. Considering only regimes that had lasted at least ten years yields perhaps 45 or 50 democratic regimes, about a third of which came to an end because of internal conflict.[20]

Four ways of overthrowing or suspending democracy can be distinguished. Weimar Germany (1919–1932) stands out as exceptional in having permitted an avowedly antidemocratic party to come to power. The Nazi party kept its promise to do away with democracy, although its means were only quasiconstitutional and much violence was involved in the last "free" elections. Lebanon stands out as a second distinct type: the collapse of all government-based order in the face of civil war. In terms of the final mechanics of democratic overthrow, each of these two instances is unique, although some of the conditions leading up to the final events are quite similar to those in other troubled democracies.

The two major forms of democratic overthrow are the internal executive coup, in which a legitimately chosen head of state acts to suspend, and perhaps eventually replace, democratic processes and freedoms, and the military coup, in which the armed forces move to

Table 8.2 Overthrow or suspension of democratic regimes through internal conflict in the twentieth century, by type of intervention.

Type of intervention	Country	Duration of democracy before intervention
Election of openly anti-democratic parties and postelection action by incumbents	Weimar Germany	1919–1933
Incumbent authorities suppress democracy	First Austrian Republic	1919–1934
	Estonia	1919–1934
	Ceylon	1948–1971[a]
	Philippines	1946–1972
	India	1948–1975[a]
	Jamaica	1962–1976[a]
Military coup or military takeover of policy making	Argentina	1906-1929
	Chile	1861–1929
	Burma	1948–1958
	French Fourth Republic	1948–1958
	Turkey	1946–1960
	Brazil	1950–1964
	Greece	1946–1967
	Uruguay	1932–1973
	Turkey	1962–1971[a]
	Chile	1932–1973
Civil war and collapse of civilian government control	(Lebanon)	(1946–1975)

Source: Regimes with competitive elections and effective legislatures according to Arthur S. Banks, *Cross-Policy Time Series Data* (Cambridge: MIT Press, 1971.) Banks covers the time to 1966, inclusive, deleting the years of World War II. I have excluded countries in which democracy lasted less than ten years, and have excluded South Africa and Portugal (1911-1925) as having overly restrictive franchises. Lebanon, whose status as a democracy is a matter of some scholarly dispute, is added for illustrative purposes.

a. Temporary suspension.

control or replace a legitimate civilian government. Executive coups occurred in the First Austrian Republic, where the Christian Social government set up an authoritarian "corporatist" regime in 1934 after defeating the Socialists in a civil war; Estonia, where Acting Chief Executive Pats used emergency powers to outlaw the authoritarian Veteran's organization and halt its antigovernment agitation, then went on to suspend elections and democratic processes in general; Ceylon (Sri Lanka), where the prime minister and her strong government instituted severe censorship and various restraints on freedoms, but did not halt the electoral process, for about five years, after the major guerrilla assaults of 1971; and India, where Mrs. Gandhi suspended constitutional rights, arrested opposition leaders, suppressed opposition state governments, and postponed national elections, when the opposition seemed likely to drive her from office in 1974.[21] A slightly less extensive curtailment of national freedoms was carried out by the majority PNP government in Jamaica before the 1976 national elections, with some constraints continuing afterwards, although elections were held on schedule and most political prisoners were freed soon afterward. And in the Philippines President Marcos proclaimed martial law and dismissed Congress in September 1972, stating that the nation was about to be overwhelmed by violent, Communist-backed, conflict; Marcos later suspended competitive elections and freedoms indefinitely, unlike Mrs. Gandhi, who restored free elections in India in 1977. In each of these cases, a chief executive with great powers and/or a strong legislative majority used these to clamp down on opposition. In each case substantial violence had occurred, more was threatened, and this threat was used as a major justification for the executive action. In each of these countries there were also either violent clashes between the party in power and some of the opposition, or some perceived likelihood that the incumbents would be driven from office.

In a slightly larger number of cases, the downfall of the democratic regime came about through action of the armed forces. In Turkey in 1960 the army acted against a government that seemed to be constricting democratic freedoms and shutting down the opposition; in 1971 the army intervened to force the government—which it did not replace—to give it a free hand to act in suppressing student and other terrorist violence. In France in 1958 the army brought about the end of the Fourth Republic in the midst of the Algerian crisis; an actual paratroop operation against Paris was called off when DeGaulle mediated an end to the Fourth Republic and establishment of the Fifth. In Greece in 1967 the army struck in anticipation of a leftist victory in the forthcoming elections and in fear of leftist penetration of the armed forces and an eventual leftist coup. In Uruguay, as described above, the armed forces intervened to control action against the Tupamaro insurgents, and eventually seized total control of government decision making; although the incumbent president was left in office, Congress was suspended and elections were proscribed. Unlike the case in Turkey, Uruguay was not returned to democratic rule after the violence had been suppressed. In the best known case of all, the army in Chile moved against the Marxist Allende government in 1973, in a sharp and bloody action in which Allende was killed and some 500 persons died, while many others were arrested and later disappeared.[22] As in Brazil in 1964, the military, having seized power, established an apparently permanent military government to replace the civilian democracy.

One facet of the military interventions is especially notable: in each case intervention had been preceded by demands from at least some prominent civilian groups and parties for military involvement. Alfred Stepan, in his excellent study of military intervention in Brazil, points out that of the five attempted coups in the late 1950s and early 1960s, each successful coup involved civilian parties calling for the military to intervene.[23] The point is not that the military answered the civilian call, but that the divisiveness of party competition reached a point where some contenders preferred military intervention to democratic competition. Hence the legitimacy of the regime was lessened; and it was possible to unite the armed forces in favor of action against the government. If the armed forces are united, they are very difficult to resist, and a military coup is likely to succeed. As long as the political parties can agree to defend democracy, and take steps to assure all citizens that democracy will be defended, it is difficult to get a military consensus on intervention. Hence the failure of military coup attempts in France in 1961, Ceylon in 1961, and Venezuela in 1966, where the parties remained loyal to the government and kept most of the armed forces from joining the rebels.[24] But in France in 1958, Turkey in 1960 and 1971, Greece, Uruguay, and Chile, important civilian factions called for the military to intervene to end violence, to prevent some party from ending democracy, to preserve national security, and so forth. Studies of military intervention suggest that efforts by the civilian regime to intervene in military command structures, or to create separate armed forces that threaten the military, or to cut military budgets drastically, can also help unify the officer corps and create conditions for a military coup.[25] But, at least in the democracies, the role of the political parties seem to be of decisive importance.

In the vast majority of cases of the overthrow of democratic government, then, the dominant incumbent forces of the regime—in the hands of the chief executive or in the hands of leaders of the armed forces—are used to replace the regime itself. Where the chief executive commands substantial independent legal powers or controls a legislative majority, the rule of democracy may be more or less legally suspended. In some cases, as in the Philippines, Austria, and Estonia, this suspension may become permanent. In cases of military intervention, the constitutional processes are likely to be more directly countervened, or reduced to formalities in response to coercion. But even the armed forces seldom overthrow a democratic regime when the major parties are united in defense of democracy. A major threat posed by organized violence is that it may undermine the confidence in democracy of the legitimate leaders themselves. The executive and military coups in the democracies did not come unexpectedly; they were preceded by serious warning signs. Among the most significant of these were renunciations of the democratic faith by its elected leaders.

Democratic Performance /
Liberty, Competition, Responsiveness

9

In Chapter 1 I identified a group of nations that claimed responsiveness to citizen demands, competitive elections, adult voting eligibility, and basic civil and political freedoms. While I used these standards to determine which countries have democratic political systems, they can also be considered as dimensions of democratic performance. In this chapter I want to address distinctively democratic performance goals: civil liberties, political competition, and responsiveness. These goals are intertwined with the very definition of democratic government and associated with democracy by historic traditions. The questions to be asked are (1) do in fact contemporary democratic countries achieve these goals? and (2) do some democracies, and some constitutional and political party arrangements, perform better than others on these criteria?

Civil Liberties

The appearance of elections with several competing political parties and general citizen eligibility is not enough. Without freedom to get information and to try to influence others, the ability of citizens to make representative democracy effective is very doubtful.[1] A free and critical press, accessible electronic media, the ability to move about and engage in political activity, freedom from arbitrary judicial action—these are characteristics intimately related to meaningful democracy in contemporary society. While the detailed study of these attributes would be a massive undertaking, we can draw on the annual "surveys of freedom" by the Freedom House organization to make some basic comparisons. The Freedom House organization rates all the nations of the world on dimensions of both political and civil rights. The political rights dimension is very close to my formal definition of democracy as free electoral competition. But the civil liberties ratings touch a dimension that I have not systematically considered. They rate nations from 1 to 7. In the nations rated 1 "the rule of law is unshaken; there is a variety of news media and freedom of expression is both possible and evident." As the numbers increase, laws and traditions impinge increasingly on such freedoms until, in the states ranked 7, "the outside world almost never hears of internal criticism except through the government's condemnation of it. Citizens have no rights vis-à-vis the state."[2] Unfortunately, these ratings were not initiated until 1973, so they cover only the end of the period of my study.

An examination of the ratings for 1976 is reassuring on the subject of civil liberties. All of the countries rated 1 are those I have selected as democracies (with the addition of a few nations too small to qualify for this study). And all of the democracies that did not have their democratic regimes overthrown were rated at least 3, and in the top third of the nations of the world in civil liberties. By contrast, the three nations toppled from the ranks of democracies—Chile, the Philippines, and Uruguay—were given scores of 5, 5, and 6, respectively. Although a few nondemocracies, such as Mexico and Maritius, scored as high as 2 or 3, the association between political rights and civil liberties was extremely strong.

Because all of the democracies do relatively well, differences between them seem less significant. Seventeen of the democracies were rated 1, three (Finland, France, and Venezuela) were rated 2, and four (India, Sri Lanka, Jamaica, and Turkey) were rated 3. As we saw in the last chapter, the level of economic development was the strongest predictor of the level of civil liberties. In 1977, however, violence led to restrictions in Germany and Italy, while curbs were relaxed to some degree in India and Sri Lanka.[3] A statistical analysis shows initially that representational parliamentary constitutions and multiparty systems were associated with more complete civil liberties. Controlling for environmental setting, particularly levels of economic development, however, makes these features less pronounced, with none of the constitutional or party system variables significant in 1976.

A slightly different approach uses the imposition of various forms of sanctions by the government, a statistic collected in the *World Handbook of Political and Social Indicators*.[4] The sanctions include all sorts of curfews, press restrictions, and the like, without regard for extensiveness, so they must be viewed cautiously. However, Hibbs's analysis of the sanctions imposed in all the countries of the world in the earlier decade did suggest that democratic countries were restrained in their imposition of sanctions, when confronted with citizen turmoil.[5] As in the analysis of civil liberties, the comparison of democracies and nondemocracies seems to favor the democracies.

A statistical analysis of sanctions within the democracies is, however, not very conclusive. As one would anticipate from Hibbs's work, the major factors leading immediately to sanctions were levels of riots and deaths. Where violence breaks out, governments tend to respond with various sanctions. In the simple comparisons, the representational parliamentary constitutions and the multiparty systems did use fewer sanctions in the decade. The Pearson correlation between legislative fractionalization and sanctions was − .26 in 1958–1967 and − .28 in 1967–1976.[6] However, once one controls for either population size or levels of deaths and riots, or both, these apparent advantages disappear. Indeed, perhaps surprisingly, the multiparty systems actually show somewhat more frequent use of sanctions in both decades. That is, in general, governments in the multiparty systems used fewer sanctions. But when confronted with violence they were even more likely to respond firmly than governments in majoritarian party systems.[7] However, we cannot be very sure about the directions of linkages here: the variables are related in complex ways, and the results are not very stable. The major conclusion to be drawn from looking at the imposition of sanctions is that within the democracies the party and constitutional variables I have been considering do not distinguish the democracies from one another very sharply.

Political Competition

I examined competition in its behavioral expression in Chapter 2. In most of the democracies there were elections that were immediately followed by shifts of the party or parties holding executive office, shifts that corresponded to the election outcomes (see table 2.1). Only in a few countries was there no recent evidence of such competitive outcomes, and one of these—India—experienced such an event in 1977. I suggested that these events constituted prima facie evidence of meaningful electoral competition.

We can go beyond this broad assessment in two ways. First, we can see which democracies did have more frequent replacement of incumbents, and whether such replacements are related to the environmental, constitutional, and party-system variables examined earlier. While seeing the impact of elections on incumbency may reassure us about the meaningfulness of competition, however, there is nothing inherently undemocratic about citizens continuing to support the same individuals and parties in office if they perform as the citizens wish. Second, we can see whether particular parties or types of parties tend to be excluded from or included in officeholding. Again, nothing in the definition of democracy prohibits permanent domination by some groups, but it is likely that such situations are undesirable to the excluded groups and from the point of view of democratic quality.[8]

Change of Government as Competition   Certainly the fact that elections bring about a change in government seems to be a mark of competitiveness. In Chapter 2 I did not attempt to explain the differences across the democracies. Table 2.1 simply shows whether at the time of each election in the 1960s and early 1970s a change in government in response to an election had taken place in the previous ten years. To expect a change at every election seemed to demand instability, rather than electoral responsiveness. To expect change to take place within a decade seemed a reasonable benchmark. We saw that in about 40 percent of the countries the voters could look back before each election and discern such a change. In only a handful of countries was there no evidence of such changes. Between these extremes stood two mixed cases: (1) countries that did experience clear-cut governmental changes in response to elections, but in which a decade or more might intervene between changes (Canada, France, and Norway, for example); and (2) countries in which the changes that occurred were related to elections only in rather complex ways (as in Finland, the Netherlands, and Italy). Broad shifts in voter support seemed to change the pattern of coalition formation, but individual parties might gain in the election and lose a role in government or vice versa.

In table 9.1 these crude estimates of competitive change are explored in a regression analysis, using the environmental, constitutional, and party-system variables that have proved important in earlier chapters. The "competitive change" variable itself is coded 4 if such changes regularly occurred; 3 if the changes were clear-cut, but less frequent; 2 if the changes were complex and hard to link; and 1 if no such changes occurred between 1960 and 1976. The top half of the table presents the analysis of competitive change, showing first the simple correlations and then the regression coefficients. The latter present environmental and constitutional variables, then add the major party-system properties of extremist support and multipartyism. The environmental heterogeneity variables are not significant, and for simplicity they are omitted here.

Table 9.1 Predicting competitive change in government and inclusion of all parties in power: correlation and regression analysis of environmental, constitutional, and party-system variables.[a]

Political competition Measure	Environmental advantages		Constitutional setting			Party-system properties	
	Small population	Level of development	Presidential executive	Majoritarian election laws	Swiss collective executive	Fractionalization of legislature	Extremist party voting support
Competitive change of government[b]							
Correlation	.21	-.15	.32	24	-.40	-.54	-.41
Regression							
($R^2 = 41\%$)	.41**	-.02	.28*	.34**	-.35**	—	—
($R^2 = 52\%$)	.31*	.01	.25*	.04	-.30*	-.35	-.13
Inclusion of All parties in power[c]							
Correlation	.22	-.33	.19	-.05	.01	-.17	-.40
Regression							
($R^2 = 20\%$)	.27	-.35*	.13	-.05	-.01	—	—
($R^2 = 44\%$)	.03	-.45**	.20	-.20	-.07	.35	-.74**

a. Regression entries are standardized regression coefficients. Population size and GNP per capita (the economic development measure) are logged, and are for 1972. Constitutional measures as in tables 4.1 and 4.4. Party-system properties of fractionalization and extremist voting measures are the averages from all elections in the 1965–1976 period. See Appendix. Analysis uses 27 countries.

b. Competitive change in government measure from table 2.1. Coded: 4 = evidence of a clear-cut change of government in response to an election outcome in previous decade present at time of each election in 1958–1976 period; 3 = evidence of such changes present at time of some elections, but not all; 2 = evidence of changes only of complex type, as in coalition rejuggling or pattern of coalition formation; 1 = no evidence of changes in national government in response to election outcomes.

c. Inclusion of all parties in power measure from table 9.2 below. Coded: 4 = no party getting over 5% of the vote in two elections (1960–1979) was excluded from government throughout the period; 3 = excluded party or parties got no more than 5–9% of the vote; 2 = excluded party or parties got no more than 10–19% of the vote; 1 = excluded party or parties got 20% or more of vote in at least two elections.

* = F level over 1.7 (significant at .10).

** = F level over 3.0 (significant at .05).

The results are easily interpreted. The level of economic development is unrelated to competitive electoral change. The smaller countries are, however, more likely to experience change, perhaps because it is easier to mobilize electoral dissatisfaction in them. The Swiss collective executive, of course, did not experience change of government, and Chapter 6 suggested that this irrelevance of national elections tends to depress voter turnout. Both presidential systems and majoritarian electoral laws, by contrast, tended to be associated with competitive changes in government. The addition of the major party-system variables renders the electoral-law variable insignificant: majoritarian electoral laws were associated with change because they encourage two-party systems in which changes in voter support are translated quite directly into government changes. At the same time, the presidency creates a potential for elections to be directly translated into changes in the chief executive regardless of the party system, and its effects are not greatly diminished in multiparty systems. (France and Venezuela provide examples of direct presidential change in such systems.)

The party-system variables behave as we might expect. The fractionalization of the legislature (multipartyism) is associated with less frequent and clear-cut changes. While massive changes in voter preference can lead to an alteration of the type of coalition formed by the parties, many smaller changes result merely in complex negotiations that produce new governments whose basis is only obscurely related to the result of the election. Even where the parties do fall along a single continuum a defeat for parties of the left may merely force them to extend their coalition toward the center, rather than bring a rightist coalition to power. Where several dimensions of voter choice are involved, it is often difficult even to estimate what a directly "responsive" change would be that could result in a coherent government.[9] Moreover, it is common in multiparty situations for votes to shift among allies. A party may lose votes to coalition partners on both right and left, yet be virtually impossible to exclude from government if the most desirable, policy-connected government is to form.

This problem seems associated with increasingly complex multipartyism. In nonmajoritarian party systems that have only three or four parties, the results may be clearer. Pre-electoral coalitions among parties can also help clarify the meaning of the election for government formation. The appearance of such coalitions in Denmark in the 1964–1971 period gave it nearly the appearance of a two-party system, as did similar events in Norway, Sweden, and Germany at various points. The natural, appealing clarity of the less fractionalized system, however, quite clearly shows through in the data.[10]

Two other party-system characteristics are worth a brief comment. The volatility of legislative representation is consistently, although not very strongly, related to competitive change in governments. In the complex multiparty systems, where the voting changes take place within a given part of the spectrum, or between spatially adjacent parties, such volatility does not necessarily enhance responsive governmental change. But in the two-party or presidential systems, it does encourage party change in response to election results. Part, but not all, of the presidential effect seems to take place because more volatile voting is typical of presidential systems. At the same time, we might expect that strong linkages between groups and parties might inhibit responses to voting change. But the converse is true, once we control for fractionalization. Given the levels of fractionalization and the constitutional arrangements, stronger linkage between groups and parties is associated with clearer linkages between election outcomes and governmental change.

Inclusion of Parties in Power as Competition   Another, complementary, way to consider party competition is to examine whether all parties have a chance to participate in governing, or whether some of them are excluded from political power for long periods—or permanently. In the simple two-party system, change of government and the opportunity of both parties to experience political power are nearly identical. But in multiparty systems it is quite possible to have substantial changes in government, yet with some parties being continually excluded.

Table 9.2 presents a rough measure of the degree of party exclusion. The measure was compiled quite simply. A list was made of all parties getting at least 5 percent of the votes in two or more elections in the 1960s and 1970s. For these parties, then, election outcomes and legislative coalitions were examined to see whether the party was ever explicitly included in a governing coalition.[11] If all parties receiving 5 percent or more of the vote in at least two elections were at some point included in a government, the country appears in the topmost category. If a party winning 5–9 percent of the vote in two elections was excluded, the country appears in the second set down the table. The third set of countries, are those in which a substantial party was excluded from power, but the excluded party received less than 20 percent of the vote. The excluded party was still, in that sense, a minor party, such as the

Table 9.2 Constitutional types and exclusion of parties from governmental power, 1960–1979.[a]

Parties excluded from power	Presidential systems	Majoritarian parliamentary systems	Representational-parliamentary systems	Collective executive systems
No party excluded getting over 5% votes in 2 elections	(Chile) Costa Rica (Philippines) U.S.	Ceylon Germany Ireland Jamaica	Belgium Netherlands	(Uruguay to 1967)
Party excluded getting 5–9% of votes in 2 elections	Venezuela (Uruguay after 1967)	Australia India	Austria Norway Sweden Turkey	Switzerland
Party excluded Getting 10–19% of votes in 2 elections	—	Canada New Zealand U.K.	Denmark Finland[b] (Greece)	—
Party excluded getting 20% or more of votes in 2 elections	France	Japan	Italy	—

Sources: See sources for table 4.2 for constitutional classification. Party vote from Mackie and Rose, *International Almanac of Electoral History; European Journal of Political Research;* and *Keesing's Archives.* Governments from *Keesing's Archives.*

a. Countries in parentheses were not democracies during the full 20 years.

b. In Finland the excluded party is the Rural party, which received 10.5% of the vote in 1970 and 9.2% in 1972.

British Liberal party or the Canadian NDP. Finally, at the bottom of the table, we see countries in which a party (or parties) receiving over 20 percent of the vote was excluded throughout two decades.[12]

Several important facts emerge from the table. First, it is noteworthy that in most countries most substantial parties did get to share power. Only in Japan, France, and Italy were large parties permanently excluded from power. (And the Communist party in Italy did gain partial sharing of legislative and policy-consultative power, although they did not hold government posts, in 1977–1979. The French Communists won some cabinet posts in the new Socialist government in June 1981.) In 19 of the 28 democracies no party with over 10 percent of the vote in two elections was permanently excluded from power. In a good many cases, however, they had to wait a substantial period, as in the long dry spell for Labour in Australia, from the end of World War II until 1972.

A second significant point is that in many cases the permanently excluded party was regarded as an "extremist" party, whose inclusion in government was both repellent in policy terms and likely to be disastrous in electoral terms for potential coalition partners. This characterization would certainly fit, for most of the time period at least, the Communists in Italy, France, Japan, Sweden, and Greece; the Socialist People's parties in Norway and Denmark; the Rural party in Finland; FIDEL/Frente Amplio in Uruguay; MAS and the National Civic Crusade in Venezuela; and the language parties in Belgium before the constitutional changes of the mid-1970s. It might even apply to the Japanese Socialists and the Komeito (although the former are not designated "extremists" in the analysis). It is not surprising that parties advocating extreme change or protest, yet failing to carry electoral majorities, will find government participation difficult to negotiate. The nonextremist parties that are excluded despite receiving substantial voting support are mostly parties operating in majoritarian electoral systems, where their actual legislative strength is much less than their voting support, as in the case of the Liberals in Britain and other "minor" parties in New Zealand, Canada, and Australia.

The division of the table into columns corresponding to the dominant constitutional arrangements suggests a third point about the exclusion of parties from power. The presidential constitutions show a good record of inclusion of parties in power. Except in France, in presidential systems all of the substantial nonextremist parties did share government power, winning the presidency directly or in coalition. Such systems also discouraged the formation or maintenance of smaller parties. The majoritarian and representational parliamentary systems had similar records in party exclusion, but the excluded parties were somewhat different. In the representational parliamentary systems, there were typically many small parties, and only extremist parties (if any) did not eventually join some government coalition. The majoritarian parliamentary systems achieved a similar general picture by discouraging the formation, support and representation of smaller parties, especially extremists. Smaller parties that did persist and win shares of the vote in the 5 percent to 20 percent range were unlikely to gain a role in government, because the electoral systems usually created simple party majorities without the need for coalitions. Where elections in these systems did not elect majorities, as pointed out in Chapter 7, the government was usually formed by the largest party and governed as a caretaker minority government until an early election.

A regression analysis based on the classification in table 9.2 appears at the bottom of table 9.1. The dependent variable is inclusion in government, coded 4, 3, 2, 1, reading down the sets of countries in table 9.2. The predominant point in the table is that extremist party support is the strongest variable limiting inclusion of parties in the government. Once account is taken of extremist-party strength, the multiparty systems are relatively more likely to include all parties in power (although the simple correlation is weakly negative). Because of their penalizing of small parties, the majoritarian electoral systems see less inclusion, although the regression coefficient is not significant. The presidential constitutions are associated with greater sharing of power. The size of the country is not related to power sharing once account is taken of extremism, despite the suggestion that small countries might find bargaining easier. And, perhaps surprisingly, the more modernized countries see more exclusion of parties. (Volatility and strength of linkages have no significant effects.)

Competition, Process, and Policy   Constitutional and party variables have some clear effects and some mixed impacts on these two aspects of competition. The presidential systems showed to good advantage according to both measures of competition. They tended to change their chief executives in direct response to elections, as they are designed to do, and they tended to bring most political parties to political power, or a share of it, at least eventually. The majoritarian arrangements also encouraged direct changes in government in response to election outcomes, but they had mixed effects on power sharing. On the one hand they inhibited the presence of extremist parties, which were likely to be excluded from power, but on the other hand they penalized minor parties (5 to 20 percent of the vote) and discouraged coalitions in general (as we saw in Chapter 7).

Similarly, the multiparty systems made clear-cut electoral impacts more difficult to trace,[13] and they were associated with extremist representation that was difficult to deal with in the legislature. But the multiparty systems did bring most of the nonextremist parties into a share of governmental power. The Swiss constitutional arrangement, from this point of view, represents an explicit institutionalization of the tendencies of multiparty systems in general. My earlier discussion of government durability showed that extremist parties accounted for almost all of the tendency of multiparty systems to be less durable. The conflicting impacts of multipartyism and extremism on exclusion from power are even more dramatic; multipartyism is an advantage for power-sharing except for the role of the extremists. Thus, the constitutional and party-system variables, which had rather little impact on civil rights and government sanctions, were quite powerful shapers of electoral and legislative competition.

The issue of competition raises important policy questions. Thus far I have been purely concerned with democratic process performance, and have ignored the question of what policies the parties have pursued when in power. Table 9.2, combined with an examination of the coalitions formed, is suggestive in this regard. Two points can be made. First, the exclusion of extremist parties from power did tend to create policy biases against their side of the political spectrum, usually the left in this period, in a number of countries. This bias is obvious in France, Japan, and Italy, each of which was dominated by parties of the political right or right-center throughout the period. Looking at the coalitions formed in the multiparty systems emphasizes the overt advantages enjoyed by parties of the center in these systems. In Belgium and the Netherlands, for example, the Catholic party was always in power, as were the Anti-Revolutionaries in the Netherlands and the DC in Italy. The Agrarian and Swedish parties in Finland were also frequent power-sharers. Center parties in Norway, Denmark, and Germany were more likely to share power than their rightist counterparts. The advantages of policy-connected coalitions (which were discussed in Chapter 7) tend to give a major role to center parties in multiparty systems, since they are available for coalitions with either the right or the left.[14]

The presidential systems and the majoritarian parliamentary systems are fairly successful in bringing a variety of parties to power and, perhaps equally useful, in removing all parties from perpetual hold on power. Those party systems with limited fractionalization, even if in a representational constitutional setting (such as Austria), do likewise. The multiparty systems seem to have more of a tendency toward systematic bias. This bias is reflected both in the systematic exclusion of most extremist parties (except in Finland) and in the systematic advantages gained by center parties. What we cannot tell from these process data is whether these patterns of party bias were associated with actual policy differences. It is quite possible, for example, that because

two-party systems face pressures to adopt more centrist policy platforms, the alternation of parties in power in these systems yields policy
consequences rather similar to the center-party advantages and extremist exclusions in multiparty systems. To begin consideration of these
problems, we must turn to looking at governmental policies, not solely
at political processes.

Policy Responsiveness

The most important identifying characteristic of a democratic system is
the assertion that the government is doing what the citizens want it to
do. Of course, such a claim is not a sufficient condition for democracy.
From the point of view of the democratic process, it is important that
the government be doing what citizens desire *and* that it be responsive
to their changes in preference. While we have seen that there is good
evidence that in most of the democracies citizens do force changes in the
parties and personnel in charge of their government, I have not shown
that the public policies adopted have any relation to such changes.

The analysis and comparison of such policy responsiveness is an
extremely difficult problem, worth several books in its own right. It is
fraught with theoretical and practical problems. At the theoretical level,
there is the deep and troubling set of problems associated with citizens'
wants: Which citizens? What if citizens themselves disagree? What if
many citizens have no opinions? What level of information do we expect
of citizens in decisionmaking? And so forth. At the most practical level,
it is very difficult to make serious comparisons about the responsiveness
of government to citizens without direct studies of citizen preferences on
issues, studies that comparably include both direction and intensity of
preference in some fashion. Such studies are not available for very many
of our democracies.

We must here be satisfied with much less than a full-scale comparison
of responsiveness. We shall have to be satisfied with demonstrating that
electoral and legislative politics does have an impact on some areas of
government policy. We can do so by distinguishing the general policy
orientation of political parties, and the electoral bases of support. These
can then be related to actual policies undertaken while the parties are in
power. If there is a clear relationship between the policy promises and
support bases of the parties in power and the chosen policies of the
governments, and if changes in the parties in power lead to changes in
government policies, we shall have demonstrated some amount of

policy responsiveness in the democracies. However, we cannot make the claim that we have seen all the policy responsiveness, because (*a*) we have not considered all types of issues, (*b*) we have not considered matters of citizen intensity, (*c*) we have not been able to deal with the way in which *all* the parties may modify their policy proposals to anticipate what citizens want. Such tasks must await further study.

Left Parties and Class Parties   In the post-World War II industrialized world, politicians and political observers have generally distinguished between parties of the right and the left in terms of their stances toward the size of government and the equalization of social conditions in a country. Parties of the left have tended to favor a larger role for government, greater equalization of income, government-supported welfare programs, and a minimization of unemployment. Parties of the right have tended to favor a more restrained role for government, maintenance of existing income distribution, private welfare, and a minimization of inflation, even at a cost in employment.[15] We do not have available platform proposals and campaign promises for most countries. But as we did in Chapter 7, we can usually identify the left parties as described by local experts. We expect that in the industrialized countries victories by such parties will be associated with expansion of the role of the national government, income equalization, and associated policies.

We can go further in identifying parties that should pursue leftist economic policies by looking at the parties' bases of political support. From the discussion in Chapter 5, we expect some leftist parties, especially where barriers to entry of new parties are low and initial voting preferences are polarized along class lines, to adopt relatively narrow and mobilizing leftist policies, appealing to well-defined groups of citizens in blue-collar, working-class occupations. Other parties, even if toward the left side of the spectrum of their party system, or even if calling themselves socialist or labor parties, will be more oriented toward the center electoral position.

Our index of class voting helps identify some of these differences, although it is based on citizens' behavior and support, not on party promises. Both the German Social Democrats and the French and Italian Socialists call themselves parties of the left. But they operate in political systems where religion has been a major cleavage. The French and Italian Socialists have major communist parties to their left as well. The class bases of these parties are more like the support of the

Democrats in the United States, rather than like support of left parties in Scandinavia. If the index of class voting is rather low, as it is in France, Italy, Belgium, Germany, the Netherlands, Switzerland, Canada, and the United States, then majority parties and coalitions both in and out of power will have more similar bases of support. It is likely that such similarity both reflects and reinforces many similarities in economic policy among parties. Where the index of class voting is higher, as in Australia, Austria, Britain, New Zealand, and all of Scandinavia, the parties should reflect and emphasize sharper economic policy choices.

As table 9.3 indicates, the industrialized democracies divide up quite evenly into countries with and without strong class voting. The top half

Table 9.3 Class voting, Left-bloc success, and economic policy in the industrialized democracies, 1960.

Class voting index	Left-bloc success, 1947–1959	Country	Economic policy measures		Income equality
			Income tax as % of GNP[a]	Government revenue as % of GDP[b]	% of total income to lower 80% (early or mid-1960s)[c]
Low (under 25)	None	West Germany Italy	6.2% 3.5 } 4.9	35% 30 } 33	47% 52 } 50
	Coalition only	Belgium France Netherlands Switzerland	6.4 3.1 8.4 6.2 } 6.0	27 34 33 22 } 29	— 46 51 — } 49
	Left majority	Canada U.S.	5.0 9.0 } 7.0	26 28 } 27	60 59 } 60
High (over 32)	None	—			
	Coalition only	Austria Denmark Finland	8.6 10.2 8.2 } 9.0	31 28 32 } 30	— 54 51 } 53
	Left majority	Australia[d] New Zealand Norway Sweden U.K.	— — 10.4 13.2 7.0 } 10.2	26 30 35 33 29 } 31	61 58 58 56 58 } 58

a. From OECD, *Expenditure Trends in OECD Countries, 1960–1980* (Paris: OECD, July 1972).
b. From World Bank, *World Tables* (Washington, D.C.: World Bank, 1976), pp. 440ff.
c. This is income after transfers but before taxes. See note 19 to this chapter.
d. Left government in the 1940s only.

of the table shows the eight industrialized democracies in which class voting was under 25. (Japan and Ireland, not fully industrialized in 1960, are excluded here, as are all the less industrialized nations, which faced a different set of policy problems and whose inclusion might bias our results.) The bottom half of the table shows the eight industrialized democracies in which the class voting index was 33 or higher. Although these class voting indices are averages, and thus do not reflect some of the changes that occurred during the postwar period, the available evidence, as noted in Chapter 6, indicates that the relative ratings did not change greatly. Some decline in Britain and Denmark, and some increase in France, apparently occurred in the 1970s. The table also indicates whether leftist parties were never in the government, were part of a government coalition only, or had executive and legislative power alone at some point between World War II and 1960. (I shall consider changes after 1960 in a moment.)

The ability to identify both the occupational divisions in support for parties and the presence or absence of leftist parties in power enables us to build upon and extend some of the fine studies of party government and policy performance among industrialized countries. Using less systematic measures and approaches, Douglas Hibbs, David Cameron and Edward Tufte have shown the association between control of the legislature and executive by socialist parties and several policies and outcomes. Hibbs related such control to a decline in strike activity, more redistributive tax policies, expansion of the public sector, and acceptance of inflation, if needed to maintain employment. Cameron looked at expansion of the public sector in the postwar period, and at the levels of income inequality. Tufte associated socialist control with greater size of the public sector by the early 1970s, and with equalizing effects of tax policy at the same time.[16] These studies examine between 10 and 14 countries. Each of them shows a clear awareness of the complexities of public policy formation and, especially, of linking policies to social outcomes. They treat the findings as suggestive; are concerned with the role of chance, given the small numbers of countries involved; and note the other factors operating on policy and consequence. Such caution is appropriate. Policies reflect a variety of beliefs, constraints, and opportunities, as well as commitments to voters and activists. For example, historical needs and conditions, as well as cultural emphases, produced a commitment to mass education far earlier, but to health and welfare much later, in the United States than in Western Europe.[17] Historical conditions after defeat in World War II seemed to compel nonleftist governments in Germany and Austria to come to the aid of industry and to support displaced populations. Above all, of course, the very different social structures and economics in the premodern and modernized nations compel their governments to pursue different policies. The age structure of the population alone creates different welfare needs.[18] Agricultural and industrial bases open up different tax possibilities and problems.

In looking at some economic outcomes of party government in the democracies, I shall first consider initial conditions, then look at the impact of the outcomes of party conflict on government policies, and finally consider broader social consequences. In doing so, however, we must keep in mind that one characteristic of contemporary government is the establishment of bureaucratic mechanisms to deal with social needs. Thus, governments typically create a set of laws and bureaucratic apparatus to deal with the needs of the unemployed and aged, as well as with the education of the young. When economic downturns, or an expansion in the number of old people, or a sudden increase in the number of children triggers these mechanisms, sharp changes in government activity will occur in response. These changes will be largely independent of the actions of the party in power, unless it specifically intervenes.

The 1960 Situation: Policy and Equality   The right-hand part of table 9.3 shows two measures of government policy outputs in 1960. It would be ideal to have data on the degree to which the governments used all their policy powers to increase equality between the workers and the better-off. Such data are not available, however, except for a few countries in the 1970s (see below). But the measures shown in table 9.3 are believed to be related to such efforts. First, the size of the personal income tax revenues collected as a percentage of gross domestic product (GDP) is compared, then the size of all government revenues as a percentage of GDP. We would expect leftist successes and the clarity of differences in support for right and left parties to be related to increases in both these measures. The table also indicates the percentage of all income received by the poorer 80 percent of the citizens, which should also be related to leftist success.[19]

I chose to consider personal income tax because tax studies indicate it is the only tax form that typically redistributes income away from the wealthiest citizens to the poorer ones. Other types of taxes, such as social security taxes, sales taxes, value-added taxes, property taxes, and even corporate taxes are usually not very redistributive, if at all.[20]

Leftist governments, especially class-based ones, should be partial to the income tax as a form of taxation, and collect a great deal of it for various programs. This turns out to be the case. Both leftist government control and the degree of class voting are associated with higher personal income tax revenue. Of the two, class voting seems the stronger factor. The contrast between countries having weak class voting and no leftist victories and countries having strong class voting and clear leftist majorities is quite stark. The latter collected income taxes that were twice as great as the former in proportion to GDP. Other factors are at work as well, but the pattern is fairly clear.

On the other hand, neither class voting nor leftist majorities seem to be related to the size of the government sector in 1960. The countries with low class-based voting had government sectors that were slightly less than 30 percent of the total economy in 1960; the countries with high class-based voting had only a fraction more. (Only the less industrialized countries—Japan and Ireland—clearly had smaller government sectors.) In 1960 the size of the government sector was not related to leftist success. Germany and Italy, where at that time leftists did not even participate in coalitions in the independent postwar governments, had large government sectors. So did Austria and France, in which Socialist parties were in government only in coalition or as unsupported minorities. Their large public sectors are primarily, it would seem, the effects of large welfare programs, financed through regressive transfer payments, and substantial government involvement in the economies being reconstructed after the war. Here is a good example of the danger of trying to predict policy outputs from consideration of party factors alone. Nonetheless, the measures of income equality—which are after transfers, but before taxes—do show substantial association between leftist success and equality.[21]

The impact of leftist success on equality, however, seems at this point to be much more associated with leftist victory than with its base in class voting or socialist programs. The results may be unduly shaped by the relative equality of the United States and Canada, with their historical experiences unfettered by the more rigid European class structure, but they are there, nonetheless. Another way of putting it is that there are several roads to income equality. As Cameron shows, equalization of educational opportunity can help, too, and this is the path taken by the United States and Canada.[22] (Multivariate regression analysis supports the finding that it is leftist majorities, as such, not class voting, that are primarily associated with equality. Across the full range of democracies, it is GNP per capita and leftist majorities that account for equality.)

Policy Changes: 1960 to 1970   Various historical circumstances, especially those associated with war and reconstruction, had sharp effects on
the levels of government involvement and equality in 1960. Looking at
the dynamic changes in the measures in the 1960 to 1970 decade
provides a clearer idea of government policy effects in their own right.
We do have to recall, though, the effects of automatic tax and welfare
mechanisms earlier instituted. Moreover, the Netherlands in particular
has made a major effort, institutionally, to insulate economic policy
from party politics in the electoral and legislative arenas.

In all the industrial democracies, the size of taxation and the size of
government increased in the 1960s (see table 9.4). Despite some
taxpayer unrest, the time had not come for tax rebellion, especially
given the general economic prosperity of the decade. Rightist parties
everywhere, from the American Republicans to the rightist coalitions in
Norway and Denmark which came to power in the last couple of years
of the decade, were struggling to slow the growth of government, rather
than to decrease its size.

Table 9.4 shows the impact of leftist success, in countries with and
without class voting, on the increases in income taxes and total
government revenue in the 1960s. It is clear that leftist success had an
impact on the degree of tax expansion in the 1960s, just as it did on the
tax levels at the beginning of the decade. Class voting also seems
important in the decade for increases in both income tax and total
revenue.[23] The middle columns of the table show the cumulative impact
on income taxes and a closely related measure, the tax rate on the
average worker (including income and social security tax, but not sales,
property, and value-added taxes).[24] These levels reflect the cumulative
effects of class-voting situations and leftist victories in the full postwar
period, and these effects are quite dramatic. Those countries with strong
class voting and continuing leftist victories had very high marginal tax
rates, even for the average worker, and relied heavily on income taxes.

Although there is much continuity from 1960 to 1970, the political
changes that occurred are interesting. In Germany the Social Democrats
gained a share of power, joining a coalition with the CDU/CSU as
junior partners. The increased legitimacy they gained as government
partner proved electorally valuable in 1969, with later policy consequences, but the effects on tax policy were limited in coalition.[25]
Similarly, the famous "opening to the left" in Italy did not really change
the base of the government very much, and the policies were seen then
and appear here as more of the same. In France, the dominance of the

Table 9.4 Class voting, Left-bloc success, and economic policy in the industrialized democracies, 1960–1970.

Class voting	Left-bloc success	Country	Economic policy changes[a] — Income tax as % of GNP: 1958–1968 increases	Economic policy changes[a] — Government revenue as % of GNP: 1960–1970 increases	Economic policy changes[a] — Income tax as % of GNP 1968[a]	Policy consequences for equality — Marginal tax rate of worker: 1972[b]	Policy consequences for equality — Tax equalization: % of income shifted away from top quintile[c]	Policy consequences for equality — % of income to lower 80%[c]
Low: under 25	None	Ireland	2.1	7.6	5.2	26%	—	—
		Japan	.2 } 1.3	1.8 } 4.4	3.9	18	1.5% } .8	59% } 56
		France	1.5	3.8	4.6	14	.1	53
	Coalition only	Belgium	1.7	7.5	8.1	24%	—	54%
		West Germany	2.0 } 1.9	1.7	8.4	26	.7 } 1.8	54 } 55
		Italy	1.6	2.8 } 5.1	5.1	23	—	57
		Netherlands	2.4	9.9	10.8	35	2.9	
		Switzerland	2.0	3.5	8.2	23	—	
	Left majority	Canada	2.9 } 2.5	8.8 } 5.5	7.9	27%	2.3 } 2.1	59% } 58
		U.S.	2.0	2.2	11.0	28	1.9	57
High: over 32	None	Australia	—	2.9 } 1.7	—	33%	.1 } .1	61% } 61
		New Zealand	—	.4	—	31	—	—
	Coalition only	Austria	1.8 } 2.4	5.8 } 5.1	10.4	23%	—	—
		Finland	2.9	4.4	11.1	38	—	—
	Left majority (or supported minority)	Denmark	4.6	14.4	14.8	54%	—	—
		Norway	2.2 } 3.9	7.8 } 11.6	12.6	42	3.6 } 2.9	63% } 62
		Sweden	5.0	13.2	18.2	62	3.5	63
		U.K.	3.8	11.1	10.8	34	1.6	61

a. Sources as in table 9.3.
b. See note 24 to this chapter.
c. Income after taxes and transfers. See note 21 to this chapter.

193

Gaullists in the new Fifth Republic worsened the position of the left, which had at least shared power in the Fourth Republic. Overall, as we would expect, changes in the countries without much class voting were not very great.

In the countries with high class voting there were both more changes and sharper implications. The left faced a decade out of power in Australia and New Zealand, with policy outputs to match. Although I have no data on income tax for Australia and New Zealand, the total revenue figures suggest that rightist parties in power in those class-voting countries were most successful of all in limiting the growth of government. In Austria, the Grand Coalition continued to 1966, followed by a Conservative OVP government to 1970, but great collaboration continued among the parties, so policy was highly stable. In Finland, the fluctuating coalitions did several times include the Communists, as well as the Socialists, but only in vastly oversize coalitions, whose electoral base was not far left of the electorate as a whole and whose more conservative members quite consciously were there to keep the Communists in check.

In two of the nations at the bottom of the table, the leftist push was dramatic. In Britain, the Labour party ended a decade in the wilderness and brought leftist class politics to power in 1964. In Denmark, the Social Democrats broke up their long-standing coalition with the Agrarian Liberals, and Danish politics took on a two-party format after 1964. The clear electoral and legislative majority enjoyed by the Social Democrats with the help of their leftist allies from 1966 to 1968 enabled them to push through major legislation. In Norway, by contrast, the left was only in power in 1960–61 and the conservative coalition restrained growth afterward. Thus the implications of electoral victory or defeat for economic policies were much more dramatic in the countries with high class voting, although victories by right or left were relevant in all the types of democracies.

Reliable data are not available on changes in income inequality over time. Such data as are occasionally presented are fraught with difficulties in comparison. But the last part of table 9.4 does present some data on the impact of taxes and transfers for a few countries, as of the late 1960s or early 1970s. The next-to-last column shows Malcolm Sawyer's analysis of the net percentage of income taken from the wealthiest fifth of the population by the tax structure. The positive numbers mean that in all cases the taxes are slightly redistributive. But the effects range from minuscule in France and Australia, to slight in

Germany, to very striking in Sweden and Norway. (Comparing the middle and right-hand columns shows that these redistributive effects are fairly closely associated with reliance on the personal income tax for revenue.) With so few cases it is hard to be confident about the results, but the equalization pattern seems quite consistent with both leftist success and class-based politics. (The Netherlands remains somewhat deviant, as noted earlier.)

The last column of table 9.4 presents for 10 of the industrialized democracies data on the equality of income distribution after both taxes and transfers as of the late 1960s or early 1970s. Here seem to be effects of both leftist success as such and leftist class politics in particular.[26]

Paths to Tax Policy   Path analysis makes it possible to pull together some elements in the discussion of the consequences of party competition for government policy. In the industrialized democracies, at least, the party systems tended to offer the voters some choice regarding policies on the economy and the size and financing of the public sector. The contrast between right and left parties was particularly sharp in countries in which voting divided along lines of occupation. Where voters put leftist parties in power the size of the government sector grew more rapidly, and government policies were financed by the more redistributive and visible income taxes. The leftist victories in countries with pronounced class voting were particularly likely to lead to higher incidence of income taxes.

Figure 9.1 adds consideration of a factor found by Cameron to have a major effect on the growth of government in the 1960s: the degree to which the economy was "open" to international trade impacts. Using the same measure Cameron used, the ratio of imports plus exports to GNP in 1960, yields similar results, as shown in the top line of the figure. The more involved the local economy was in international trade, the greater the growth of the government sector in the 1960s. These data are consistent with the proposal that where economies are more internationally vulnerable, the government will tend to play a larger role in attempting to control them. As suggested by the direct path in the diagram, the effects here are not related to internal leftist victories or class voting, although various such indirect models have been suggested.[27]

When we take account of the openness of the economy, class voting as such has insignificant effects on government growth, but the success of leftist parties does have a powerful impact on government expansion

Figure 9.1   Paths to tax policies in the industrialized democracies. Reduced standardized regression coefficients, the 1960s.[a]

Demographic and constitutional conditions	Party-system outcomes	Tax policy changes in the 1960s

Openness of the economy: Exports + imports/GNP (1) — +.53 → Increase in government revenue as % of GDP, 1960–1970 (9)

GNP per capita (log) (2) +.68

Catholic population (3) −.33 → Success of left-bloc parties 1960–1969 (8)

Majoritarian election laws (4) −.41 → Magnitude of class voting (6)

−.63

+.42

+.34 → Increase in income tax revenue as % of GNP, 1958–1968 (10)

+.40

[+.26]

[+.26]

Success of left-bloc parties 1946–1959 (5) — +.57 →

+.47

Income tax as % of GNP, 1960 (7) — +.57 → Visible tax rate on average worker, early 1970s (11)

a. The arrows and path coefficients represent the standardized regression coefficients significant at the .10 level in a set of recursive regression equations. As indicated by the direction of the arrows, the model assumes that variables with smaller identifying numbers are causally prior to variables with larger identifying numbers. Success of left-bloc parties 1946–1959 (5) and size of income tax in 1960 (7) are not included in equations to predict variables (9) and (10). Specific equations, variables, and sources are described in the Appendix.

in this period. As I suggested in examining tables 9.3 and 9.4, class voting did not have as much impact on the size of government as upon the nature of its revenue structure. Below the increase in the size of all government revenue, at the right of figure 9.1, is shown the increase in the size of income tax as a percentage of GNP. Here class voting and left bloc success are about equally important, while economic openness is irrelevant. The redistributive efforts of the leftist parties in the countries with high class voting are again manifest.

As the left-hand part of the figure shows, the more economically developed countries among the industrial democracies in this period were more likely to give support to leftist parties. The countries with large Catholic populations were somewhat less likely to support leftist parties. The election laws had little significant impact on leftist success, but were clearly related to class voting. As suggested in Chapter 5, class voting was more likely in the industrialized countries that were non-Catholic and ethnically homogeneous and had proportional representation electoral laws. The Catholic countries had strong linkages between groups and parties, but these were usually based on religion rather than on social class. The double links from a Catholic population to more conservative government policy in this time period show up clearly in figure 9.1. The European Catholic countries both were less likely to support leftist parties and had less clear-cut class voting. Both effects produced more conservative economic policies.

The bottom of the figure indicates a prelude to the antigovernment discontent that was to appear in some of the most progressive European nations in the 1970s. In the mid-1970s the OECD prepared an analysis of the visible tax rates experienced by the average worker, married with two children, when his or her income increased 10 percent. These rates included both income taxes and social security taxes, but not the various sales and value added taxes.[28] This figure, which was shown for each country listed in table 9.4 and ranged from 14 percent in France to over 60 percent in Sweden, is the absolute level, not the increase in the decade. Hence, the bottom line of the table shows the size of the visible tax burden as a function of the income tax rate in 1960, as well as a function of the increased income taxes of the 1960–1970 period, and of the growth of government in that time. All of these factors contribute significantly. Income tax levels in 1960 were themselves consequences of earlier leftist victories and class voting. Class voting and leftist victories in the 1960s alone account for over 65 percent of the variance in the visible tax rates. As the very substantial tax magnitudes, especially visible tax magnitudes, were thus in large measure a product of voters' backing of class-based leftist parties, it is not surprising that those successes should have eventually brought about an antitax reaction in a number of nations.

Did the democracies in general live up to their promise of freedom, competition, and responsiveness? Did some constitutional or party arrangements perform better than others on these democratic dimensions?

The answer to the first question seems to be yes. Although we have no absolute standards by which to judge, the democracies were much more likely than other nations to uphold civil liberties and freedom of the press. They were less likely to use repression when confronted with citizen discontent. Most of the democracies experienced changes in the parties controlling the government in response to citizens' electoral choices. In most of the democracies, all parties receiving substantial voting support (over 20 percent of the vote) did eventually attain at least a share of government power. The few exceptions were largely parties calling for extreme changes in social and political structure. By these measures the performance in areas of civil liberties and competition seems relatively impressive.

Examining the responsiveness of policies concerning government growth and income redistribution, I found substantial evidence that electoral support and election outcomes made significant differences. Not only did it matter whether parties of the right or left received enough electoral support to come to power, but the class bases of the support for political parties was also highly relevant. An analysis of the impact of party control on abortion policies, not presented here, also suggests important impact of parties and elections.[29] There is substantial evidence, then, that the democracies are responsive, although no standards exist by which to judge the absolute degree of responsiveness. Moreover, the absence of data on citizen preferences means that this evidence does not include consideration of the pressures that elections put on *all* political parties to adopt policies favored by citizens.[30]

Comparisons among the democracies were less definitive, except in the dimension of competition. The civil rights measure did not discriminate greatly, except to suggest the greater limitations on civil rights, on average, in less economically developed countries and in all democracies where deadly violence breaks out. The use of sanctions was primarily shaped by the amount of rioting and deaths. The constitutional arrangements had little direct effect. Multiparty systems were less likely to experience turmoil, but perhaps more likely to use sanctions when faced with it.

The effects of constitutional and party arrangements on competition were more clear-cut. The presidential systems were quite successful at encouraging changes in the chief executive and at providing the opportunity for all parties to hold major office Majoritarian parliamentary systems had similar, but weaker, effects, because of their tendency to limit the number of political parties.

Multiparty systems, indeed, performed less well by these measures of competition.[31] They complicated the impact of electoral changes on government, as the intervening coalition process often bore only indirect marks of election outcomes. Such complex interactions between vote, representation, and government formation were particularly evident in very fractionalized party systems. In simple correlations and in regression, fractionalization of the legislature was the strongest inhibitor of clear-cut connections between changes in a party's share of the vote and changes in its share of government power.

In the exclusion of parties from power, as with governmental durability, support for extremist political parties played the key role. Because extremist parties were more common in multiparty systems, these systems showed more exclusion. But the multiparty systems were very successful at bringing about sharing of power among all nonextremist parties: they were less likely to exclude legitimate minor parties with voting strength in the area of 10–20 percent of the vote, as often happened in majoritarian parliamentary and party systems. The Swiss collective executive system presented in extreme and "constitutional" form the advantages and disadvantages of multiparty systems from the point of view of competition and exclusion—no impact of elections on the party makeup of government; all substantial nonextremist parties given a role.[32] It is unclear what the appearance of strong extremist parties would do to this system. It seems likely that they would be excluded from power.

Without a good comparative measure of policy responsiveness, there is no simple way to judge the relative responsive capacity of the different democratic arrangements. Our data suggest that in the systems with strong linkages between occupational groups and parties, the effects of leftist parties in coming to power or being excluded from it were more dramatic. That is, in such systems the immediate policy impacts of the party and electoral process seemed greater. It seemed to make more difference which parties shared political power. Within the systems with high class voting, the correlation (and regression coefficients) between the type of party in power (left or right) and growth of government was much greater than in the systems with low class voting.[33] Over time, the policy impacts might or might not even out, if different parties came to power.

Unfortunately for purposes of study, in the time period covered there were relatively few dramatic shifts in power. The broad cross-sectional comparisons emphasize above all the contrast between rightist or leftist groups occupying predominant positions for long periods of time. Because many other factors also affect policy outcomes, it is, indeed, such long-run dominances as those of the left in much of Scandinavia and Canada, versus those of the right in France, Italy, Australia, and

New Zealand, that we would expect to have the clearest impact on policy.

The dramatic impacts of leftist parties in power in the countries with high class voting do not mean that representational constitutions and/or multiparty systems automatically create strong electoral effects on redistributive policies. These systems do, as discussed in Chapter 5, encourage stronger linkages between groups and parties. At least half of the multiparty systems had low *class* voting, because of the power of religious and ethnic cleavages in those societies. Where such divisions were politicized, they often overshadowed class politics, or encouraged blurred centrist coalitions, or both, limiting the impact of party changes in government on redistributive policies. Thus, the association between representational constitutions (and/or multiparty systems) and class voting, although positive, was not very strong across the full set of democracies. Similarly, the impact of leftist victories on leftist policies was not much greater (if at all) in the countries with representational constitutions and multiparty systems than in their majoritarian counterparts.[34]

The exploration in this chapter has indicated that in a basic sense the democracies do seem to fulfill their claims to be free, competitive, and responsive. Relative to other nations, their maintenance of freedom is impressive. Most are competitive by several measures, with the presidential and majoritarian parliamentary systems showing to particularly good advantage. (However, small, nonextremist parties were more likely to share power in the multiparty systems and representational parliamentary settings.) For various reasons, above all the absence of data on citizens' preferences, I have only been able to suggest some directions in comparing the relative performance of democracies in the critical area of responsiveness to citizens' wishes. I did find substantial evidence that in the democracies elections and their outcomes made important differences in public policies.

Conclusion / Constraint and Creativity in Democracies

10

I began this book with a question: Why does the political process work more successfully in some democracies than in others? In the initial chapters I developed the question more specifically, focusing on three dimensions of democratic performance: voting participation, government stability, and political order. Each of these forms of performance has been the subject of substantial research, research that has yielded expectations about how a nation's social and economic conditions, constitutional setting, and party system shape its political process.

I tested these expectations against the experience of 29 contemporary democracies. The analysis was carried out in two general stages. In Chapters 3 to 5 I developed measures of the various social, constitutional, and party conditions and examined their ability to explain the different dimensions of performance in simple and controlled statistical comparisons. In Chapters 6 to 8 I traced in more detail the connections between general conditions and performance outcomes, using theories about the processes linking setting to performance. In Chapter 9 I briefly considered some other, specifically democratic, forms of performance.

This concluding chapter has three objectives: to summarize what we have learned thus far; to consider the possibilities of leadership and political creativity; and to indicate limitations and future directions in the study of political performance. The findings of Chapters 3 to 5 will be further explored to address one remaining puzzle: the relationships among the performance dimensions. The findings of Chapters 6 to 8 will be restated as the backdrop of ongoing processes against which creative leadership must operate.

Relationships among the Dimensions of Performance

As I pointed out in Chapters 1 and 2, democratic theorists disagree about the compatibility of the three dimensions of political performance: participation, stability, and order. A major disagreement focuses on participation. One line of thought emphasizes the legitimacy-enhancing virtues of citizen voting participation; the other emphasizes the destabilizing pressures created by citizen involvement. A second disagreement focuses on the relationship between stable government and political order. One approach favors stable governments as critical symbols of continuity as well as prerequisites for effective problem solving. Other scholars point out the danger that strong and stable majority governments may abuse their power and may cause disadvantaged minorities to reject legitimate political channels.

The factor analysis in Chapters 2 and 4 suggested that higher voting turnout is strongly associated with higher levels of political order (fewer riots and deaths), but also with less government stability. Moreover, the dimensions of government stability and political order are themselves virtually unrelated. It was not clear, however, whether these relationships among voting turnout, stability, and order are the product of immediate causal effects or of other environmental conditions. Table 10.1 presents additional regression analysis to attempt to answer this question about the relationships between the performance dimensions.

Table 10.1 serves first to remind us that some environmental conditions do help to account for differences in political performance. As noted earlier, a number of variables suggested by previous theoretical and empirical work do not appear as significant in the equations with the full set of environmental conditions. Among the variables omitted here are such promising conditions as Catholic-protestant religious divisions, income inequality, and even average economic growth rates. These conditions may, of course, play a role under some circumstances. But across the full set of democracies they are not as important as the variables shown in Table 10.1. Moreover, no one characteristic of the general setting is equally important for all types of performance. Population size affects rioting and deaths; economic development level affects voting participation and deaths; ethnic homogeneity affects executive stability and deaths; constitutional factors affect voting, executive stability, and deaths. The different dimensions of performance require different explanatory equations and different variables.

If we think of the characteristics of the party system as in part a product of environmental and constitutional conditions and in part as a product of historical events and leadership decisions, it is appropriate to enter them in the equations after the environmental and constitutional variables. The second row of regression coefficients listed for each dependent performance measure shows the addition of the significant party variables from Chapter 5 to the environmental measures. This line of coefficients reveals not only the significance of the party measures but the decline in strength of some environmental coefficients whose effects operate through the party systems.

Party-system characteristics are important for voting (not shown here), executive durability, and riots, but not for politically related deaths. Strong linkages between groups and parties seem to be the major connection between economic development and voting turnout. These linkages also account for some of the constitutional effects on voting turnout, although other constitutional effects are linked to turnout through voting laws and competition. The strength of extremist parties is the major explanator of executive instability, along with presidential (and Swiss collective executive) constitutions. The strength of extremist parties plays the major role in linking ethnicity and electoral laws to executive instability; after the extremism variable is in the equation, ethnicity and electoral laws are barely significant (if at all), and their coefficients are more than halved. Extremist-party support also encourages rioting, while multipartyism (legislative fractionalization) seems to inhibit it, although population size continues to be the major factor accounting for riots. None of the party-system characteristics is significantly related to deaths, once the environmental and constitutional characteristics are in the equations.

These findings about environmental, constitutional, and party effects on political order are supported by a new source of data concerning the decade 1967–1976. The second-decade measure of riots and deaths had been collected from *Keesing's Archives* and *Facts on File,* and were admittedly not as complete as the measures for the first decade, which were drawn from Taylor and Hudson's *World Handbook.* As this book was being completed, however, new data from the *World Handbook III* were generously made available, and could be used to check on these measures.[1] Thus, table 10.1 shows both my own measures of riots and deaths and the measures from the new *Handbook.* The coefficients are very similar (with one exception discussed below), a result that lends support to the analysis in previous chapters.

The last columns in table 10.1 show the effects of adding voting turnout and executive stability to analysis of the other performance measures. Because of the complexities of analysis and the concern about possible causal direction of interactions, these results must be treated

Table 10.1 Regression analysis adding voting turnout and executive durability to strongest environmental, constitutional, and party variables, 1967–1976.[a]

Durability of executive — 19 parliamentary systems

Performance measure	Major environmental measures from Chapters 3–4: standardized regression coefficients		Major party variable from Chapter 5: standardized regression coefficients	Addition of performance measures: standardized regression coefficients
	Ethnic homogeneity	Majoritarian election laws	Extremist party seats	Voting turnout
	+.40**	+.70**	—	—
	+.19	+.27*	-.68**	—
	+.20	+.27	-.68**	-.02
(15 parliamentary systems, developed countries)	(+.21)	(-.05)	(-.79**)	(-.28*)

Low rioting — 27 systems, Powell data

Performance measure	Major environmental measures from Chapters 3–4: standardized regression coefficients	Major party variable from Chapter 5: standardized regression coefficients		Addition of performance measures: standardized regression coefficients	
	Small population (log)	Extremist vote	Legislative fractionalization	Voting turnout	Executive durability
	+.77**	—	—	—	—
	+.65**	-.30**	+.36**	—	—
	+.60**	-.24*	+.36**	+.20*	+.23*

204

	Small population (log)	GNP/capita 1972 (log)	Ethnic homogeneity	Representational constitution			
27 systems, World Handbook III data	+.78**				−.49**	+.49**	—
	+.61**				−.52**	+.46**	—
	+.58**						+.16*
							+.01
Low deaths 27 systems, Powell data	+.27*	+.53**	+.06	+.21*			
	—	—	—	—			
	+.24*	+.53**	+.05	+.25*			
27 systems, World Handbook III data	+.37**	+.51**	+.12	+.14			—
	—	—	—	—			+.10
	+.36**	+.50**	+.13	+.20			+.12
							—
							−.05
							+.07

Sources: All independent variables from sources and coded exactly as in tables 4.4 and 5.7, except that representational constitutions are coded: presidential = 1; majoritarian = 2; Germany, Ireland, and Japan = 3; parliamentary representational = 4. (See Chapter 4 for explanation.) Dependent rioting and death variables truncated to ninetieth percentile. Use of log transformed variables yields very similar results. Dependent variables collected from *Keesing's Archives, Facts on File,* and other sources. Additional riot and death data for comparison are from Charles Taylor and David Jodice, *World Handbook of Political and Social Indicators,* III (New Haven: Yale University Press, 1982).

a. Each line of numbers presents the standardized regression coefficients for the variables that were significant predictors of the given performance measure (stability, rioting, deaths) in Chapters 4 and 5. The first line shows the coefficients when the equation contains only the socioeconomic and constitutional variables; the second line shows the coefficients when the equation contains also the party variables (if any); the third line shows the coefficients when the equation contains the environmental, party, *and* participation and stability variables.

* = F level over 1.7 (significant at .10).

** = F level over 3.0 (significant at .05).

with caution. But they reflect interestingly upon the debates about relationships among the performance dimensions. Several points are quite clear.

The most straightforward point concerns deaths by political violence: neither voting turnout nor executive stability adds anything to the effects of the environmental and constitutional setting. The strong association between high voting participation and low levels of deadly violence seems to be a statistical artifact of the conditions that shape each of them. (In the new data, for example, the simple correlation of $+.31$ between voting turnout and low deaths actually becomes insignificantly negative in the regression equation.) This finding reinforces the idea that deadly violence in these countries is largely an elite-dominated phenomenon, not greatly affected by citizen involvement or choices in the party and electoral processes. Nor does executive durability have any simple part to play here. (While government strategies for meeting deadly violence may well be important, recall from Chapter 9 that multiparty systems are as likely as majoritarian ones to respond to violence with sanctions.)

Levels of rioting are more closely tied than deaths to the electoral, party, and legislative processes. The table shows very clearly the importance of the party-system characteristics of extremist voting support and legislative fractionalization. It also suggests quite consistently that while part of the strong association between high voting turnout and low rioting is caused by other variables affecting each of them, higher voting turnout does have a significant dampening effect on the likelihood of rioting. In both my own data and the *World Handbook III* data the initial correlation of $+.33$ between voting participation and low rioting is cut nearly in half by introducing controls for population size and the party system, but the regression coefficient remains significant (at the .10 level used throughout this book). Although the dampening effect is not very powerful, it is consistent and robust, holding up when the data are log transformed, or when we look only at the more economically developed countries; weaker in the first decade than in the second, but present nonetheless. The effects of voting turnout and the party system on rioting support the idea that citizen involvement in legitimate political channels inhibits mass turmoil. To this extent the data favor the theorists who believe that citizen involvement enhances legitimacy.

The other implications to be drawn from the table are less clear-cut. The argument about government stability and political order, for example, is unresolved. Government stability has no significant effects on deadly violence. In my own data, the weakly positive correlation between stability and less rioting becomes stronger and significant in the regression equation. But in the *World Handbook III* data the relationships are completely trivial, in both correlation and regression, across the 27 countries. As the newer data are likely to be more reliable, these findings do not support the theorists who favor government stability as a factor enhancing civil order. Yet, if we look only at the 18 economically developed nations, the coefficients do become significant in the regression analyses in both data sets. (Other variables remain significant also.) Unlike most of our findings, these results are weakened when we use log transformations rather than truncating the riot variable. In short, there is no evidence that executive stability in itself encourages turmoil. There is some mixed evidence suggesting that it may be associated with less turmoil once other factors of environment, party system, and citizen involvement are accounted for. But closer investigation is needed.

The results concerning the effect of citizen participation on government instability are complex. It is very clear that much of the strong negative association of participation and executive stability is a consequence of the way each is affected, directly and indirectly, by the constitutional arrangements and party systems. Across the full set of parliamentary systems (or all the countries, if we add variables for the presidential and Swiss constitutions), the negative association is reduced to almost nothing, once we take account of extremist-party strength and majoritarian electoral laws. It seems that high levels of citizen participation are not additionally destabilizing, once we take account of extremist party strength. Yet this conclusion cannot stand by itself without embellishment. First, considering only the 15 economically developed parliamentary systems, as shown in the table in parentheses, yields a much stronger correlation between participation and instability, and the regression coefficient is still significant, although greatly reduced, after we take account of extremist-party strength. Second, close analysis of extremist-party support suggests that higher voting turnout may have some impact on levels of vote for extremist parties.[2] Thus, while the effects are not very strong, the data suggest that higher levels of citizen voting involvement, at least in the more modernized societies, may indeed create some destabilizing pressures on government, in part through bringing discontented citizens to the polls where they may support extremist parties.

This analysis, then, clarifies some of the interactions among participation, government stability, and order, but it does not resolve the disagreements. It seems that deadly violence is not greatly affected by the other performance dimensions. Rioting and turmoil are inhibited to some extent, by citizen electoral involvement, and perhaps by government stability. Across the full set of countries, participation does not seem related to executive stability, once we take account of the properties of the party system. But in the economically developed countries, high levels of participation do seem to have some destabilizing effect, both directly and through encouraging the representation of protest parties. The intricacies of the role of voting participation in the writings of theorists are thus in part matched by its empirical role, weakening stable governments even while it enhances civil order.

Above all, it is important to keep in mind that most of the associations between performance measures are created by effects of the socioeconomic, constitutional, and party-system environments that shape each of them. Their interactive effects are less powerful in comparison. Further insight into the interaction among performance measures will require close examination of the dynamic processes of politics in different contexts, and particularly of the choices made by political leaders.

Executive Control and Economic Manipulation

It will be helpful to gain additional insight into the usual consequences of executive control. While executive control creates opportunities for creative leadership on the part of presidents and prime ministers, it also creates temptations for manipulation of government power for party and personal advantage. Although democracies allow citizens to punish leaders retrospectively for abuse of power, some forms of manipulation are not easily discerned. The manipulation of the economy for short-run electoral advantage is one good example of the abuse of executive power.

Edward Tufte has described many ways in which governments attempt to control their economies. Some of these approaches require new legislation, such as tax and welfare policies. Others can be based on manipulation in the short run of fiscal and monetary policy. Tufte convincingly demonstrates that in the American system, at least, executive power can be used even without control of the legislature to expand personal disposable income temporarily.[3] An excellent example of this possibility was provided by the 1972 presidential election, in which the incumbent was able to concentrate veterans' benefits, government aid to states and localities, and other transfer payments at election time. Regardless of their broader policy commitments, it is tempting to all incumbents to manipulate the economy immediately before elections.

The likelihood that incumbents will manipulate the economy will depend on a variety of factors, such as available fiscal and monetary tools, the external dependence of the economy, the personal philosophy of the incumbents, and the stake incumbents see in the given election. Broadly speaking, we would expect short-term expansions in personal income of citizens to be associated with election years rather than nonelection years across all the democratic systems. Tufte found that this is, indeed, the case. In 19 of the 27 democracies he studied, between 1961 and 1972 the growth in real disposable income accelerated more often in election years, and the differences were sometimes striking.[4]

Some systems tend to generate clear party control of the executive, while other systems do not. In the presidential systems, the constitutional rules give undivided executive control to a single party. Usually, substantial independent powers accompany that control. It is difficult to deprive the president of his office, even if his party does not enjoy a legislative majority. Thus we should expect some economic manipulation in most presidential systems.

In the parliamentary systems, by contrast, the strength of the executive depends on control of the legislature. A single party that controls the legislature, and hence controls the prime ministership, can manipulate the economy fairly freely, if it wishes to do so. A coalition government enjoying a legislative majority may be able to manipulate the economy, but only with the agreement of the parties in the coalition. Because each party in the coalition is competing with the others, as well as with opposition parties, getting such agreement may be quite difficult. As noted in Chapter 5, flows of votes from one party to another usually take place between parties that are adjacent on the political spectrum. As seen in Chapter 7, it is just such adjacent parties that form the government coalitions. Hence, this intense competition between neighbors in the multiparty systems should help restrain economic manipulation by coalition governments. Minority governments, which are dependent on outside support of other parties in the legislature, usually adjacent parties with which they compete, should be even more restrained.

Table 10.2 divides the democracies studied by Tufte according to their legislative-executive arrangements and their creation of single-party legislative majorities in the parliamentary systems. At the top of the table are the five presidential systems. Each of the presidential systems except the Philippines (whose manipulations of budget deficits have been described by scholars),[5] experienced more growth in election years. The aggregate difference was quite striking, with growth in 71 percent of election years and 47 percent of nonelection years—a

Table 10.2   Control of the executive and manipulation of the economy: growth of real disposable income in election years and nonelection years, 24 democracies, 1961–1972.[a]

Type of constitution and party majorities[b]	%of years in which the rate of growth of real disposable income increased[c]		
	Election years	Nonelection years	Difference
Presidential systems	71%	47%	+24%
Chile, Costa Rica,			
France, Philippines,			
United States			
Parliamentary systems			
Always a single-party majority	78	39	+39
India[d], Jamaica, Japan			
New Zealand, United Kingdom			
Mixed election outcomes	67	57	+10
Australia, Austria, *Canada,*			
Ireland, *Sweden*			
Always a coalition or minority government	54	48	+ 6
Belgium, Denmark, *Finland*			
Germany, Italy,			
Netherlands, *Norway*			
Collective executive systems	50	50	0
Switzerland, Uruguay			

Sources: Tufte, *Political Control of the Economy,* p. 12, for growth data. Election outcome data from *Keesing's Archives.*
   a. Data not available for Ceylon, Lebanon, Turkey, Venezuela.
   b. Italicized countries had more growth in election years than in nonelection years.
   c. See Tufte, *Political Control of the Economy,* Appendix I, for coding details and original sources.
   d. India is included in this category, as Tufte shows only two elections, presumably those of 1962 and 1967.

difference of 24 percent. The next group of countries in the table includes the five parliamentary systems in which a single party was always in majority control of the legislature and executive. Here the effects are even more impressive, as might be expected from the strong position enjoyed by the party in power in such situations. All these countries showed more frequent income growth in election years, and the difference between election years and nonelection years was a huge 39 percent. Such systems were twice as likely to have growth in election years.

In the countries with mixed election outcomes of majorities and minorities or coalitions, the difference between election and nonelection years was only 10 percent, and two of the five countries did not experience greater growth in election years. In the seven countries in which there was always a coalition or minority government, there was little difference between election years and nonelection years, and over half of those countries showed more growth in nonelection years. The two countries with collective executives, shown at the bottom of the table, seem to resemble coalition governments: there is little evidence of manipulation. Growth spurts were more typical in Switzerland in election years, although not in Uruguay, but the differences are slight. Given the limited electoral competition in Switzerland, discussed in Chapter 6, we might expect limited efforts to manipulate the economy for electoral purposes.

The data in table 10.2 are powerful evidence that single-party control of the executive is a great temptation to economic manipulation. We would not want to press the argument about the mechanisms too far without knowing more about the processes operative in each country. It may be that the multiparty systems are restrained in part by the likelihood that most parties will serve in subsequent coalitions, as well as by the checks the parties impose on one another. Moreover, according to Lijphart, in the Netherlands decisions about economic policy have long been distanced from cabinet policies, with a major role played by the Economic and Social Council, on which all major parties, as well as experts and representatives of business and labor, sit.[6] The absence of economic fluctuations linked to elections in that nation may result from this insulation from the electoral process, rather than from specific inhibitions facing a given coalition government. Mechanisms of this kind may be present in various countries and effective to different degrees. In the interests of stable and effective economic policy, they may be quite desirable, although they insulate policy from voters' preferences to some degree, as well as from electoral temptations. Thus, the typical patterns of majoritarian or consultative politics in a country may be more important than single election outcomes.

Institutionalizing Compromise: Consociational Practices

The theories of party strategies assume that leaders act primarily to seek electoral success and governmental office. Predictions based on these assumptions of self-interest hold up quite well across a range of cultures and settings. However, a theme that has emerged from the analysis of political performance is the importance of deliberate choices by political leaders, especially by political incumbents, to use their aggregated political resources to sustain the democratic system. Some of these choices, such as the formation of coalitions to defend the political system against assault or to minimize interparty conflict, seem to run counter to the short-run electoral and governmental interests of some of the parties involved.

While we have little direct data about the bases of such leadership decisions, we can draw upon Lijphart's discussion of "consociational" practices to examine further the effects of elite choices. Lijphart suggests that in some political systems the elites have consciously adopted a set of unwritten rules to help sustain democracy against the threat of group divisiveness.[7] They have rejected the majoritarian ideas that view democracy as the expression of majority elections and coalitions in favor of an emphasis on consultation and accommodation of all major groups. While representational constitutions and multiparty, nonmajoritarian party systems (discussed in Chapters 4 and 5) encourage such consociational practices and may reflect values that facilitate their adoption, consociationalism goes beyond them to guarantee directly a significant accommodation among all major groups. In its pure form, consociationalism would give each group a veto over all decisions affecting its interests.

Looking back to the origins of present Dutch political arrangements, Lijphart saw the Netherlands in 1913–1917 as a society so riven by class and religious differences as to stand on the brink of civil war. Strenuous elite negotiation, bargaining, and compromise led to a solution that would avert the disaster and guarantee all the contending factions present security, satisfaction of some major demands, and a future role in political decision-making. In subsequent decades the bones of the 1917 settlement were fleshed out with a variety of institutional arrangements and policy practices to create a system of accommodation that remained vitually unchanged until at least the 1970s.

The basic elements of the Dutch system were the creation of "grand coalitions" of all parties to make major substantive decisions and to carry through major changes in the constitution; provision of a veto to any group faced with an unacceptable policy; proportionate sharing of government expenditures and patronage; and substantial autonomy for each party to regulate and control its supporters. Mechanisms for ensuring that these elements endured included the Social and Economic Council, on which elements of government, labor, and business shared decisionmaking responsibility; deep embedding of proportionate-spending policies in the bureaucracy and the policy-making organizations; and adoption of a set of elite "rules of the game" to keep policy-making relatively secret so as not to mobilize citizens around divisive issues.

Lijphart and other scholars have identified similar consociational practices in other political systems.[8] Not surprisingly, Lijphart also sees federalism as frequently containing consociational elements, when its pattern of state autonomy and national representation effectively serve to guarantee the maintenance of and bargaining between regionally based political forces.[9] Specific instances of political elites working together to develop and sustain policies that will provide security to all the political groups in the society, meet their most salient demands, and generally dampen and control potentially intense divisions can be found in a number of societies, regardless of the formal constitutional arrangements. In addition to the Netherlands, the best examples of such consociationalism being institutionalized among the democracies seem to be Switzerland, postwar Austria, Belgium in 1958 and the 1970s, and Venezuela in the late 1950s. Lijphart also cites examples of consociational practices in India, and in Canada, where the inclusion of at least some French-speakers in every cabinet was carried on even with great difficulty by the Conservatives in 1979.[10]

Some very impressive achievements have been created under the auspices of these consociational practices. The tense relations between the formerly warring parties, or their descendants, in postwar Austria were brought under control in the elaborate interparty agreements and power-sharing arrangements of the 1953–1966 period, and arrangements for party consultation were continued afterwards.[11] Similarly, the parties that had been primarily responsible for the breakup of the abortive attempt at democracy in Venezuela between 1945 and 1948 worked out a proportionate solution to religious and educational policy when democracy was reestablished in the late 1950s, successfully kept the most explosive issues in the hands of behind-the-scenes party negotiators, and joined in support of policies to sustain the regime against both military coup attempts and guerrilla warfare in the 1960s.[12] The major parties in Belgium worked out an elaborate and successful all-parties agreement to end religious strife in 1958, an accommodation involving proportionate expenditure and control relationships and support by all factions for a return to peaceful politics. In the 1970s strenuous efforts were made to incorporate linguistic differences similarly.[13] In Switzerland the pattern of interparty agreement has been institutionalized in the collective executive and its rotating chairmanship, with all major parties participating since 1943.[14]

The successes of these examples of consociational practice cannot be ignored, but two important warnings are in order. First, the willingness of all the parties to work toward accommodative bargains is critical in the success of consociational democracy. Success requires the discovery of substantive and procedural solutions that will secure the interests of all parties. Examination of the range of successful consociational examples offers suggestions for types of substantive accommodation and continuing procedural guarantees of security that might be considered, but their worth in each case depends on the demands and fears of the parties in question. They cannot be blindly applied. Indeed, the very nature of the elements proposed by Lijphart suggests the problems.[15] Participation by all parties and mutual vetoes indicate that one recalcitrant group can block any new policies, to the great advantage of the supporters of the status quo and the disadvantage of the have-nots. Proportional expenditures and patronage often, at least initially, mean sacrifices by those presently receiving benefits or holding income advantages; but they may not satisfy the demands of others. Control by group leaders over their followers may perpetuate unsatisfactory intragroup relationships. If the groups are regionally based, as in a federalist approach, local minorities may be suppressed (as was the case for Southern blacks in the United States for many years).

The second warning is equally important. Accommodation among leaders will not be enough if they cannot sustain the support of their followers. And if large sections or groups of citizens are not mobilized at all, then the emergent consociational system is vulnerable to new elites making new promises. The efforts of some leaders to introduce consociational government and policies in Northern Ireland have foundered repeatedly because moderate Protestant leaders have quickly been outflanked by extremist leaders, unwilling to accept any compromise and able to back up their position by strikes and votes.[16] One of the impressive elements in the Swiss form of accommodation is the use of mechanisms to see that citizen voices are not shut out. National referenda to bring important issues to the national consciousness, and even to override party stands, offer a legitimate channel for grievances that parties may ignore. And the formation of a new canton in the 1970s over the linguistic disagreement between French and German speakers in the Bern region is an impressive example of the effort to get consent on important issues, with areas and even towns having multiple opportunities to vote on their fate under the new arrangements.

An effort to bring consociational practices directly into the statistical analysis of this book yields suggestive, if ultimately inconclusive, results. The major problem is the absence of systematic studies of consociational practices in all of the democracies. In the absence of such studies we face the double danger of failing to identify some countries with important consociational practices and of tending to ascribe successful governmental outcomes to "consociationalism" that is no more than accident or elite negotiation similar to such efforts in many countries. With this firm warning about limitations on data, the analysis reported in table 10.3 is nonetheless interesting. Lijphart identifies Austria, Belgium, the Netherlands, and Switzerland as consociations, and Canada and India as semiconsociations. With these coded 3, 2, and 1 (1 for nonconsociations), a variable for consociational practices can be added to regression equations containing the environmental and party variables found significant in Chapters 3 and 5. From the changes in variance explained and from the standardized regression coefficients in the last column, we can see whether Lijphart's attribution of consociational practices—based on his analysis of decision-making in these countries—is improving our predictive power and/or having a significant effect.[17]

Examining the coefficients in the last column of the table, we can see, first, that the consociational practices variable does not help explain either executive stability or rioting. The variables discussed earlier are dominant here: extremist voting for executive stability in parliamentary systems; population size, legislative fractionalization, and extremist voting for the level of rioting. It is worth noting that although consociational practices are associated with legislative fractionalization, it is the latter that inhibits rioting in the regression analysis. I do not

Table 10.3 Consociational practices, government effectiveness, and control of violence: standardized regression coefficients with controls.[a]

Performance measures	Variance explained	Environmental advantages[b]			Party-system outcomes[c]		
		Small population	Ethnic homogeneity	Modernity (GNP/capita)	Extremist party vote	Legislative fractionalization	Consociational practices
Government performance (19 parliamentary systems)							
Executive stability	59%	—	—	—	-.77**	—	—
	59	—	—	—	-.77**	—	-.07
Executive control of legislature	12	—	—	—	—	-.34*	—
	23	—	—	—	—	-.42*	+.35*
Containment of violence (27 democracies)							
Low riots							
1958-1967	69	+.68**	—	—	-.27*	+.33*	—
	69	+.67**	—	—	-.28*	+.26*	-.02
1967-1976	67	+.65**	—	—	-.30*	+.33*	—
	67	+.67**	—	—	-.26*	+.30*	+.09
Low deaths							
1958-1967	76	+.34**	+.40**	+.46**	—	—	—
	79	+.31**	+.47**	+.42**	—	—	+.17*
1967-1976	61	+.29*	+.10	+.64**	—	—	—
	64	+.23*	+.21	+.58**	—	—	+.20*

a. Only coefficients shown are in the regression equations. Others eliminated earlier. Violence analysis uses 26 cases for 1958–1967. Standardized regression coefficients are shown for two equations explaining each dependent variable. The first equation includes all environmental and party variables that were significant in the final analysis in Chapter 5. In the second equation, the consociational variable is added. Comparing the first and second equations shows the additional explanatory power of the consociational variable.

b. From Chapter 3.

c. From Appendix.

* = F level over 1.7 (significant at .10).

** = F level over 3.0 (significant at .05).

want to be too assertive about this point, given the small number of cases and the difficulties in measurement, but the presence of consociational practices as measured here does not help us to explain executive stability or rioting.

Consociational practices *are* related to the formation of majority cabinets in the parliamentary systems (as suggested in Chapter 7). Table 10.3 shows that adding the consociational practices variable to legislative fractionalization definitely increases our ability to explain executive control of the legislature in these countries. What is operating here apparently is the tendency of the consociational systems to avoid minority governments. Where minimum winning coalitions cannot be created, the leaders in these systems are more likely to choose oversize coalitions than minorities—as Belgium and the Netherlands did during part of the period of this study. Such coalitions are not necessarily durable, but they do provide temporary majorities. Including the collective executive systems of Switzerland and pre-1967 Uruguay in this part of the analysis would make these patterns even more pronounced. Since Lijphart identified systems as consociational partly because of the simultaneous bargaining, negotiation, or involvement of all groups, these regressions reemphasize the leadership component as much as they provide a new test. But they help confirm the distinctiveness of consociational patterns.

Most important, the positive impact of consociational practices on restraining deaths by political violence, which appears in the significant coefficients for both the 1958–1967 and 1967–1976 decades, is not likely to be mere measurement artifact. In both decades the consociational countries had fewer deaths by violence, even after taking account of environmental conditions. The relationship between ethnic division and consociational practice is especially interesting. Such practices are more likely to be employed in countries with ethnic divisions ($r = +.31$ between ethnic fractionalization and consociational practices). The unmeasured presence of these practices helps hide the conflictual tendencies of the ethnic variable itself, especially in the second decade. As can be seen by comparing the ethnicity coefficients, each is more powerful as a variable when the other is specified in the equation.

Nonetheless, these findings must be taken as merely suggestive; not conclusive. A comparison of these relationships with those reported in table 10.1 shows that the consociational variable is about as strong as the "representative constitutions" variable in explaining deaths by violence. When both are entered in the regression analysis, each becomes statistically insignificant, although the coefficients continue to be in the correct direction. In fact, consociational practices are strongly associated with representative constitutions (+.33 in the first decade, +.44 in the second). We cannot disentangle the constitutional, cultural, and leadership effects that are involved here. Without better measurement of consociational practices, it would be folly to try. At this point we can only look forward to better future research on the presence of consociational practices in democracies.

Requirements for Performance and Survival

Each of the constitutional arrangements has some advantages and disadvantages for the attainment of participation, political order, and government stability. The advantages and disadvantages result from the opportunities and constraints placed on political parties who enter the electoral and legislative arena under the respective constitutional rules. The rules can, if need and willingness arise, be circumvented by deliberate efforts of the parties themselves. What leaders must do to enhance performance varies under the different constitutional arrangements.

Presidential Constitutions   The major characteristic of the presidential system is the selection of a strong chief executive for a fixed term, usually in a direct election. Such rules do lead to the highest degree of executive durability among any of the constitutional arrangements. No variable is more powerful than a presidential executive in predicting executive stability. This stability enhances the possibility of responding with vigorous action to short-term emergencies and of using the very considerable powers of a chief executive to create continuity in policy.

A second aspect of the presidential system, the separation of the legislative and executive bases of power, has mixed implications. It may well help prevent executive overthrow of democratic regimes when the executive does not control the legislature through a party majority. The history of the presidential systems reveals no cases of executive overthrow of democracy without majority legislative control by the executive, although in many countries the emergency powers of the president are so substantial that such action is conceivable. However, the division of executive and legislative authority often makes it difficult to create and implement coherent, positive programs to deal with national problems. Students of American politics are familiar with the frequent deadlocks of the presidential and legislative branches. Not only are such deadlocks common when the party controlling the presidency is in the legislative minority—a frequent occurrence in all the presidential systems—but the differing constituency bases of president and legislators seem to hinder the development of coherent, disciplined national party systems and to create policymaking tensions even when the same party controls both. It is probably no accident that the presidential systems tend to have rather smaller governmental sectors than we might expect, although there are too few cases, and too many of them are poor countries, to determine the respective roles of weak party discipline, limited class-party linkages, and executive limitations in policy control.

As noted earlier, in the presidential systems the chief executive apparently is consistently able to manipulate short-term economic cycles for electoral advantage. The presidential systems have in some respects the disadvantages of each of the other types: the executive is strong enough to use governmental powers for party or personal advantage; yet frequently the executive faces a hostile majority in the legislature. The price paid for pure executive stability is a substantial one. Moreover, since the situation of the same party controlling both legislature and executive also arises frequently, there is often a tension-filled and unpredictable set of transition possibilities, which can be highly threatening to the security of losing parties. The security of a minority presidency can suddenly become the domination of a majority presidency. Majority presidents can even replace a democratic regime when they are threatened, as happened in the Philippines.

The presidential regimes are likely to do well, by their very constitutional rules, in sustaining a durable chief executive. Their negative effect on strong linkages and the pressure for the parties to move to the center to win national presidential elections also makes turnover of power quite likely in these political systems. However, the attainment of other democratic objectives requires a combination of constructive elite efforts. In the case of majority presidencies, the requirements are tolerance and accommodation on the part of the incumbents, and patience on the part of the opposition. These are not impossible to achieve, especially if the incumbent recognizes the need. In the case of minority presidencies, the requirements are accommodation on both sides, as the president must work out a modus vivendi with the legislature in order to make effective national policy. This possibility is enhanced by the usual weakness of party linkages to special groups in such systems, but constrained by the rather different electoral interests of president and legislators. Venezuela and Costa Rica provide good examples of rather successful accommodation between minority presidents and legislatures dominated by opposition parties in the early 1970s. The bitter conflict between the Allende government and the Congress in Chile, especially in 1972–1973 when the president increasingly used rule-by-decree and the legislature impeached cabinet members, illustrates the other extreme, and certainly contributed to the breakdown in governmental legitimacy in Chile.

Majoritarian Parliamentary Systems   Parliamentary systems, in which the chief executive serves subject to sustaining at least passive support from the legislature, rather than for a fixed term, are found in two-thirds of the democracies. They divide in practice into two rather different constitutional situations. In the majoritarian systems the rules of legislative representation act to keep smaller parties out of the legislature and to benefit the largest party or parties. The most common device creating such outcomes is the single-member-district electoral constituency, although other rules can be used in addition to or rather than the single-member district.

As we saw in Chapters 4 and 7, such rules make it likely that stable governments controlling legislative majorities will appear much of the time. The majoritarian rules discourage smaller parties, especially ones unable to form electoral coalitions, from entering elections in the first place. In the elections, such smaller parties as do compete are unlikely to win many seats unless their support is geographically concentrated or they can join in pre-election coalitions with other parties. Single-party majorities after the election can usually form stable and disciplined governments. Pre-election coalitions that become minimum winning governmental coalitions can also be very durable and effective. The exclusion of smaller extremist parties assists in the construction of stable, connected, minimum winning governments of great durability.

Hence, the majoritarian legislative systems tend to perform well in terms of stability and effectiveness. Their major weakness in this respect is that when elections fail to create a majority, parties in the majoritarian systems are often inclined to choose a caretaker minority government and wait for a new election, rather than to build a stable coalition. Some majority parties are also somewhat internally incohesive, especially in the less modernized countries. Instability was created by intraparty divisions in India and Turkey in the late 1960s and early 1970s, for example, and such divisions can also lead to less effective legislative control.

At the same time, the majoritarian systems have some of the vices of their strengths. As shown in table 10.2, single-party majority governments in parliamentary systems are even more likely to manipulate the short-term economic forces for party advantage than are presidential governments. The majoritarian systems also have more serious violence than the representational ones. As we saw in the analysis of citizen turmoil in Chapter 6, merely shutting out small extremist parties does not guarantee an absence of rioting and protest. On the contrary, majority control seems to make diffuse, nonparty rioting much more likely. There is no question that minorities can be severely disadvantaged under these majoritarian systems if they are permanently distinctive and unable to form coalitions with part of the majority. Northern Ireland is a clear example, with the Catholics in permanent minority status and faced with a variety of forms of government-backed discrimination from the autonomous provincial government controlled by Protestants. Efforts to turn outside the usual electoral and legislative arenas to use protests and pressure met with repressive response from both private and quasigovernmental Protestant groups; the result was a rapidly escalating violent conflict, exacerbated by historical and international conditions.

Moreover, these strong majority governments face little restraint upon them between elections. It is quite possible to use the powers of government to constrain or even to eliminate democratic government. This abuse of executive power can be even easier to achieve in such systems than under presidential government, as the party system is stronger and agreement between legislative and executive more likely. The most frequent suspensions of democratic freedoms were found, as we saw in Chapter 8, in majoritarian legislatures, usually of the parliamentary form: India, Sri Lanka, Jamaica, (even Canada in 1969 might be included, with the use of State of Emergency powers to limit freedoms in Quebec). In each of these cases the suspensions proved temporary, and the governments in question did eventually allow free elections. But the concern about strong executive authority, such a strong tradition in American historical thought, is not without foundation.

What is needed from elites to enhance democratic performance in these systems seems clear. The systems will tend to generate stable majority governments much of the time, through the natural operation of their rules and incentives. But efforts must be made, first, to secure the involvement and support of minority groups through major parties with a chance to share power. If linkages between parties and groups are weak, or some groups excluded, cycles of violence are likely. Parties must develop the flexibility to recognize new pressures and trends, even without the presence of successful minority parties to point the way. The general tendency of electoral competition to force parties to move toward the political center to win majority elections in such systems, pressures counterbalanced in part by the demands of activist party organizers, can be an advantage in stabilizing governments, but can also frustrate the groups who do not find themselves at the center.

The other great requirement for democratic performance in the majoritarian systems is to sustain mutual respect among the parties and support for the general democratic rules. The majority must be willing to avoid abuse of power, to keep in touch with the minority and recognize its grievances, and to surrender power in its turn. The minority must be willing to wait and to work democratically for its chance, forming coalitions to meet electoral needs, avoiding the use of violence to enhance its position. Both the security of minority elites, so that the majority will be willing to surrender power when it loses elections, and the avoidance of interparty violence will depend in part on the willingness and ability of the party leaders to work with each other behind the screen of majority control. Various studies of decision-making in Britain suggest again and again the role of consultation and compromise in smoothing the way for use of the awesome powers of parliamentary majority.[18] Where these practices of consultation are forgotten or rejected, the specters of separatism, interparty violence, majority abuse of power, and serious threat to democracy appear.

Representational Parliamentary Systems   The representational parliamentary systems facilitate easy entry to the legislature for small and new political parties, including extremists. (However, parties overtly espousing an end to democratic government are forbidden in many systems.) The executive depends on legislative support to remain in office. These arrangements facilitate the mobilization of small parties, as parties can target potential supporters of particular interests throughout the nation, without having to worry about being defeated by majorities in each district. When many parties emerge or when barriers to entry of new parties are low, parties also have an incentive to adopt representational strategies of campaigning, in which they seek to mobilize well-defined support groups, even if these have no chance of constituting popular majorities, in order to gain consistent legislative representation from which to bargain for government participation. Hence representational systems encourage close linkages between groups and parties, as well as multiple parties.

The advantage of the representational parliamentary system is that it facilitates entry through the legitimate political processes, even for relatively small and distinct minorities. (In a few countries, special rules or very strong party organizations inhibit fractionalization, leading these systems to work in practice more like majoritarian systems, as in post-1966 Austria.) Once in the national legislative arena, minorities gain a national forum and their leaders become more closely tied to incentives of democratic involvement. Other groups can then bargain with them in a democratic context. Voting participation tends to be quite high in this group of political systems, both because of the party-group linkages developed in the party system, and because the legislatures tend to adopt participation-facilitating voting laws. Representation is relatively equitable. As long as existing parties do not dominate new entry too thoroughly when new issues emerge, working through the electoral system is more common than protest demonstration. Both legislative fractionalization and high voting turnout discourage rioting, as was apparent in Chapter 6 and in table 10.1. Although extremist-party activity is encouraged by the possibilities of representation in these systems, and constitutes a major difficulty for government stability when discontent rises, the association of extremism and citizen turmoil is notably outweighed by effects of participation and representation.

Serious violence is less frequent in these representational systems (although environmental factors were predominant). While the lower violence of these systems reflects in part the tendency for the systems to have been introduced in countries that now face less serious environmental tensions, the countries of Western Europe, the regression analysis suggested less frequent deadly violence in representational systems even after taking account of the economic and cultural environment. The generally more negotiation-oriented pattern of politics does seem to inhibit deadly violence.

The serious performance defects in these systems appear most glaringly in the level of government stability. In half of them, during the period studied, the average government lasted only two years or less, before it was defeated, reorganized, or forced to call an election. As we saw in Chapter 7, this instability resulted above all from the presence of extremist parties, which made the construction of durable, connected, minimum winning coalitions quite difficult. Even when coalitions were constructed, the presence of the extremist parties and general polarization weakened their ability to survive. Under such conditions, oversize and minority governments tended to fail quickly. The extremist parties themselves were very often excluded from participation in government, limiting power sharing.

Government weakness is not without compensations. Table 10.2 suggested that governments in countries with coalition and minority governments were much less likely to manipulate the economic cycles for electoral advantage than were those in countries with single-party majorities or presidential executives. Moreover, in none of the countries did coalition or minority governments use executive power to overthrow or suspend democratic processes. The representational systems did, for the most part, work as their design suggests: bringing most groups into the political arena, giving them some policymaking role, and emphasizing the linkages between all citizens and the democratic processes of government.

But the problem of political deadlock in the representational parliamentary systems cannot be ignored. The development of governments depends on negotiation among the political parties. As these systems encourage strong linkages between parties and groups, it is difficult for electoral reasons to form coalitions with parties that are not close together on the most important issue continuum. Yet the adjacent parties are those competing intensely with each other for votes. At the ends of the continuum may often be extremist parties whose wishes are by definition threatening to other party contenders. Strong tensions involving the extremists can either threaten to deadlock the system, or perpetually push the formation of center governments whose weak durability, policy immobilism, and limited political accountability are themselves frustrating to those wishing change in the society. Italy represents these tendencies in extreme form, with the problems made more difficult by the special role of the Catholic church and by the strength of the Communist party, derived historically from its role in the World War II Resistance.

When one party or an extremist-linked coalition shows signs of developing a majority, the very clarity of party alignments encouraged by the representational system creates a threatening situation, and it may be difficult for a new majority of this type not to abuse its unaccustomed position. The bitter conflicts over religious issues that emerged in Belgium in the early 1950s were in part generated by the unusual appearance of Catholic party majorities, and the seesaw of sharp policy transitions between Catholic and Liberal-Socialist governments spilled over into street violence. Similarly, in much more extreme form and under more difficult conditions, the emergent majoritarian situation in Austria in the late First Republic was difficult to bear under an intensely socially bifurcated party system.

A final problem is that the representational parliamentary systems can be quite vulnerable to military intervention if the major parties cannot act together to support the system. Under conditions of represented extremist parties and legislative deadlock, the danger of military intervention following an appeal by some parties to the armed forces is substantial. The military's usual dislike of turmoil and the fear of extremist electoral victories facilitate intervention when encouraged by civilian groups. Greece, Brazil, and Turkey provide examples of military intervention under such conditions.

The critical role of elite cooperation and negotiation, which is present, but often hidden, in the majoritarian systems, is manifest in the representational ones. Failure of the elites to accommodate a variety of parties and groups in constructing stable governments is obvious in short-lived executive durability, periods of negotiation with no government at all, or frequent minority governments. In such countries as Italy, Denmark, and Turkey, all three of these symptoms manifested themselves in the 1970s. In other systems it was possible for party negotiations to ease these difficulties and/or to develop recognized rules for accommodation of represented interests. The appearance of consociational practices was more likely (or at least more easily recognizable) in the representational systems, and, as seen in table 10.3, such practices made minority deadlock less likely. The Swiss system, with its standing decision to allow the four largest parties a proportionate representation on the collective executive, presents an extreme institutionalization of such practices. While interparty compromise is important in the presidential and majoritarian parliamentary systems, especially to contain tensions and keep the stakes of defeat from getting too high, it has symbolic as well as practical implications in the representational systems. In addition to whatever real costs are experienced in terms of failure to take effective policy steps, the mere presence of short-lived governments, minorities, and deadlocked negotiation without a government encourages a loss of confidence. Policymaking is a complicated business; it may be a long time before the final outcomes are seen. But the persistent failure of parties to form and support a government acts as a continuing signal that all is not well with the democratic system.

Comparative Analysis: Limits and Directions

It seems to me that the most important lesson to be drawn from this investigation is cautionary. There are many ways to organize a working democracy. The different approaches tend to have different advantages and disadvantages. The implications of a given approach depend in part on what sorts of performance are most strongly desired. Creative political leadership can help to mitigate the undesirable qualities, or undermine the benefits, in any type of setting. It is important not to draw too sweeping inferences about the effects of proportional representation, or political extremism, or citizen participation from their presence in one particular country or another.

In this vein it is appropriate to add some cautionary notes about the enterprise in general. It shares with most studies some serious limitations. Some of these are inherent in the necessary choices made to pursue one strategy of investigation rather than another in seeking to answer important and complex questions. These limitations constitute challenges and opportunities for future study, as well as warnings against too facile acceptance of the present findings.

One limitation is that the present conclusions are based primarily on comparisons across nations during a particular historical time period. Such comparisons need to be supplemented by and extended with over-time analysis within and across countries. It is essential that such analyses begin to incorporate time periods when different international conditions, economic and political, subjected democratic regimes to much more severe strains than most nations experienced in the 1960s and 1970s. The period between the two world wars is one place to extend the present analysis; the 1980s may be another.

A second limitation is that in the attempt to make rigorous statistical use of the experiences of all the democratic countries, much detail about individual conditions has been sacrificed. The individual conditions and the choices citizens and leaders have made in response to them provide the richness and complexity of experience from which the patterns we have been analyzing are distilled. They are important for many reasons, and any careful reading of the present work will suggest a number of critical directions in which detailed, but theoretically oriented, work can build. One of the most important of these is the variety of attitudes about issues and about democracy involved in the designation of some groups and parties as "extremist." I have suggested in passing that parties representing diffuse protest do not always create the same type of problems as parties representing ideological challenges to democratic regimes. Including and going beyond that point is the need to understand the transformations of extremist parties over time, both in self-perception and as described by others.[19] It seems clear that such changes will have major impacts on the system of political parties and on democratic performance. While these changes are not easily measured statistically, their presence must be recognized and explained if we are to understand the dynamics of party systems.

Similarly, the present study merely begins to touch upon the role of creativity in leadership, and upon the critical intertwining of process and policy in shaping democratic performance. While I have focused on aspects of process, it is clear that to some extent solutions must be found to major policy disagreements, as well as to recognized common problems, if the democratic political system is to thrive. We also need much more information about the role of cultural values and assumptions as these shape the operations of the political process. Intraparty negotiations and structural arrangements, as well as policy stances, are worthy of far more attention than I have been able to give them here. While the political party has proven to be a powerful and useful unit of analysis in this study, the analysis of intraparty factions is essential for understanding certain problems. I have also assumed that the political process is relatively homogeneous, but various studies have suggested that in different issue areas, and in different parts of the system, the processes of rule and negotiation may vary markedly.[20] Understanding of the broader patterns of political decisionmaking requires continually aggregating and disaggregating our analyses of the components.

Yet a third limitation is that I have here considered only three areas of performance across the democratic systems. Of course there are other aspects of the political process worthy of attention. While participation, stability, and order have received most attention in the literature, such particularly democratic aspects of performance as competitiveness, responsiveness, representation, and accountability are exciting areas for future work.[21] Moreover, in analyzing participation I have dealt only with voting turnout, while various studies have demonstrated that other forms of citizen involvement have a powerful role to play.[22] Quite clearly, the role of the political process in achieving such citizen-backed policy goals as economic stability and full employment is also a major area for study. Given some current doubts about the viability of democracy itself, some systematic analyses of the record of democratic and types of nondemocratic regimes would seem very much in order.[23]

Too frequently assaults upon democracy have been justified in the name of social goals—equality, justice, civic rectitude, economic growth, political order—that have proved unobtainable by the nondemocratic successor. The concern in these pages should not blind us to the successes and failures of democracies, under various conditions, in comparison to other alternatives of the present and future.

Appendix

Notes

Index

Appendix

Science is a social activity. Analyses by a single scholar should be susceptible to replication, amplification, and modification by others. Throughout this book I have attempted to present materials in a fashion that will facilitate further exploration of the problems of participation, government stability, and violence in the contemporary democracies. The dependent variables used to measure these dimensions of political performance, and the arguments underlying their selection, are presented in Chapter 2, with the original sources indicated in the notes. The major independent variables, their theoretical origins and practical measurement, are presented in Chapters 3–5. For the most part, the specific values used in the analyses are shown in tables in those chapters.

This appendix is designed to supplement those tables by providing relevant data on national average scores for the 1967–1976 decade not completely available in the text. The appendix also provides details on the equations and variables used in the path diagrams in the figures. Space does not permit presentation of data for individual years, elections, or cabinets that are used in Chapters 5 to 7 to supplement the basic analysis of average scores for decades.

Measures of violence, 1967–1976. Table 2.3 in the text shows the average numbers of riots and deaths by political violence per year for the democratic nations with the largest numbers of violent events. Statistical analysis uses the full range of events, including those in the countries shown in table 2.3 as having "less severe conflict by these measures." The data for 1958–1967 were calculated from Taylor and Hudson's *World Handbook*[1] by simply adding up the events during the years in which the nation was a democracy during the decade and dividing by the number of years. All the countries except Greece and Turkey were counted as democracies throughout the decade. The data for 1967–1976 were collected by me from *Keesing's Archives* and *Facts on File*. These new data are presented in columns two and three of table

A.1. I counted the nations in the table as democracies for the full 10 years except for the following: Chile, 7 years; India, 8 years; Philippines, 6 years; Turkey, 8 years; Uruguay, 6 years. (Despite some post-1971 censorship, Ceylon is counted as a democracy for 10 years, as elections continued; this choice does not affect the data analysis, because of the distribution and magnitude of violent events.)

As these data were collected by a single scholar from only two sources, they must be considered less complete and reliable than the data for the earlier decade. However, after completion of most of the

Table A.1 Supplemental data on violence and party-system characteristics.

	Measures of violence[a]		Measures of party systems[b]	
Country	Riots per year 1967–1976	Deaths per year 1967–1976	Extremist-party vote: Average 1965–1976	Fractionalization of parties in legislature: Average 1965–1976
Australia	.1	0	0%	61
Austria	0	0	1	54
Belgium	.6	.1	21	76
Canada	.4	.3	0	63
Ceylon	.4	121.1	13	67
Chile	1.4	87.3	30	73
Costa Rica	.2	0	2	58
Denmark	.1	0	18	79
Finland	0	0	25	81
France	3.3	.7	25	71
West Germany	1.9	2.7	3	57
India	56.8	328.4	18	60
Ireland	.3	4.0	0	61
Italy	7.4	8.9	37	73
Jamaica	.6	17.9	0	45
Japan	2.9	2.7	16	60
Netherlands	.3	.2	13	84
New Zealand	0	0	1	49
Norway	0	0	9	72
Philippines	2.0	332.7	0	49
Sweden	0	0	5	69
Switzerland	.3	0	8	81
Turkey	4.4	18.1	9	63
U.K.	11.7	160.0	3	53
U.S.	42.7	20.7	0	48
Uruguay	2.7	18.2	12	61
Venezuela	4.5	5.9	12	72

a. Includes only years when nation was a democracy.

b. Averages based on national legislative elections. Some small parties receiving under 2 percent of vote may not be included. Fractionalization averages calculated after each election.

present study, preliminary data collected for the new *World Handbook* III[2] were generously made available to me by David Jodice and Charles Taylor. Agreement is quite high between the two estimates. The correlations are .78 between average riots in table A.1 and the *World Handbook* III riot average, and .71 between the two figures for deaths. More important, when the data are transformed to lessen the impact of extreme outliers, as was done in data analysis throughout the text, agreement is much higher. Truncating both sets of figures back to the ninetieth percentile yields correlations of .88 and .96 for riots and deaths respectively, while using a log transformation (as employed by Hibbs)[3] yields correlations of .90 and .94. Moreover, as shown in table 10.1 in the text, the use of the *World Handbook* III data serves to strengthen those relationships that emerged as significant from the text analysis, particularly those involving the party-system variables.

Measures of average party-system characteristics, 1965–1976. The data presented in Chapter 5 describing party fractionalization and support for extremist parties are shown for the party systems of the early 1960s. However, much of the data analysis from table 5.7 on uses the average characteristics of the party systems for 1967–1976. In practice these begin with the last election immediately before 1967 if no election took place in 1967; typically three or four elections are included. These data are calculated by me from original materials in Mackie and Rose's *International Almanac of Electoral History*,[4] the *Europe Yearbook*, the *European Journal of Political Research*, and *Keesing's Archives*.

The *fractionalization* score is the average party fractionalization of legislative seats following the elections: the probability, multiplied by 100 to give whole numbers, that any two legislators are of different parties. The formula is based on that of Rae: $F = 1 - (\Sigma_1^N T^2)$, where N is the number of parties and T is the party's decimal share of the vote in the legislature.[5]

The vote for extremist political parties is the vote received on average in national legislative elections of the period. In principle, I judged parties to be "extremist" if they seemed to represent any of the following: (*a*) a well-developed nondemocratic ideology; (*b*) a proposal to break up or fundamentally alter the boundaries of the nation; (*c*) diffuse protest, alienation, and distrust of the existing political system.[6] As pointed out in the text, these different bases did seem to have somewhat different consequences, and the nature of party extremism is an important area for future research, as is the dynamics of its continuation or change. For purposes of the analysis here, all Communist parties were considered extremist, and Communist parties are included in the averages for Austria, Belgium, Ceylon, Chile, Denmark, Finland, India (both CPI and CPI-Marxist), Italy, Japan, the Netherlands, Norway, Sweden, Switzerland, and Venezuela. In addition, the following parties were considered extremist. Belgium: the language parties. Ceylon (Sri Lanka): the LSSP and the MEP. Chile: the Socialists and the far left. Costa Rica: PAS. Denmark: Socialist People's party, Left Socialists, Progress, Single Tax. Finland: Rural party. France: far left parties. Germany: NPD. India: Jan Sangh. Italy: PSIUP, Monarchists, MSI. Japan: Komeito. Netherlands: BP, PSP, GPU, Democrats '66 (1967 and 1971 only). New Zealand: Values. Norway: Socialist People's Party, Lange's Party, and the Socialist Electoral Alliance. Switzerland: the Republican Movement and National Action. Turkey: Turkish Labour party, National Action, and National Salvation. United Kingdom: the Scottish and Welsh Nationalists. Uruguay: FIDEL and Frente Amplio. Venezuela: MAS and National Civic Crusade.

Variables, sources, and equations for figures. Six of the figures in the text present path diagrams, showing the results of regression analysis that assumes a hierarchical causal relationship among the variables. Many of the same variables appear in these equations, although their equation numbers may vary because of different numbers of variables in some of the different models. The identifying labels are, however, the same from figure to figure for the same variable, as are the coding rules.

The following sources and coding rules apply each time a variable appears in one of the figures: Population size (log) in 1965 or 1972 from table 3.1. GNP per capita (log) in 1965 or 1972 from table 3.2. Ethnic fractionalization from table 3.3. Agricultural minority: percentage employed in agriculture in 1965 from table 3.2; coded under 20 percent = 1; 20–49 percent = 3; over 49 percent = 2 (as in table 5.6). Catholic minority from Taylor and Hudson, *World Handbook,* coded as in agricultural minority. Catholic population is percentage Catholic from Taylor and Hudson, *World Handbook.* Openness of economy (exports + imports)/GNP calculated from Organization for Economic Cooperation and Development, *National Accounts for OECD Countries, 1960–70* (Paris: OECD, 1973). Representational constitution coded presidential = 1; majoritarian parliamentary = 2; West Germany, Ireland, and Japan = 3; representational parliamentary = 4; from table 4.1. Majoritarian election laws coded single-member district = 3; West Germany, Ireland, Japan = 2; others = 1; from table 4.1. Presidential executive coded parliamentary = 0; presidential = 1; from table 4.1. Extremist-party voting support from Appendix for 1967–1976; from table 5.4 for earlier decade. Party system with strong cleavage alignments is larger of two index numbers in table 5.3. Magnitude of class voting is class alignment index from table 5.3. Legislative fractionalization from Appendix for 1967–1976; from table 5.2 for earlier decade. Voting participation of eligibles from table 2.1. Mobilizing voting laws from table 6.1, combining compulsory voting and registration laws. Riots from Appendix for 1967–1976; from Taylor and Hudson, *World Handbook* for earlier decade. Deaths from Appendix for 1967–1976; from Taylor and Hudson, *World Handbook* for earlier decade. Protests from Taylor and Jodice, *World Handbook* III for 1967–1976; from Taylor and Hudson, *World Handbook* for earlier decade. For riots, deaths, and protests extreme cases are truncated to ninetieth percentile to prevent bias; log transformation yields similar results. Success of left-bloc parties 1946–1959 is from table 9.3 and coded none = 1; coalition only = 2; majority = 3. Success of left-bloc parties 1960–1969 is from table 9.4 and coded as in the preceding variable. Income tax as percent of GNP in 1960 from table 9.3. Increase in government revenue as percent of GDP 1960–1970 from table 9.4. Increase in income tax revenue as percent of GDP, 1958–1968, from table 9.4. Visible tax rate on average worker, early 1970s, from table 9.4.

The following equations and sources were used in computation of the coefficients in the figures:

Figure 6.1. The arrows represent the standardized regression coefficients from the set of recursive equations:

$$X_5 = X_1 B_{15} + X_2 B_{25} + X_3 B_{35} + X_4 B_{45}.$$

$$X_4 = X_1 B_{14} + X_2 B_{24} + X_3 B_{34}.$$

$$X_3 = X_1 B_{13} + X_2 B_{23}.$$

Coefficients not significant at the .10 level are deleted from the figure and arrows corresponding to them are not shown.

Figures 6.2, 6.3, 8.1. The arrows leading to party-system measures in these figures indicate standardized regression coefficients significant at .05 level in table 5.6. The coefficients in brackets are for 1958–1967; others are for 1967–1976. Coefficients shown in the tables are from the reduced equations predicting riots, protests, or deaths. The reduced equations include the coefficients significant at the .10 level in equations predicting riots, deaths, or protests with all independent variables in the figure. The specific reduced equations are:

$$\text{Riots } (X_{10}) = X_1B_{1,10} + X_8B_{8,10} + X_9B_{9,10}.$$

$$\text{Protests } (X_{10}) = X_1B_{1,10} + X_2B_{2,10} + X_8B_{8,10} + X_9B_{9,10}.$$

$$\text{Deaths } (X_9) = X_1B_{19} + X_2B_{29} + X_3B_{39} + X_4B_{49}.$$

Figure 9.1. The arrows represent the significant standardized regression coefficients from the set of recursive equations:

$$\begin{aligned}
X_{11} = {} & X_1B_{1,11} + X_2B_{2,11} + X_3B_{3,11} + X_4B_{4,11} + X_5B_{5,11} \\
& + X_6B_{6,11} + X_7B_{7,11} + X_8B_{8,11} + X_9B_{9,11} \\
& + X_{10}B_{10,11}.
\end{aligned}$$

$$\begin{aligned}
X_{10} = {} & X_1B_{1,10} + X_2B_{2,10} + X_3B_{3,10} + X_4B_{4,10} + X_6B_{6,10} \\
& + X_8B_{8,10} + X_9B_{9,10}.
\end{aligned}$$

$$\begin{aligned}
X_9 = {} & X_1B_{19} + X_2B_{29} + X_3B_{39} + x_4B_{49} + X_6B_{69} \\
& + X_8B_{89}.
\end{aligned}$$

$$\begin{aligned}
X_8 = {} & X_1B_{18} + X_2B_{28} + X_3B_{38} + X_4B_{48} + X_6B_{68} \\
& + X_7B_{78}.
\end{aligned}$$

$$X_7 = X_1B_{17} + X_2B_{27} + X_3B_{37} + X_4B_{47} + X_5B_{57} + X_6B_{67}.$$

$$X_6 = X_1B_{16} + X_2B_{26} + X_3B_{36} + X_4B_{46}.$$

Coefficients not significant at the .10 level are omitted from the figure, and arrows corresponding to them are not shown. The analysis is based on 16 countries: those in table 9.4, less Australia and New Zealand for which data were missing.

Figure 7.2. The arrows in this figure are based on analyses of two subsets of data. The arrows leading to electoral outcomes represent the significant standardized regression coefficients from the set of recursive equations:

$$\begin{aligned}
X_{10} = {} & X_1B_{1,10} + X_2B_{2,10} + X_3B_{3,10} + X_4B_{4,10} + X_5B_{5,10} + X_6B_{6,10} \\
& + X_7B_{7,10} + X_8B_{8,10} + X_9B_{9,10}.
\end{aligned}$$

$$\begin{aligned}
X_9 = {} & X_1B_{19} + X_2B_{29} + X_3B_{39} + X_4B_{49} + X_5B_{59} + X_6B_{69} \\
& + X_7B_{79} + X_8B_{89}.
\end{aligned}$$

$$\begin{aligned}
X_8 = {} & X_1B_{18} + X_2B_{28} + X_3B_{38} + X_4B_{48} + X_5B_{58} + X_6B_{68} \\
& + X_7B_{78}.
\end{aligned}$$

$$X_7 = X_1B_{17} + X_2B_{27} + X_3B_{37} + X_4B_{47} + X_5B_{57} + X_6B_{67}.$$

The regressions were computed on 60 elections, with each country weighted equally (57 weighted elections in 19 parliamentary systems). The sources are those used in compiling table A.1. The computation formulas for fractionalization and volatility are those given in tables A.1 and 5.5. Extremist parties are those shown in table A.1. Extremist-party strength, single-party majorities, fractionalization, and volatility represent the situation at the beginning of the new legislative session. Coefficients not significant at the .10 level are omitted from the figure, and arrows corresponding to them are not shown.

The arrows leading to cabinet outcomes represent the significant standardized regression coefficients from the set of recursive equations:

$$X_{12} = X_7 B_{7,12} + X_8 B_{8,12} + X_9 B_{9,12} + X_{10} B_{10,12} + X_{11} B_{11,12}.$$

$$X_{11} = X_7 B_{7,11} + X_8 B_{8,11} + X_9 B_{9,11} + X_{10} B_{10,11}.$$

These regressions were computed on 84 cabinets, with each country weighted equally (57 weighted cabinets in 19 parliamentary systems). Minimum winning coalition governments include both single-party majorities and multiparty connected minimum winning coalitions, in about a 2-to-1 ration, as in table 7.2. Cabinet durability in months calculated as in table 2.2; cabinets lasting longer than 36 months scored as 36 months. Coefficients not significant at the .10 level are omitted from the figure, and arrows corresponding to them are not shown.

Notes

1. Introduction: Democracy, Parties, and Performance

1. To cite only a few examples: Seymour Martin Lipset discussed the problem of stable democracy in *Political Man* (Garden City: Doubleday, 1960), chs. 2–3. William H. Riker introduced the systematic study of strategic calculations and suggested their impact on political stability in *The Theory of Political Coalitions* (New Haven: Yale University Press, 1962). Gabriel A. Almond and Sidney Verba argued the importance of citizens' values for democratic participation and political stability in *The Civic Culture* (Princeton: Princeton University Press, 1963) and have elsewhere discussed parties, leadership, and elite values. Samuel Huntington has written compellingly of the importance of political institutions, especially party systems, for political order in *Political Order in Changing Societies* (New Haven: Yale University Press, 1968). Arend Lijphart has been a major spokesman for the role of leaders in accommodating potential conflict, most recently in *Democracy in Plural Societies* (New Haven: Yale University Press, 1978). Robert Dahl summarized his own and many other comparative analyses of effects of social and cultural environment, political institutions, and the beliefs and strategies of leaders in *Polyarchy: Participation and Opposition* (New Haven: Yale University Press, 1971).

2. See especially the fine work by Douglas A. Hibbs, Jr., *Mass Political Violence* (New York: John Wiley, 1973), which reviews a large number of previous studies and makes original contributions.

3. My own analysis suggests that even ignoring the question of women's suffrage, there were only about 9 democracies among the 48 nations in 1902, 22 democracies among the 64 independent nations in 1920, 21 democracies among the 65 nations in 1929–30, 29 democracies among the 121 nations in 1960. This analysis draws upon Arthur Banks, *Cross-Polity Time Series Data* (Cambridge: MIT Press, 1971), for estimates of the selection bases and effectiveness of legislatures and upon a variety of sources for estimates of electoral suffrage, especially Stein Rokkan, "Mass Suffrage, Secret Voting and Political Participation," *Archives European de Sociologie* 2 (1961): 132–152, and Thomas T. Mackie and Richard Rose, *The International Almanac of Electoral History* (New York: Free Press, 1974).

4. The tradition of such analysis is an ancient one. A brilliant empirical study written at the point of early democratic expansion in the twentieth century is James Bryce, *Modern Democracies*, 2 vols. (New York: Macmillan, 1921).

5. For another discussion of criteria, see Dahl, *Polyarchy,* ch. 1. For a theoretical discussion distinguishing the concept of representative democracy from its structural mechanisms, see Carl Cohen, *Democracy* (New York: Free Press, 1971), ch. 3.

6. A discussion of alternative twentieth-century versions of democracy, stressing the difference between responding to the wishes of the people and acting in their interests, can be found in Giovanni Sartori, "Democracy," in David Sills, ed., *International Encyclopedia of the Social Sciences,* vol. 4 (New York: Macmillan and Free Press, 1968), pp. 112–121.

7. Dahl, *Polyarchy,* pp. 231–249.

8. Dankwart A. Rustow, *A World of Nations: Problems of Political Modernization* (Washington: Brookings Institution, 1967), pp. 290–291.

9. Banks, *Cross-Polity Time Series.*

10. David Butler, Howard R. Penniman, and Austin Ranney, eds., *Democracy at the Polls: A Comparative Study of National Elections* (Washington: American Enterprise Institute, 1981), pp. 2–5.

11. See Gabriel A. Almond and G. Bingham Powell, Jr., *Comparative Politics: System, Process and Policy* (Boston: Little, Brown, 1978), p. 225, for a summary of regime types and sources of classification. Butler, Penniman and Ranney, *Democracy at the Polls,* p. 4, report a similar distribution in 1979.

12. Some questions could be raised about the voting eligibility of illiterates (excluded in the Philippines and in Chile until 1970), women (excluded in Switzerland until the early 1970s at the national level), and adults not born in a given nation (especially the Indian-born Tamils in Ceylon). Despite concern about these limitations, I think that each of these countries provides a relevant democratic experience in the time period I am discussing, and I have followed the general consensus by including them.

13. Although Israel is included here, trying to analyze political order in Israel raises some very difficult problems in the assessment of the "domestic" and "international" sources of conflict. Particularly after 1967, the two become very difficult to disentangle in Israel, to a degree unique among the democracies of this period. For practical reasons of comparability, Israel is excluded from much of the statistical analysis in subsequent chapters.

14. I shall, however, occasionally draw upon evidence from the Brazilian experience, particularly concerning military intervention in democratic politics. See Chapter 8.

15. On the elitist nature of "parties" in Lebanon, see Michael Hudson, *The Precarious Republic: Political Modernization in Lebanon* (New York: Random House, 1968). Hudson argues that "Lebanon may have parties, but it does not have a party system" (p. 249). Similarly, see Michael W. Sulieman, *Political Parties in Lebanon* (Ithaca: Cornell University Press, 1967); John P. Entelis, *Pluralism and Party Transformation in Lebanon: Al'Kataib, 1936–1974* (Leiden: S. J. Brill, 1974); and Abdo I. Baaklini, *Legislative and Political Development: Lebanon, 1942–1972* (Durham: Duke University Press, 1976).

16. Hibbs, *Mass Political Violence,* pp. 186–187.

17. For example, Gabriel A. Almond, "Introduction," in Gabriel A. Almond and James Coleman, eds., *The Politics of the Developing Areas*(Prince-

ton: Princeton University Press, 1960); and Huntington, *Political Order*. Also see the references in Chapter 5 below.

18. Harry Eckstein, *The Evaluation of Political Performance: Problems and Dimensions* (Beverly Hills: Sage Publications, 1971); Ted Robert Gurr and Muriel McClelland, *Political Performance: A Twelve Nation Study* (Beverly Hills: Sage Publications, 1971).

19. On other forms of participation and their role in shaping concurrence between the attitudes of citizens and those of elites, see Sidney Verba and Norman H. Nie, *Participation in America* (New York: Harper and Row, 1972), esp. pp. 299–333. Also see Heinz Eulau and Kenneth Prewitt, *Labyrinths of Democracy* (New York: Bobbs-Merrill, 1973), pp. 218–304.

20. Almond and Powell, *Comparative Politics: System, Process and Policy*, ch. 2, present a discussion of secularization and legitimacy.

21. The importance of violence and of stability of top governmental roles is clearly spelled out in the operationalization discussion in Gurr and McClelland, *Political Performance*. The correlation between "Government Continuation-Changes" and "Authority Maintenance" is .91 for their 21 polities, while the latter correlates at .64 or better with all other dimensions (p. 70). Indeed, across their set of systems, which includes both democracies and nondemocracies, the correlations across performance dimensions seem higher than within the contemporary democratic universe examined here. See Chapter 2 below.

22. Dahl, *Polyarchy*, p. 123.

23. Almond and Powell, *Comparative Politics: System, Process and Policy*, pp. 46–51, 104–107.

24. For argument that security and order are valued by all, or at least most, contemporary societies, see J. Roland Pennock, "Political Development, Political Systems and Political Goods," *World Politics* 18 (April 1966): 415–434. Pennock cites welfare, security, liberty, and justice as his principal "political goods." At the individual level, see A. H. Maslow, *Motivation and Personality* (Oxford: Oxford University Press, 1938), pp. 80–98, for a discussion of primary and secondary universal human needs.

2. Political Performance: The Initial Comparison

1. The time frame varies slightly with different dimensions examined. In the case of riots and deaths, data from Charles L. Talor and Michael C. Hudson, *World Handbook of Political and Social Indicators* (New Haven: Yale University Press, 1972), were used for 1958–1967. I collected additional data for 1967–1976, using primarily *Keesing's Archives* and *Facts on File*, and deliberately overlapped the year 1967 to check source comparability. For an update on the violence data, see table 10.1 and the Appendix.

2. For example, see Carl Cohen, *Democracy* (New York: Free Press, 1971), chs. 1–2.

3. Cohen, *Democracy*, pp. 224–231. Also see J. Roland Pennock, *Democratic Political Theory* (Princeton: Princeton University Press, 1979), p. 442.

4. See, for example, the arguments summarized in Thomas R. Dye and L. Harmon Zeigler, *The Irony of Democracy,* 5th ed. (Belmont, Calif.: Wadsworth Press, 1978), especially chs. 1 and 5.

5. In the strong presidential systems, such as the United States and Chile, where legislative elections were held apart from presidential ones, turnout was almost always higher in the latter. In the mixed French system, legislative elections are shown, because turnout levels are more consistent from election to election, but median levels are similar.

6. The calculation of turnout is more complex than one might expect because of varying practices in reporting registration figures and turnout percentages in different countries. The most comparable figures are for actual voters as a percentage of the voting-age population. For these data the raw turnout figures are largely from Thomas Mackie and Richard Rose, *The International Almanac of Electoral History* (New York: Free Press, 1974), the *European Journal of Political Research, Keesing's Archives,* and various individual country studies, especially the American Enterprise Institute's excellent "At the Polls" series. Ages of eligibility are primarily derived from Mackie and Rose; Valentine Herman, ed., *Parliaments of the World* (New York: De Gruyter, 1976); and United Nations Secretary General's Report, *Constitution, Electoral Law, and Other Legal Instruments Relating to the Political Rights of Women.* The population of voting age is calculated from United Nations *Demographic Yearbook 1970* and later editions. In the Philippines and pre-1970 Chile, illiterates are excluded, as are the Indian Tamils in Ceylon. In general, see G. Bingham Powell, Jr., "Voting Turnout in Thirty Democracies," in Richard Rose, ed., *Comparative Electoral Participation* (Beverly Hills: Sage Publications, 1980), pp. 5–34.

7. In the elections shown in table 2.1, fewer than one-third of the shifts in turnout from one election to the next were as large as 5 percent. In only about one-sixth of the cases was the shift 6 percent or more. Many of the latter cases involved changes in registration laws or penalties for not voting. The median shift from election to election was about 2.5 percent of the eligible electorate; the median standard deviation ws 2.25 percent across the 29 countries. Less economically developed countries tended to show more variation from election to election.

8. Sidney Verba, Norman H. Nie, and Jae-on Kim, *The Modes of Democratic Participation* (Beverly Hills: Sage Publications, 1971); and Sidney Verba, Norman H. Nie, and Jae-on Kim, *Participation and Political Equality* (Cambridge: Cambridge University Press, 1978).

9. Richard Rose, *Citizen Participation in the Electoral Process* (Glasgow: University of Strathclyde Center for the Study of Public Policy, 1978).

10. See Gabriel A. Almond and Sidney Verbá, *The Civic Culture* (Princeton: Princeton University Press, 1963).

11. That is, the column reports whether, at the time of a given election, any election outcome in the previous ten years had led to a transition of government power. In determining whether an election "led to" such a transition, I looked at the make-up of the government before and after each election. In most cases where the new government had different party composition than the old—the

definition here of "power transition"—the connection was obvious. In a few cases, as discussed in the text, the linkages were quite complex, and parties lost strength but entered the government, or vice versa. Such complex or dubious connections were found in Italy, Finland, the Netherlands, Belgium after 1958, and Sweden before the 1970s.

12. See Jurg Steiner, *Amicable Agreement versus Majority Rule: Conflict Resolution in Switzerland* (Chapel Hill: University of North Carolina Press, 1974).

13. For a fine study of the complexities of Italian governmental coalition formation and policy, see Guiseppi DiPalma, *Surviving without Governing: The Italian Parties in Parliament* (Berkeley: University of California Press, 1976).

14. See Douglas A. Hibbs, Jr., *Mass Political Violence* (New York: John Wiley, 1973), pp. 9–16.

15. These sketches of violence in various countries are drawn primarily from *Keesing's Archives,* supplemented by various country-specific sources. See Chapter 8 for additional discussion and references.

16. See Cohen, *Democracy,* and Pennock, *Democratic Political Theory.*

17. See Dye and Ziegler, *Irony of American Democracy.*

18. See Almond and Verba, *Civic Culture.*

19. Karl Dietrich Bracher, "The Problem of Parliamentary Democracy in Europe," *Daedalus* (Winter 64), pp. 178–198, rpt. in Andrew J. Milnor, ed., *Comparative Political Parties: Selected Readings* (New York: Thomas Y. Crowell, 1969), p. 356. Also see Robert A. Dahl, *Polyarchy: Participation and Opposition* (New Haven: Yale University Press, 1971), pp. 122–123.

20. See the references cited in Chapter 4, note 13; Chapter 5, note 13; and Chapter 10, note 10. A rejection of party "tyranny" has also been a theme in the debates about proportional representation in Britain. See Samuel J. Finer, *The Changing British Party System 1945–1979* (Washington: American Enterprise Institute, 1980), ch. 6.

21. A serious problem in these analyses is created by extreme "outlier" cases, such as the large number of deaths in the Philippines in the first decade, or riots in the United States. To stabilize the correlation and regression analysis, the highest values for deaths and riots were truncated back to the ninetieth percentile values (looking at both decades), which were about 40 deaths per year and 9 riots per year. These were the maximum values used in the econometric analyses here and in subsequent chapters. This procedure is described in Sidney Verba and Norman H. Nie, *Participation in America* (New York: Harper and Row, 1972), p 392. Per capita figures, where analyzed, are also truncated. As a check against bias, an alternative means of treating outliers, using a log transformation of the dependent variable, was used to recheck all final analyses of riots and deaths; see Hibbs, *Mass Political Violence,* p. 10. Very similar results appear in almost all cases—exceptions will be noted where appropriate—although the results are slightly less stable for the log transformation approach.

22. As I am calculating these coefficients on the universe of democracies available in this time period, the usual meaning of statistical significance may not apply. If the objective were purely to describe the democracies, all the

coefficients would be meaningful and no statistical significance discrimination would be necessary. Insofar as the objective is to test theories applying to all democracies of past, present, and future, it is unclear what sort of a sample this set of democracies may be. But, following the usual custom, I shall calculate significance at the .05 and .10 levels as if these cases were a random sample of democracies. The reader can then, at least, more easily distinguish those relationships which are particularly powerful and noteworthy.

3. The Social and Economic Environment

1. For example, Aristotle's discussion of the types of constitutions appropriate for and appearing in societies dominated by the "poor" farmers, the middle class, and so forth. *The Politics of Aristotle,* trans. Ernest Barker (New York: Oxford University Press, 1958), pp. 184–186.

2. See the discussion of alternative approaches in Douglas A. Hibbs, Jr., *Mass Political Violence* (New York: John Wiley, 1973), ch. 1.

3. However, a good recent discussion of some of the reasons why small nations should be more easily governable is Arend Lijphart, *Democracy in Plural Societies* (New Haven: Yale University Press, 1978), pp. 65–70.

4. At the cross-system level, see the arguments and references in Robert A. Dahl and Edward Tufte, *Size and Democracy* (Stanford: Stanford University Press, 1973), ch. 4. Also see Sidney Verba and Norman H. Nie, *Participation in America* (New York: Harper and Row, 1972), ch. 13; Sidney Verba, Norman H. Nie, and Jae-on Kim, *Participation and Political Equality: A Seven-Nation Study* (New York: Cambridge University Press, 1978), pp. 269–285; and Nancy E. McGlen, "Strategy Choices for Political Participation: The Case of Austria," (Ph.D. diss., University of Rochester, 1974).

5. Verba, Nie, and Kim, *Participation and Political Equality,* pp. 119–123.

6. Various studies of U.S. politics have emphasized the difficulties of building strong and unified party organizations in such a large country. And a comparative study of party centralization found geographically large countries were more likely to have decentralized parties. See Robert Harmel, "The Relative Impact of Country-Level and City-Level Factors on Party Decentralization" (Paper delivered at the 1978 Annual Meeting of the Southwestern Political Science Association, Houston, Texas).

7. Val Lorwin, "Segmented Pluralism: Ideological Cleavages and Political Cohesion in the Smaller European Democracies," *Comparative Politics* (Jan. 1971); and see the discussion and sources cited in Lijphart, *Democracy in Plural Societies,* pp. 65–70.

8. Lijphart, *Democracy in Plural Societies,* and see Hibbs, *Mass Political Violence,* p. 25.

9. Hibbs, *Mass Political Violence,* pp. 171, 232–238.

10. See, for example, the excellent collection of essays in Jason L. Finkle and Richard W. Gable, eds., *Political Development and Social Change,* 2nd ed., (New York: John Wiley, 1976), as well as Gabriel A. Almond and G. Bingham Powell, Jr., *Comparative Politics: A Developmental Approach* (Boston: Little,

Brown, 1966); Samuel P. Huntington, *Political Order in Changing Societies* (New Haven: Yale University Press, 1968); and Barrington Moore, Jr., *Social Origins of Dictatorship and Democracy* (Boston: Beacon Press, 1966).

11. See the analysis in Bruce Russett et al., *World Handbook of Political and Social Indicators* (New Haven: Yale University Press, 1964).

12. The best known analysis of the ratio of economic development to social mobilization is that in Huntington, *Political Order.* Huntington usefully distinguishes three approaches to interpreting the political impact of the transition from agrarian to industrial society: those contrasting the levels, those emphasizing different starting points, and those analyzing various disruptive aspects of the process of change. See Samuel P. Huntington, "Post-Industrial Politics: How Benign Will It Be?" *Comparative Politics* 6 (Jan. 1974): 163–192. Empirically, however, it is very difficult to distinguish among those approaches with the present data and set of countries. My analyses from necessity emphasize the contrast in levels. Rates of change, it may be noted, have little consistent impact. This does not mean that growth rates are unimportant, but their impacts are not consistent among the countries and in the range here studied.

13. A factor analysis of (log)GNP/capita, percentage of the work force employed in agriculture, percentage of adults literate, and dependence of economy on exports (see sources in table 3.2) for 28 democracies in 1965 yielded only a single strong factor, accounting for 73 percent at the variance. (log)GNP/capita was the most strongly related to the principal factor and correlated $-.86$, $+.86$, and $-.51$ with the other three variables respectively. It is thus extremely difficult to determine any independent effects of these variables, apart from the general level of modernization. Where such effects occurred, they will be discussed, but the continuing use of (log)GNP/capita should be understood as representing the general level-of-modernity dimension.

14. See Richard Musgrave, *Fiscal Systems* (New Haven: Yale University Press, 1969) for a historical review of the evidence, and see the discussion in Gabriel A. Almond and G. Bingham Powell, Jr., *Comparative Politics: System, Process and Policy* (Boston: Little, Brown, 1978), pp. 290–292.

15. On social mobilization see Karl W. Deutsch, "Social Mobilization and Political Development," *American Political Science Review* 55 (Sept. 1961): 493–514; and Daniel Lerner, *The Passing of Traditional Society* (New York: Free Press of Glencoe, 1958).

16. For evidence on the higher levels of political information and involvement created by education, media exposure, and modern working conditions see Alex Inkeles and David M. Smith, *Becoming Modern: Individual Change in Six Developing Countries* (Cambridge: Harvard University Press, 1974). For data on such effects within more modernized countries, see Gabriel A. Almond and Sidney Verba, *The Civic Culture* (Princeton: Princeton University Press, 1963). On the linkages between awareness and involvement and participation, see Norman H. Nie, G. Bingham Powell, Jr., and Kenneth Prewitt, "Social Structure and Political Participation: Developmental Relationships," *American Political Science Review* 63 (June and Sept. 1969), pp. 371–378, 808–832; and Verba, Nie, and Kim, *Participation and Political Equality.*

On group and party transformation see John Duncan Powell, "Peasant Society and Clientelist Politics," *APSR* 64 (June 1970): 411–425; Carl H. Lande, "Networks and Groups in Southeast Asia," *APSR* 67 (March 1973): 103–127; and James Scott, "The Erosion of Patron-Client Bonds and Social Change in Rural Southeast Asia," *Journal of Asian Studies* 32 (Nov. 1972): 5–38.

17. Russett et al., *World Handbook*.

18. Enrique Baloyra, "Public Attitudes toward the Democratic Regime," in John D. Marz and David J. Myers, *Venezuela: The Democratic Experience* (New York: Praeger, 1977), p. 51.

19. See Almond and Powell, *Comparative Politics: System, Process and Policy,* p. 290, and the references cited there. On the development of governmental bureaucracy and capacities in Europe, see the essays in Charles Tilly, ed., *The Formation of National States in Western Europe* (Princeton: Princeton University Press, 1978).

20. See for example Huntington, *Political Order.*

21. In general this point is consistent with Hibbs's failure to find strong crossnational effects of ratios of mobilization and capacity; *Mass Political Violence,* ch. 4. Of course, the data do not mean that the curvilinear effects are never present, only that across this set of nations the most severe forms of violence are on average found in the poorest and least developed countries. As we shall see in Chapter 5, support for extremist parties is more prevalent in the somewhat more developed countries, although deadly violence is not.

22. See Seymour Martin Lipset and Stein Rokkan, *Party Systems and Voting Alignments* (New York: Free Press, 1967), "Introduction."

23. See Alvin Rabushka and Kenneth Shepsle, *Politics in Plural Societies* (Columbus, Ohio: Merrill, 1972).

24. See Robert A. Dahl, *Polyarchy: Participation and Opposition* (New Haven: Yale University Press, 1971), ch. 7; Lijphart, *Democracy in Plural Societies;* Hibbs, *Mass Political Violence,* ch. 5.

25. Dahl, *Polyarchy,* p. 108.

26. See Donald L. Horowitz, "Direct, Displaced and Cumulative Ethnic Aggression," *Comparative Politics* 6 (Oct. 1973): 1–16.

27. Despite their historic importance as bases of conflict, I have not included Catholic-Protestant divisions in this index of subcultural divisions. Except in Northern Ireland such divisions are not a major base of violent conflict, nor statistically associated with it, and their inclusion here obscures the impact of other subcultural divisions. The impact of Catholic-Protestant and secular-Catholic divisions on parties and policy is discussed in Chapters 5, 7, and 9 below. The impact of these divisions on the contemporary performance levels in general is insignificant in comparison to the other environmental factors, although they greatly affect the process in some countries.

28. Hibbs, *Mass Political Violence,* ch. 5, found ethnicity linked to violence through the effects of ethnic separatism, across the full set of independent nations, and the data for the democracies here seem consistent with his analysis.

29. Hibbs found little direct relationship between ethnic division and his "protest" dimension, which included rioting (ibid.).

30. If we divide the countries in table 3.4 at the median level of ethnicity,

for example, the correlation between riots and deaths is .45 in the first decade in more homogeneous countries, .54 in more ethnically divided ones. In the second decade the correlations are .51 and .65. Even controlling for population size, we find this relationship to hold up.

31. On peasant rebellions see Moore, *Social Origins;* and Anthony Oberschall, *Social Conflict and Social Movements* (Englewood Cliffs: Prentice-Hall, 1973).

32. Data are from Hollis Chenery et al., *Redistribution with Growth* (New York: Oxford University Press, 1974), pp. 8–9; and Felix Paukert, "Income Distribution at Different Levels of Development," *International Labour Review* 108 (Aug.–Sept. 1973): 97–128. In cases of disagreement, the higher estimate of inequality was used.

33. However, studies of the tax system in several countries suggest that its impact on income distribution is not significantly great in most cases. It is transfer payments—in the form of social security, unemployment benefits, and the like—that show most governmental impact on income distribution. See Malcolm Sawyer, "Income Distribution in OECD Countries," *OECD Economic Outlook, Occasional Papers,* July 1976.

34. For a vivid account of class divisions in Weimar Germany, see William S. Allen, *The Nazi Seizure of Power* (Chicago: Quadrangle, 1965).

35. In fact, the very poorest nations have often only moderate inequality; with much of the income produced and consumed on the peasant farm, there is some barrier to high accumulation and concentration. We see here the medium position of India and Ceylon in income equality. As modernization gets well under way, the divergence of modern and traditional sectors, and the accumulation of capital for development, very typically mean sharply increasing income inequality and immense discrepancies between the rich and poor within a nation. Then, at the highest levels of modernization, the diffusion of education and occupational specialization and the appearance of a large middle class usually means a moderation of inequality. Government policies can, of course, affect this process. See Chenery, *Redistribution,* ch. 1. As we shall see in Chapter 9, it is no coincidence that continuing domination by conservative coalitions in France and Italy is associated with policies preserving more inequality than in most other democracies.

36. As we shall not return to them until Chapter 5, it should be pointed out here that adding variables for two other measures of possible subcultural divisions, Protestant-Catholic divisions and agricultural minorities, does not substantially change the results from multivariate regression analysis of riots and deaths by political violence. Nor does it change the conclusions from the analysis of all the performance measures using population size, economic development level, ethnicity, and the constitutional variables shown in table 4.4. Except for a moderately strong relationship between the presence of agricultural minorities and less government stability, neither variable is significant as predicted when added to the regressions shown in table 4.4. These variables will, then, be ignored until Chapter 5, where their effects through the party system are discussed.

37. For several reasons it is preferable to enter the dependent variables on

an absolute rather than a per capita basis. As Hibbs points out, the use of per capita measures like GNP per capita as independent variables could create artificial correlations with per capita dependent variables (*Mass Political Violence*, n. 25). Moreover, as seen in the table, population size is much more powerfully related to riots than to deaths; per capita measures could lead us to overlook or distort these important differences.

38. A log transformation approach is the one used by Hibbs (*Mass Political Violence*, p. 10). The transformation is made by simply computing log of (the variable +1). The truncated variables seem slightly more robust in that emergent relationships are less easily altered by addition or deletion of a few cases. But throughout the analysis I have compared the truncation and log transformation approaches in an attempt to obtain the most reliable results. Some relationships do tend to be affected by a few extreme outliers if the riot and death variables are not transformed by one of these procedures.

4. The Constitutional Setting

1. For similar usage, see Gabriel A. Almond and G. Bingham Powell, Jr., *Comparative Politics: System, Process and Policy* (Boston: Little, Brown, 1978), chs. 9 –10.

2. More complete discussions of executive-legislative relations can be found in Gerhard Loewenberg and Samuel Patterson, *Comparing Legislatures* (Boston: Little, Brown, 1979); Michael Mezey, *Comparative Legislatures* (Durham: Duke University Press, 1980); and in the notes to Chapter 7 below. Details of constitutional arrangements in most parliamentary systems are provided in Inter-Parliamentary Union, *Parliaments of the World*, prepared by Valentine Herman with Françoise Mendel (London: Macmillan, 1976). (Subsequently cited as Herman, *Parliaments*.) Also see Arthur Banks, *Political Handbook of the World, 1976* (New York: McGraw-Hill, 1976).

3. For the purposes of this study I am going to ignore the potentially important realm of relations between the judicial branch and other decision-making structures. For a brief discussion, see Almond and Powell, *Comparative Politics: System, Process and Policy,* and the sources cited there.

4. Following the usual custom in parliamentary systems, I use the term "the government" to refer to the prime minister and the cabinet—or the political parties sharing cabinet positions—not to the democratic regime itself.

5. The 1970s presented some notable changes in the circumstances under which a British government was expected to resign. Governments continued in several instances despite legislative defeats that might, earlier, have precipitated resignation. See Philip Norton, *Dissension in the House of Commons, 1945–1974* (London: Macmillan, 1975) and *Dissension in the House of Commons* (Oxford: Clarendon Press, 1980). In 1979, however, the government was forced to resign after losing a vote of confidence.

6. See Ergun Ozbudun, *Party Cohesion in Western Democracies* (Beverly Hills: Sage Publications, 1970), and the sources cited there.

7. Maurice Duverger, *Political Parties,* trans. Barbara North and Robert

North (New York: John Wiley, 1954). Douglas Rae, *The Political Consequences of Electoral Laws* (New Haven: Yale University Press, 1967). An interesting discussion of the historical origins of the idea before its statement by Duverger is William H. Riker, "The Two-Party System and Duverger's Law: An Essay in the History of Political Science" (Paper presented at the American Association for the Advancement of Science, Washington, D.C., January 1982).

8. See Giovanni Sartori, *Parties and Party Systems* (New York: Cambridge University Press, 1976), ch. 4; and Alan Zuckerman, *The Politics of Faction: Christian Democracy in Italy* (New York: Yale University Press, 1979).

9. Rae, *Electoral Laws*. The pre-1960 Turkish system, with multimember districts, but with the winning party in each district getting all of the seats, illustrates the need for PR as well as multimember districts. The pre-1960 Turkish rules produced the same tendency toward overrepresentation of the majority party and single-party legislative majorities as do single-member districts. See Frederick W. Frey, *The Turkish Political Elite* (Cambridge: M.I.T. Press, 1965), pp. 423–437.

10. For discussion of variations, see Rae, *Electoral Laws*, and Herman, *Parliaments*. F. A. Hermans remarks that "prominent supporters of proportional representation insist that the number of representatives per district should be at least five." "The Dynamics of Proportional Representation," in Andrew J. Milnor, ed., *Comparative Political Parties* (New York: Thomas Y. Crowell, 1969), p. 220.

11. Rae, *Electoral Laws*.

12. A curious combination of rules also appears in Uruguay. Under the Uruguayan "double simultaneous vote" system voters could support groupings and subgroupings of candidates, yet the totals for all the groupings associated with a party were accumulated toward that party's representation. See Russell H. Fitzgibbon, *Uruguay: Portrait of a Democracy* (New Brunswick: Rutgers University Press, 1954), pp. 153–155.

13. Eric A. Nordlinger, *Conflict and Conflict Management in Divided Societies* (Cambridge: Harvard Center for International Studies, 1972), p. 117. Although often not stated directly in terms of arguments about constitutions, the debate about the advantages and disadvantages of party majorities also applies here (see Chapter 5). And see the discussion of the problem of simple-majority decision rules in J. Roland Pennock, *Democratic Political Theory* (Princeton: Princeton University Press, 1979), pp. 363–437.

14. Information about constitutional arrangements upon which these classifications are based is drawn from a large number of individual country studies and from Banks, *Political Handbook;* Herman, *Parliaments;* and Thomas Mackie and Richard Rose, *The International Almanac of Electoral History* (New York: Free Press, 1974).

15. Hermans, "Dynamics of PR," p. 220.

16. Entering both riots per capita and deaths per capita into the factor analysis creates some multicollinearity as each original measure has been divided by the same quantity. See Douglas A. Hibbs, Jr., *Mass Political Violence* (New York: John Wiley, 1973), p. 25, n.11.

17. The principal component factors in the analysis of all 27 countries in

Chapter 2 yielded eigenvalues of 1.86, 1.30, 1.00, .46, and .37. In the analysis of the 19 parliamentary systems, the comparable eigenvalues are 2.18, 1.37, .82, .41, and .22. Not only the usual cut-off point of 1.0, but also the distance between values suggests the difference between the three- and two-factor solutions.

18. In some cases these designs were worked out at a single constitutional convention, as in the United States, or by a single piece of parliamentary legislation such as the British North American Act, for Canada, or by a designer and his advisers, as in DeGaulle's constitution for the Fifth Republic France. In other cases, as in Britain, the constitution reflects a long history of experience and reworking.

19. On the concept of political culture, see Almond and Powell, *Comparative Politics: System, Process and Policy,* ch. 2 and the references cited there.

20. For example, see Arend Lijphart's account of the Dutch adoption of proportional representation as part of the 1917 settlement in *The Politics of Accommodation* (Berkeley: University of California Press, 1967), and the essays in Robert A. Dahl, ed., *Political Oppositions in Western Democracies* (New Haven: Yale University Press, 1966).

21. See Rae, *Electoral Laws,* on the cultural differences in perception of appropriate representation between British and American majoritarianism and continental European proportionality.

22. Val Lorwin, "Segmented Pluralism: Ideological Cleavage and Political Cleavage in the Smaller European Democracies," *Comparative Politics* 3 (Jan. 1971); Gerhard Lehmbruch, "A Non-Competitive Pattern of Conflict Management," in Kenneth D. MacRae, ed., *Consociational Democracy* (Toronto: McClelland and Stewart, 1974), pp. 90–97; and Arend Lijphart, *Democracy in Plural Societies* (New Haven: Yale University Press, 1978), pp. 65–70.

5. Party Systems and Election Outcomes

1. For example, Gabriel A. Almond, "Introduction: A Functional Approach to Comparative Politics," in Gabriel A. Almond and James S. Coleman, eds., *The Politics of the Developing Areas* (Princeton: Princeton University Press, 1960); Maurice Duverger, *Political Parties* (New York: John Wiley, 1954); Samuel P. Huntington, *Political Order in Changing Societies* (New Haven: Yale University Press, 1968); Avery Leiserson, *Parties and Politics* (New York: Knopf, 1958); Seymour Martin Lipset and Stein Rokkan, *Party Systems and Voter Alignments* (New York: Free Press, 1967); Sigmund Neumann, *Modern Political Parties* (Chicago: University of Chicago Press, 1956); Giovanni Sartori, *Parties and Party Systems* (New York: Cambridge University Press, 1976).

2. This has been the traditional "pluralist" American view of political parties. An especially good discussion is Leon D. Epstein, *Political Parties in Western Democracies* (New York: Praeger, 1967), pp. 15–16, 355ff.

3. A more complete discussion of different lines of thought about strong party systems is presented in G. Bingham Powell, Jr., "Party Systems and Political System Performance in Contemporary Democracies," *American Po-*

litical Science Review 75 (Dec. 1981): pp. 861–879. In that paper I distinguish aggregative, responsible, and representational images of strong parties, and typologize contemporary party systems in terms of those visions. The analysis in the present and subsequent chapters reaches similar substantive conclusions, using continuous variables rather than the system types.

4. David E. Butler and Donald E. Stokes, *Political Change in Britain* (New York: St. Martin's Press, 1969).

5. See especially Duverger, *Political Parties*.

6. See especially Lipset and Rokkan, *Party Systems*, and Sartori, *Parties and Party Systems*.

7. On party images and their reinforcement, see Philip Converse, "Of Time and Partisan Stability," *Comparative Political Studies* 2 (1969): 139–171; Butler and Stokes, *Change in Britain;* and the essays in Ian Budge, Ivor Crewe, and Dennis Farlie, eds., *Party Identification and Beyond* (New York: John Wiley, 1976).

8. Lipset and Rokkan, *Party Systems*, "Introduction," esp. pp. 50ff.

9. On "cross-cutting cleavages," see David Truman, *The Governmental Process* (New York: Knopf, 1951); Seymour Martin Lipset, *Political Man: The Social Bases of Politics* (Garden City: Doubleday, 1960); G. Bingham Powell, Jr., "Political Cleavage Structure, Cross-Pressure Processes, and Partisanship," *American Journal of Political Science* 20 (Feb. 1976): 1–23.

10. At the formal theoretical level, see Harold Hoteling, "Stability in Competition," *Economic Journal* 29 (1929): 41–57; and Anthony Downs, *An Economic Theory of Democracy* (New York: Harper and Row, 1957), ch. 8.

11. An exceptionally clear and forceful statement of this position is Huntington, *Political Order,* ch. 7. For the alternative view, see Epstein, *Political Parties in Western Democracies.*

12. See E. E. Schattschneider, *Party Government* (New York: Holt, Rinehart and Winston, 1940); American Political Science Association Committee on Political Parties, "Toward a More Responsible Two-Party System," *American Political Science Review* 44 (Sept. 1950), supplement; James McGregor Burns, *The Deadlock of Democracy* (Englewood Cliffs: Prentice-Hall, 1963). Also see comments in Duverger, *Political Parties,* and Sartori, *Parties and Party Systems,* and for a more complete exposition, see Powell, "Party Systems and Political Performance." As strong linkages are in fact usually associated with multiparty systems, this type is fairly unusual across the world's democratic party systems.

13. See Hans Daadler, "The Netherlands: Opposition in a Segmented Society," in Robert A. Dahl, ed., *Political Opposition in Western Democracies* (New Haven: Yale University Press, 1966), pp. 188–236; Arend Lijphart, *Democracy in Plural Societies* (New Haven: Yale University Press, 1977); Arend Lijphart, "Majority Rule versus Democracy in Deeply Divided Societies," *Politikon* 4 (Dec. 1977): 113–126; Gerhard Lehmbruch, "A Non-Competitive Pattern of Conflict Management in Liberal Democracies," in Kenneth D. McRae, ed., *Consociational Democracy* (Toronto: McClelland and Stewart); Jurg Steiner, *Amicable Agreement versus Majority Rule: Conflict Management in Switzerland* (Chapel Hill: University of North Carolina Press,

1974). Lijphart explicitly rejects the majoritarian arguments in divided societies; *Democracy in Plural Societies,* pp. 61–65.

14. Huntington, in *Political Order,* is particularly critical of fractionalized party systems without strong linkages to groups in the society, and argues that most multiparty systems in the Third World are of this type. It is important to recognize that among the contemporary democracies almost none of the Third World countries have multiparty systems, a fact that supports Huntington's argument that such systems unstable, but makes it impossible to investigate them here. The increased fractionalization in Turkey in the mid-1970s, in a context of presumably weak linkages between parties and social groups, was associated with intensified conflict. The subsequent findings about multiparty-ism would be even stronger if Venezuela, the nearest approximation to Huntington's "fractionalized" type, were deleted. For a test of the weakness of elite fractionalized systems in Africa, see Robert W. Jackman, "The Predict-ability of Coups d'Etat," *American Political Science Review* 72 (Dec. 1978): 1262–1275.

15. Karl Dietrich Bracher, "The Problems of Parliamentary Democracy in Europe," in Andrew J. Milnor, ed., *Comparative Political Parties* (New York: Thomas Y. Crowell, 1969), pp. 340–364, esp. p. 356. Also see Robert A. Dahl, *Polyarchy: Participation and Opposition* (New Haven: Yale University Press, 1971), p. 122.

16. See the excellent discussion by Sartori, *Parties,* pp. 185ff., on the different lists of "two-party" systems formulated by various theorists.

17. Douglas Rae, *The Political Consequences of Electoral Laws* (New Haven: Yale University Press, 1967), pp. 53ff. For an analysis based on party legislative majorities, see Powell, "Party Systems and Political Performance."

18. The fractionalization scores based on vote are probably slightly less reliable than those for seats, as sources vary in the accuracy of reporting for small parties.

19. Duverger, *Political Parties,* p. 217; in general see his discussion on pp. 206–255. A major argument to the contrary is John G. Grumm, "Theories of Electoral Systems," *Midwest Journal of Political Science* 2 (1958): 357–376. Grumm examines the historical experience of several European countries whose multiparty systems predate the introduction of proportional representation. He raises some important questions that can be answered only by a more complete examination of party dynamics in premodern or partially modernized societies. See note 48 below.

20. The hypothesis that voters do not vote for parties whose chance of winning is low has been the subject of some controversy. For the British case, see Peter H. Lemieux, "The Liberal Party and British Political Change: 1955–1974" (Ph.D. diss., M.I.T., 1977) and Bruce E. Cain, "Strategic Voting in Britain," *American Journal of Political Science* 22 (Aug. 1978): 639–655. For positive evidence from Canada, see Jerome S. Black, "The Multicandidate Calculus of Voting: Application to Canadian Federal Elections," *American Journal of Political Science* 22 (Aug. 1978): 609–639.

21. Pre-electoral coalitions do seem more prevalent in single-member-district or majority-enhancing systems. Such coalitions have been formed in

France, Ceylon, India, Australia, Germany, and Ireland in recent years, for example, and are now being attempted in Britain. (However, Denmark, Norway, and Sweden have also experienced some elections with pre-election coalitions.) Systems in which multiple parties compete in single-member districts, as in Ceylon and France, find the pre-electoral coalitions critical for election outcomes. The French system of two-stage balloting for single-member districts may, as Duverger suggests, encourage both multiple parties and their pre-electoral coalitions. Duverger, *Political Parties,* pp. 239ff.

22. Ibid., p. 205.

23. Stein Rokkan, "Electoral Systems," in his *Citizens, Elections, Parties* (New York: David McKay, 1970), p. 162. However, the number of representatives per district and the specific form of PR are nuances much more likely to follow from party-strategic decisions. I have not, therefore, used such features in characterizing constitutional arrangements in Chapter 4 or in the subsequent analysis. The basic majoritarian-versus-PR distinction is more safely treated as a factor "prior" to the party system than are those more subtle variations.

24. Rae, *Electoral Laws.*

25. Downs, *Economic Theory of Democracy.*

26. My attention to the importance of agricultural minorities was stimulated by Kautsky's work on bases of Communism. See John H. Kautsky, *Political Change in Underdeveloped Countries: Nationalism and Communism* (New York: John Wiley, 1962), and Roger W. Benjamin and John H. Kautsky, "Communism and Economic Development," *American Political Science Review* 62 (March 1968): 110–123.

27. Lipset and Rokkan, *Party Systems,* pp. 51–52.

28. See Richard Rose and Derek Urwin, "Social Cohesion, Political Parties and Strains on Regimes," *Comparative Political Studies* 2 (April 1969): 7–67; Arend Lijphart, *Class and Religious Voting in the European Democracies,* Occasional Paper no. 8, (Glasgow: Survey Research Center, University of Strathclyde, 1971); Richard Rose, ed., *Electoral Behavior: A Comparative Handbook* (New York: Free Press, 1974).

29. See James C. Scott, *The Moral Economy of the Peasant* (New Haven: Yale University Press, 1976).

30. A large literature on clientelism and parties has developed in the last decade. See, for example, John Duncan Powell, "Peasant Society and Clientelist Politics," *American Political Science Review* 64 (June 1970): 411–425; Carl H. Lande, "Networks and Groups in Southeast Asia," *APSR* 67 (March 1973): 81–113; and Scott, *Moral Economy of the Peasant.*

31. The calculation of the measure of party-group alignment was based for the most part on tables of social class, ethnicity, occupation, income, and so forth and their relationship to party support that have been published in a variety of different studies. Indices were calculated from tables in Rose, *Electoral Behavior,* for Australia, Belgium, Canada, Finland, Germany, Norway, Italy, Ireland, Netherlands, and Sweden; from tables in Sten Berglund and Ulf Lindstrom, *The Scandinavian Party System(s)* (Lund: Studentlitteratur, 1978), for Denmark, Finland, Norway, and Sweden; from tables in Ronald Inglehart, *The Silent Revolution: Changing Values and Political Styles among*

Western Publics (Princeton: Princeton University Press, 1977), for Belgium, France, and Germany. Tables from the following were also used: Austria— Lijphart, *Class and Religious Voting;* Powell, "Political Cleavage Structure". Canada—John Meisel, *Cleavages, Parties, and Values in Canada* (Beverly Hills: Sage Publications, 1974). Chile—James W. Prothro and Patricio E. Chapperio, "Public Opinion and the Movement of the Chilean Government to the Left," *Journal of Politics* 36 (Feb. 1974): 2–43. Denmark—Eric Damgaard, "Stability and Change in the Danish Party System over Half a Century," *Scandinavian Political Studies* 9 (1974): 103–125. France—"Religion et politique," *Sondage* 29, no. 2 (1967): 25; "Les Elections des 4 et 11 Mars, 1973," *Sondage* 35, no. 1 (1973): 26; India—D. L. Sketh, "Social Bases of Party Support," in D. L. Sketh, ed., *Citizens and Parties: Aspects of Campaign Politics in India* (New Delhi: Allied Publications, 1975), pp. 135–164. Italy—Giacomo Sani, "The Italian Electorate in the Mid-1970's," in Howard Penniman, ed., *Italy at the Polls: 1976* (Washington: American Enterprise Institute, 1977), pp. 31–122. Jamaica—Carl Stone, *Class, Race, and Political Behavior in Urban Jamaica* (Jamaica: University of the West Indies, 1973). New Zealand—Austin Mitchell, *Politics and People in New Zealand* (Christchurch: Whitecombe and Tombs, 1969). Switzerland—Henry H. Kerr, Jr., *Switzerland: Social Cleavages and Partisan Conflict* (Beverly Hills: Sage Publications, 1974). United Kingdom— Ivor Crewe, Bo Sarlvik, and James Alt, "Partisan Dealignment in Britain," *British Journal of Political Science* 7 (April 1977): 129–190. United States— Gerald Pomper, *Voters' Choice* (New York: Dodd, Mead, 1974). Data for the Philippines were drawn from tables in Harry Averch, John E. Koehler, and Frank H. Denton, *The Matrix of Policy in the Philippines* (Princeton: Princeton University Press, 1971), adjusting the marginals for size of population groups according to demographic data. Data for Japan were generously provided by Norman H. Nie and Sidney Verba; for their study see Sidney Verba, Norman H. Nie, and Jae-on Kim, *Participation and Political Equality: A Seven-Nation Comparison* (New York: Cambridge University Press, 1978). Tables for Venezuela were kindly contributed by Enrique Baloyra and John D. Martz; see their *Political Attitudes in Venezuela: Societal Cleavages and Public Opinion* (Austin: University of Texas Press, 1979). Where equivalent data were available from several sources, or for several years, these were averaged to get the best estimate.

32. Robert R. Alford, *Party and Society: The Anglo-American Democracies* (Chicago: Rand McNally, 1963); Lijphart, *Class and Religious Voting.*

33. See especially Carl H. Lande, *Leaders, Factions, and Parties: The Structure of Philippine Politics* (New Haven: Yale University Southeast Asia Studies, 1965). Also see Jean Grossholtz, *Politics in the Philippines* (Boston: Little, Brown, 1964); Ando Hirofumi, "Voting Turnout in the Philippines," *Philippines Journal of Public Administration* 12 (Oct. 1969): 424–441; and Averch, Koehler, and Denton, *Policy in the Philippines.*

34. Lipset and Rokkan, *Party Systems;* Lijphart, *Class and Religious Voting;* Rose, *Electoral Behavior.*

35. Downs, *Economic Theory of Democracy.*

36. For a discussion of how strong national centralization, plus the role of

activists in less competitive districts, can increase the strength of linkages in a two-party system, see David Robertson, *A Theory of Party Competition* (London: Wiley, 1976). Downs, in *Economic Theory of Democracy,* also points out that the need to mobilize voters prevents parties from becoming identical, even in two-party situations. Various studies have pointed out that a two-stage process of candidate selection, if the first stage consists of activists from opposite sides of the spectrum clustered behind each party, will pull parties away from the median voter. See the review in Dennis C. Mueller, *Public Choice* (New York: Cambridge University Press, 1979).

37. The importance of extremist parties has been emphasized by many scholars and observers. See especially Huntington, *Political Order,* p. 412; Duverger, *Political Parties,* pp. 419–420; Sartori, *Parties and Party Systems,* ch. 6.

38. Obviously these parties represent not only a wide range of issue positions, but a substantial variety of positions in regard to change in the political structure of the society. In a number of cases, such as the Italian Communists and the Japanese Komeito in the 1970s, there is substantial disagreement as to the "true" position of the party, both in intention and as viewed by voters and other parties. These differences can be of critical importance in the politics of individual countries. However, I think that in general most observers would roughly accept the judgments in table 5.4 and the Appendix.

39. See Benjamin and Kautsky, "Communism and Economic Development," and John H. Kautsky, *Communism and the Politics of Development* (New York: John Wiley, 1968).

40. Barrington Moore, Jr., *The Social Origins of Dictatorship and Democracy* (Boston: Beacon Press, 1966).

41. This formulation was taken from Lawrence C. Dodd, *Coalitions in Parliamentary Governments* (Princeton: Princeton University Press, 1976), p. 88. Dodd credits Przeworski and Sprague with the concept.

42. See the references in notes 35 and 36 above, and Duverger, *Political Parties.*)

43. For some empirical evidence of how voters shift support among spacially adjacent parties in multiparty systems, see the chapter on Finland in Rose, *Electoral Behavior.* Also see Berglund and Lindstrom, *Scandinavian Party Systems.*

44. On changes in the traditional Dutch party system, see Arend Lijphart, *The Politics of Accommodation,* rev. ed. (Berkeley: University of California Press, 1974). Also see Inglehart, *Silent Revolution,* and for Britain, Crewe, Sarlvik, and Alt, "Partisan Dealignment in Britain."

45. Although the inflation variable has statistically significant impact on extremist-party growth, close analysis shows that this impact is completely determined by the cases of Chile and Uruguay. As in much of the analysis of short-term economic factors, only very extreme changes seemed to have major effects. Moreover, in both Chile and Uruguay the inflation was only one of multiple economic problems of great intensity. See, for example, Arturo Valenzuela, *The Breakdown of Democratic Regimes: Chile,* vol. 4 of Juan Linz

and Alfred Stepan, eds., *The Breakdown of Democratic Regimes* (Baltimore: Johns Hopkins Press, 1978); and Martin Weinstein, *Uruguay: The Politics of Failure* (Westport: Greenwood Press, 1975).

46. On the rise of the Progress party in Denmark, see Berglund and Lindstrom, *Scandinavian Party Systems;* and Hans Jorgen Nielsen, "The Uncivic Culture: Attitudes toward the Political System in Denmark and Vote for the Progress Party," *Scandinavian Political Studies* 11 (1976): 147–163.

47. Scattered evidence on party-group linkages, for which consistent over-time data were not available, suggests fairly stable levels in most countries, but some decline in Britain (Crewe, Sarlvik, and Alt, "Partisan Dealignment") and Denmark (Damgaard, "Stability and Change"; Berglund and Lindstrom, *Scandinavian Party Systems*). Neither Britain nor Denmark changes very greatly in comparative ranking, however. Turkey becomes consistently more frac-tionalized and less majoritarian in this period. Substantial increases in extremist-party support appear in Belgium and Denmark; substantial temporary increases appear in the Netherlands and Norway.

48. The table does not attempt to untangle the relationships between party system properties. Considerable efforts to do so have convinced me that the rewards are not worth the costs in complexity of presentation. It is true that fractionalization and extremism are associated, and not all of that relationship can be accounted for by the environmental and constitutional variables in the present model. This relationship might be caused by the presence of intense issue minorities (not captured by our heterogeneity measures) enhancing both fractionalization and extremism under facilitative, representational constitu-tions. Or it may be that extremist strategies are encouraged in fractionalized conditions. Or perhaps the presence of extremist candidates facilitates divisions of other parties. The interactive relationships among the party-system proper-ties remain an important problem for study. The point made in the text about the apparent absence of strong centrifugal effects in comparing elections in the 1960s and 1970s remains significant. For the purposes of the text discussion, it is notable that adding respective party variables to equations for other party variables does not cause the significant coefficients shown in the table to disappear. The effects shown in the table are in this respect robust. These coefficients are also very similar if the analysis is replicated using only the 57 elections in more economically developed countries (GNP per capita over $1300 in 1972).

49. See especially Samuel P. Huntington, "Post-Industrial Politics: How Benign Will It Be?" *Comparative Politics* 6 (Jan. 1974): 163–192. Various arguments emphasizing the problems of post-industrial societies are summarized and reviewed in G. Bingham Powell, Jr., "Social Progress and Liberal Democracy," in G. A. Almond, M. Chodorow, and R. H. Pierce, eds., *Progress and Its Discontents* (Berkeley: University of California Press, forthcoming). Also see the essays in Richard Rose, ed., *Challenge to Governance* (Beverly Hills: Sage Publications, 1980).

50. The source for data on percentage employed in agriculture in 1970 is *Food and Agriculture Organization of the United Nations,* vol. 27 (New York: United Nations, 1975), pp. 17–18.

51. The simultaneous regression equations using the majoritarian election law variable as well as all three party-system variables tend to substantial multicollinearity. Hence, the election law analysis is postponed until we examine the causal models involving subsets of the party variables in Chapters 6 and 7. None of the inferences about party effects are changed if we add majority election laws (and all of the other variables in table 4.4) to the equations shown in table 5.7. However, some changes in magnitude do occur.

52. Powell, "Party Systems and Performance."

6. Citizen Involvement: Participation or Turmoil

1. Sidney Verba, Norman H. Nie, and Jae-on Kim, *The Modes of Democratic Participation* (Beverly Hills: Sage Publications, 1971). See the overview and references to various studies of modes of participation in the United States and other countries in Sidney Verba, Norman H. Nie, and Jae-on Kim, *Participation and Political Equality: A Seven-Nation Comparison* (New York: Cambridge University Press, 1978), pp. 310–339.

2. Angus Campbell, Philip E. Converse, Warren E. Miller, and Donald E. Stokes, *The American Voter* (New York: John Wiley, 1960), pp. 105–106.

3. Herbert Tingsten, *Political Behavior: Studies in Election Statistics* (Totow, N.J.: Bedminster Press, 1963; originally issued in 1937).

4. See Giorgio Galli and Alfonso Prandi, *Patterns of Political Participation in Italy* (New Haven: Yale University Press, 1970), pp. 28–32; and Raphael Zariski, *Italy: The Politics of Uneven Development* (Hinsdale, Ill.: Dryden Press, 1972), p. 75.

5. On the new compulsory voting provision, see Marvin Weinstein, *Uruguay: The Politics of Failure* (Westport, Conn.: Greenwood Press, 1975), pp. 125–126.

6. For a detailed comparison of the registration laws in 22 of these democracies, see Inter-Parliamentary Union, *Parliaments of the World,* prepared by Valentine Herman with Françoise Mendel (London: Macmillan, 1976). For a discussion of other facilitating devices see Ivor Crewe, "Electoral Participation," in David Butler, Howard R. Penniman, and Austin Ranney, *Democracy at the Polls* (Washington: American Enterprise Institute, 1981).

7. Ann Spackman, "Electoral Law and Administration in Jamaica," *Social and Economic Studies* 18 (March 1969): 1–53.

8. Kelley, Ayers, and Bowen found that differences in registration laws were a major factor in explaining turnout differences across cities, as did Kim, Petrocik, and Enokson across states. Rosenstone and Wolfinger estimate that voting turnout in the 1972 presidential election might have been about 9 percent higher if all states had registration laws as facilitating as those in a few states. It is certainly likely that automatic registration would have increased turnout even further. Stanley Kelley, Jr., Richard Ayers, and William J. Bowen, "Registration and Voting: Putting First Things First," *American Political Science Review* 61 (March 1967):359–379; Jae-on Kim, John R. Petrocik, and Stephen N. Enokson, "Voter Turnout among the American States," *APSR* 69 (March 1975):107–123; Steven J. Rosenstone and Raymond Wolfinger, "The Effect of Registration Laws on Voter Turnout," *APSR* 72 (March 1978):22–45. Also see

Campbell et al., *American Voter,* pp. 108–109, and Richard Rose, *Citizen Participation in the Electoral Process* (Glasgow: University of Strathclyde, Center for the Study of Public Policy, 1978).

9. See G. Bingham Powell, Jr., "Political Cleavage Structure, Cross-Pressure Processes and Partisanship," *American Journal of Political Science* 20 (Feb. 1976):1–23.

10. Robert R. Alford, *Party and Society: The Anglo-American Democracies* (Chicago: Rand McNally, 1963), p. 302.

11. Seymour Martin Lipset and Stein Rokkan, *Party Systems and Voter Alignments* (New York: Free Press, 1967), pp. 1–64. Also see Richard Rose and Derek Urwin, "Persistence and Change in Western Party Systems Since 1945," *Political Studies* 18 (Sept. 1970):287–391; Alan Zuckerman and Mark Irving Lichback, "Stability and Change in European Electorates," *World Politics* 29 (July 1977): 523–555; and Chapter 5 above.

12. For a discussion of the strength and impact of such organizations in Austria see G. Bingham Powell, Jr., *Social Fragmentation and Political Hostility: An Austrian Study* (Stanford: Stanford University Press, 1970); and Verba, Nie, and Kim, *Participation and Political Equality,* ch. 10. My measure here does not discriminate between the organizational properties of party systems and their perceived connections with social groups in the society, although in principle the distinction is important and worthy of much additional study. Nor do I have any direct measures of the strength or intensity of citizens' sense of partisanship.

13. For an analysis of these data that examines several measures of party-group linkages, see G. Bingham Powell, Jr., "Voting Turnout in Thirty Democracies," in Richard Rose, ed., *Electoral Participation: A Comparative Analysis* (Beverly Hills: Sage Publications, 1980), pp. 5–34. Also see Crewe "Electoral Participation," and a qualitative analysis of participation in 10 nations that reaches similar conclusions: Peter Lange, "Voter Turnout in Advanced Industrial Democracy" (Paper prepared for the Committee for the Study of the American Electorate, Sept. 1979).

14. Ivor Crewe, Bo Sarlvik, and James Alt, "Partisan Dealignment in Britain," *British Journal of Political Science* 7 (April 1977): 129–190.

15. Adam Przeworski, "Institutionalization of Voting Patterns," *American Political Science Review* 69 (March 1975): 49–67.

16. See Jurg Steiner, *Amicable Agreement versus Majority Rule: Conflict Resolution in Switzerland* (Chapel Hill: University of North Carolina Press, 1974), and Henry Kerr, *Switzerland: Social Cleavages and Partisan Conflict* (Beverly Hills: Sage Publications, 1974).

17. For a somewhat more detailed discussion of party competition in theory and in relation to the measures applied in this analysis, see Powell, "Voting Turnout."

18. As discussed in Chapter 4, I do not have the data to investigate directly the effects of cultural values on both constitutional and legal variables.

19. Douglas A. Hibbs, Jr., *Mass Political Violence* (New York: John Wiley, 1973), ch. 1.

20. David Bayley, "Public Protest and the Political Process in India," *Pacific Affairs* 42 (Spring 1969): 5–16. Also see the review of the literature on

crowds in Anthony Oberschall, *Social Conflict and Social Movements* (Englewood Cliffs: Prentice-Hall, 1973), and the essays in James F. Short and Marvin B. Wolfgang, eds., *Collective Violence* (Chicago: University of Chicago Press, 1972).

21. See G. Bingham Powell, Jr., "Party Systems and Political Performance in Contemporary Democracies," *American Political Science Review* 75 (Dec. 1981): 861–869. Also see the references in Chapter 5, note 13.

22. Hibbs, in *Mass Political Violence,* found that Communist party membership was related to citizen turmoil; when such a variable is included here, it is significant in the first decade but not quite in the second, and it does not change the significance of other variables in figure 6.2, although, naturally, it weakens the extremism coefficient. I have chosen to treat it as a more particular case of the latter, although Communist parties are likely to be associated with all the problems here associated with extremist parties.

23. See Maurice Duverger, *Political Parties* (New York: John Wiley, 1954), p. 420; and Giovanni Sartori, *Parties and Party Systems* (New York: Cambridge University Press, 1976), pp. 292–293.

24. For details of classification and a typology of countries, see Powell, "Party Systems and Political Performance."

25. The full list of extremist parties is given in the Appendix. Of these, I classify the following as "protest" parties in the regression analysis described in the text: Denmark—Progress, Single Tax; Finland—Rural; Japan—Komeito; Netherlands—PSP, D '66; New Zealand—Values; Norway—Lange's party; Switzerland—Republican Movement and National Action.

26. Charles Taylor and David A. Jodice, *World Handbook of Political and Social Indicators,* III (New Haven: Yale University Press, 1982). The new *Handbook* also makes it possible to check my riots and death analyses; see table 10.1 and the Appendix.

27. See Susan Welch, "Dimensions of Political Participation in a Canadian Sample," *Canadian Journal of Political Science* 8 (Dec. 1975):553–557, for characteristics related to protest activity in Canada. For data concerning protest propensities, but not actual behavior, in five countries, see Samual H. Barnes, Max Kaase, et al., *Political Action: Mass Participation in Five Western Democracies* (Beverly Hills: Sage Publications, 1979).

28. Peter Eisinger, "Racial Differences in Protest Participation," *American Political Science Review* 68 (June 1974):592–606.

29. I have not dealt with labor unrest, but an interesting analysis of the relationship between Socialist parties, governmental control, and labor unrest that is quite consistent with this analysis is Douglas A. Hibbs, Jr., "Industrial Conflict in Advanced Industrial Societies," *American Political Science Review* 70 (Dec. 1976):1033–1058; also see Douglas A. Hibbs, Jr., "On the Political Economy of Long-Run Trends in Strike Activity," *British Journal of Political Science* 8 (1978): 153–175.

7. Government Performance: Executive Stability

1. The major theoretical stimulus has been the work of William H. Riker, *The Theory of Political Coalitions* (New Haven: Yale University Press, 1962). A

summary and an analysis of efforts to apply his theory to cabinet formation are presented in Abram DeSwaan, *Coalition Theories and Cabinet Formation* (Amsterdam: Elsevier, 1973). A somewhat different theoretical approach is Robert Axelrod, *Conflict of Interest* (Chicago: Markham, 1970). For my analysis of the durability of cabinets, influential descriptive studies are Jean Blondel, "Party Systems and Patterns of Government in Western Democracies," *Canadian Journal of Political Science* 1 (June 1968): 180–203; and especially Michael Taylor and Valentine Herman, "Party Systems and Government Stability," *American Political Science Review* 65 (March 1971): 28–37. A splendid theoretically based study of cabinet durability drawing on Riker's work is Lawrence C. Dodd, *Coalitions in Parliamentary Governments* (Princeton: Princeton University Press, 1976). Also see Paul Warwick, "The Durability of Coalition Governments in Parliamentary Democracies," *Comparative Political Studies* 11 (Jan. 1979): 465–498.

2. See G. Bingham Powell, Jr., "Party Systems and Political Performance in Contemporary Democracies," *American Political Science Review* 75 (Dec. 1981): 861–869.

3. Of course, specific parliamentary constitutions vary in exact rules and procedure. West Germany requires a "constructive vote of no confidence," in which a chancellor can be ousted only by a positive vote for his replacement. In other countries, it is only necessary to defeat the incumbent government on some designated motion or critical piece of legislation, such as the yearly budget.

4. On intraparty factions, their causes and consequences, see. Alan Zuckerman, *The Politics of Faction: Christian Democratic Rule in Italy* (New Haven: Yale University Press, 1979); and Giovanni Sartori, *Parties and Party Systems* (New York: Cambridge University Press, 1976), ch. 4.

5. This statement follows, for parties, what Riker, *Theory of Political Coalitions,* calls the "size principle."

6. This formulation of a generally recognized point is similar to that developed in Gabriel A. Almond, Scott Flanigan, and Robert Mundt, eds., *Crisis, Choice and Change* (Boston: Little, Brown, 1973). Also see Axelrod, *Conflict of Interest;* DeSwaan, *Coalition Theories;* and Warwick, "Durability of Coalition Governments."

7. This analysis of the factors shaping coalition preferences does not take into account attitudes of party leaders toward risk. For analyses applying this potentially important factor, for which I here have no measures, see Bruce Bueno de Mesquita, *Strategy, Risk, and Personality in Coalition Politics* (New York: Cambridge University Press, 1975).

8. This definition follows Dodd's formulation of Riker's size principle theory. See Dodd, *Coalitions in Parliamentary Governments.*

9. See Axelrod, *Conflict of Interest,* and DeSwaan, *Coalition Theories.*

10. This point combines Axelrod's argument with the line of thought developed in Almond, Flanigan, and Mundt, *Crisis, Choice and Change.*

11. Ceylon's oversize coalition of 1965 was actually not oversize when formed: a special provision of the constitution gave the prime minister authority to appoint six additional members of parliament *after* the government was formed and had received a vote of confidence.

12. Although I have considered the Irish coalition of Labor and the Fine Gael in 1973 as connected, A. S. Cohen argues, in an interesting analysis, that it was not. "The Open Coalition in the Closed Society," *Comparative Politics* 11 (April 1979): 319–338. Cohen stresses that coalitions in countries where the policy space is ambiguous and/or the parties primarily personalistic and localized are not subjected to as many internal stresses as are nonconnected coalitions in systems where the parties are clearly differentiated along a policy space (as in Italy and Finland). On the policy space in Italy, see Samuel Barnes, "Right, Left and the Italian Voter," *Comparative Political Studies* 4 (1971): 157–175. For data on party spaces in several countries see Ronald Inglehart and Hans D. Klingemann, "Party Identification, Ideological Preference and the Left-Right Dimension among Western Mass Publics," in Ian Budge, Ivor Crewe, and Dennis Farlie, eds., *Party Identification and Beyond* (New York: John Wiley, 1976). In making judgments about connected coalitions I only consider coalitions as unconnected in countries where the party space permits such a designation, or where, as in Turkey, elite discussion when the coalition was formed made its unconnectedness clear. In practical terms, I did not consider a coalition unconnected (without evidence from elite reactions) where the index of linkages between groups and parties was under 30 in table 5.3

13. DeSwaan, *Coalition Theories,* p. 288.

14. As noted in table 7.1, I consistently count the permanent coalition between the Country and National parties in Australia as a single-party government for purposes of this analysis.

15. For a discussion of minority governments roughly consistent with the present one, see Valentine Herman and John Pope, "Minority Governments in Western Democracies," *British Journal of Political Science* 3 (April 1973): 131–212.

16. On the use of such tactics in majority-controlled Austrian community governments, see G. Bingham Powell, Jr., with Rodney P. Stiefbold, "Anger, Bargaining, and Mobilization as Middle-Range Theories of Conflict Behavior," *Comparative Politics* 9 (July 1977): 379–398. An interesting account of opposition parliamentary and pressure tactics in Japan is Robert Ward, *Japan's Political System,* 2nd ed. (Englewood Cliffs: Prentice-Hall, 1978), pp. 97ff.

17. See Harry Eckstein, *Pressure Group Politics* (Stanford: Stanford University Press, 1958), and J. J. Richardson and A. C. Jordan, *Governing under Pressure* (London: Martin Robinson, 1979).

18. See Riker, *Theory of Political Coalitions,* and Dodd, *Coalitions in Parliamentary Governments.)*

19. *Dodd,* Coalitions in Parliamentary Governments.

20. Taylor and Herman, in "Party Systems and Government Stability," also found extremist-party representation to be the major factor associated with cabinet instability. Dodd, in *Coalitions in Parliamentary Governments,* uses a general index of party polarization with similar results. Dodd's approach has the advantage of capturing intense differences between parties which, given their general support for the political structure, would not be called extremist. The intense conflict between the major parties in Turkey is the best example of such nonextremist tension in the contemporary democracies. However, much greater

information is required for such analysis, and it is beyond my capability here. In the long run it is desirable to integrate analysis of extremism and other forms of policy disagreement, and to develop a clearer understanding of the components of policy disagreement and perceived electoral constraint that make extremism such a difficult problem for coalition formation. One interesting effort, focusing on the way extremism adds an additional issue dimension, is Subrata K. Mitra, "A Theory of Government Instability in Parliamentary Systems," *Comparative Political Studies* 13 (July 1980): 235–263.

21. Dodd, *Coalitions in Parliamentary Governments.*

22. Here the findings differ somewhat from those of Dodd, which are substantially shaped by the interwar period. Dodd reports that in the more conflictual and polarized environments the nondurability of cabinets was primarily due to their minority tendencies, while in less conflictual settings oversize cabinets were the greater problem. Among the democracies in 1967–1976, virtually the reverse was true. Only in the conflictual settings were many oversize cabinets present. Ibid., p. 181.

23. On executive-legislative relations in Costa Rica, see Charles F. Denton, *Patterns of Costa Rican Politics* (Boston: Allyn and Bacon, 1971); Christopher E. Baker, "The Costa Rican Legislative Assembly," in Weston H. Agor, ed., *Latin American Legislatures* (New York: Praeger, 1971), pp. 53–111; Ronald H. McDonald, *Party Systems and Elections in Latin America* (Chicago: Markham, 1971); and Kenneth J. Mijeski, "Costa Rica: The Shrinking of the Presidency," in Thomas V. DiBacco, ed., *Presidential Power in Latin America* (New York: Praeger, 1977), pp. 56–71.

24. See John D. Martz, "The Venezuelan Presidential System," in DiBacco, *Presidential Power,* pp. 96–116.

25. See Carl H. Lande, *Leaders, Factions and Parties: The Structure of Philippines Politics* (New Haven: Yale University Southeast Asia Studies, 1965), pp. 56ff.

26. Maurice Duverger, *Political Parties* (New York: John Wiley, 1954), pp. 393ff.

8. Managing Violence and Sustaining Democracy

1. See Rudolph J. Rummell, "Dimensions of Conflict Behavior Within and Between Nations," *Yearbook of the Society for General Systems Research* 8 (1963): 1–49; Raymond Tantor, "Dimensions of Conflict Behavior Within and Between Nations, 1958–60," *Journal of Conflict Resolution* 10 (March 1966): 41–64; Douglas P. Bwy, "Dimensions of Social Conflict in Latin America," *American Behavioral Scientist* 11 (March–April 1968): 39–50; Douglas A. Hibbs, Jr., *Mass Political Violence* (New York: John Wiley, 1973), ch. 2.

2. Of course, when civil violence escalates into full-scale civil war, large numbers of individuals become involved. But in the democracies considered here, most of the deaths seem to be the consequence of various forms of organized terrorist activity and/or small-scale guerrilla assaults. In her review of the literature on terrorism, Martha Crenshaw concludes that "Terrorism per se

is not usually a reflection of mass discontent or deep cleavages in society. More often it represents the disaffection of a fragment of the elite, who may take it upon themselves to act on the behalf of a majority unaware of its plight, unwilling to take action to remedy grievances, or unable to express dissent." "The Causes of Terrorism," *Comparative Politics* 13 (July 1981): 396.

3. For a discussion of alternative bases of elite conflict behavior, and a test of their impact on conflict activities in Austrian community politics, see G. Bingham Powell, Jr., with Rodney P. Stiefbold, "Anger, Bargaining and Mobilization as Middle Range Theories of Elite Conflict Behavior," *Comparative Politics* 9 (July 1977): 379–398.

4. But see the warning against stereotyping terrorists in Paul Wilkinson, *Political Terrorism* (London: Macmillan, 1974), pp. 132–133. Crenshaw, in "Causes of Terrorism," also cites studies indicating that terrorists represent many different types of personalities and motivations. The major work building upon general frustration-aggression models of the causes of violence is that of Ted Robert Gurr; see particularly "Psychological Factors in Civil Violence," *World Politics* 20 (Jan. 1968): 245–278; and *Why Men Rebel* (Princeton: Princeton University Press, 1971). Gurr's book combines an individual-level theory of frustration and aggression with sophisticated consideration of various societal factors shaping opportunities for action and success.

5. See William J. Crotty, ed., *Assassinations and the Political Order* (New York: Harper and Row, 1971); I. K. Feierabend, R. L. Feierabend, and B. Nesvold, "The Comparative Study of Revolution and Violence," *Comparative Politics* 5 (April 1973): 393–424.

6. That the problem of minority groups desiring to establish their own community is an extremely fundamental one in democratic theory is emphasized by Carl Cohen, *Democracy* (New York: Free Press, 1971), ch. 4. Also see Chapter 3 above, notes 23–26.

7. Hibbs, *Mass Political Violence,* chs. 5 and 8.

8. On the multiple crises in the Philippines, see Lela Garner Noble, "The Moro National Liberation Front in the Philippines," *Pacific Affairs* 49 (Fall 1976): 401–423; Justus M. van der Kroef, "Communism and Reform in the Philippines," *Pacific Affairs* 46 (Spring 1973): 29–58; and David Wurfel, "The Philippines Agrarian Crisis," *Pacific Affairs* 45 (Winter 1972–73): 582–585.

9. See, for example, Lester A. Sobel, ed., *Political Terrorism* (New York: Facts on File, 1975), for lists of incidents of terrorism in a wide variety of countries in the late 1960s and early 1970s.

10. On the connections between public disorder and military intervention, see the empirical analysis by William R. Thompson, *The Grievances of Military Coup-Makers* (Beverly Hills: Sage Publications, 1973), p. 45; the general theoretical discussions and overviews of Samuel P. Huntington, *Political Order in Changing Societies* (New Haven: Yale University Press, 1968), ch. 4; and Eric A. Nordlinger, *Soldiers in Politics: Military Coups and Governments* (Englewood Cliffs: Prentice-Hall, 1977), pp. 90–95.

11. See Ronald H. McDonald, "Electoral Politics and Uruguayan Political Decay," *Inter-American Affairs* 26 (Summer 1972): 25–46; R. Moss, "Urban Guerrillas in Uruguay," *Problems of Communism* 20 (Sept.–Oct. 1971): 14–23;

and Martin Weinstein, *Uruguay: The Politics of Failure* (Westport, Conn.: Greenwood Press, 1975).

12. See Feroz Ahmad, *The Turkish Experiment in Democracy, 1950–1975*(Boulder, Colo.: Westview Press, 1977); Ergun Ozbudun, *Social Change and Political Participation in Turkey* (Princeton: Princeton University Press, 1976); Sabri Sayari, "The Turkish Party System in Transition," *Government and Opposition* 13 (Winter 1978): 39–57.

13. *Keesing's Archives,* 1977.

14. An excellent summary and analysis of the events in Italy in this period is provided by Sidney Tarrow, "1976–1979: Three Years of Italian Democracy," in Howard Penniman, ed., *Italy at the Polls: 1979* (Washington: American Enterprise Institute, 1980).

15. Further violence took place at the time of the 1980 election. Nonetheless, the incumbent PNP government, which lost the election, peacefully turned over power to the opposition.

16. A splendid account of this process at the local level is William Sheridan Allen, *The Nazi Seizure of Power: The Experience of a Single German Town, 1930–1935* (Chicago: Quadrangle Books, 1965). On the German and Austrian cases in the 1920s and 1930s, see the essays in Juan J. Linz and Alfred Stepan, eds., *The Breakdown of Democratic Regimes: Europe* (Baltimore: Johns Hopkins University Press, 1978): M. Rainer Lepsius, "From Fragmented Party Democracy to Government by Emergency Decree and National Socialist Takeover: Germany," pp. 34–79; Walter B. Simon, "Democracy in the Shadow of Imposed Sovereignty: The First Republic of Austria," pp. 80–121.

17. Party involvement in violence is coded 0, 1, 2 as shown in table 8.1: 0 if there is no party involvement, 1 if there is limited party involvement or support, and 2 if violent clashes take place between supporters. The classifications are based primarily on accounts in *Keesing's Archives,* and should be taken as suggestive, rather than definitive. The dependent variable is continuity of democratic regime, coded 0, 1, 2, as shown in table 8.1. Northern Ireland is not included in the regression analysis, as it is not an independent country. Numbers in parentheses in the text are standardized regression coefficients. Number of deaths (constrained) and party involvement in violence explain 85 percent of the variance in continuity of democratic regime. (Considering only the cases with more than one death per year, these two variables explain 80 percent of the variance in continuity of the democratic regime.)

18. Linz argues that "the conditions leading to semiloyalty, or even suspicion of semiloyalty, by leading participants in the political game, opposition and government parties alike, account for the breakdown process almost as much as the role of the disloyal oppositions." Juan J. Linz, *Crisis, Breakdown and Reequilibration,"* vol. 1 of Juan J. Linz and Alfred Stepan, eds., *The Breakdown of Democratic Regimes* (Baltimore: John Hopkins University Press, 1978), p. 38.

19. One of the elements in the continuing failure to find solutions in Northern Ireland has been the inability of moderate Protestant leaders to maintain the support of their parties and voters when they seek accommodation. See Richard Rose, *Northern Ireland: Time of Choice* (Washington: American

Enterprise Institute, 1976): Arend Lijphart, "Review Article: The Northern Ireland Problem," *British Journal of Political Science* 5 (April 1975): 83–106; and Arend Lijphart, *Democracy in Plural Societies* (New Haven: Yale University Press, 1977), pp. 134–141.

20. The major source for this historical survey is Arthur S. Banks, *Cross-Polity Time Series Data* (Cambridge: M.I.T. Press, 1971). I have included regimes of the twentieth century with competitive elections and effective legislatures, according to Banks's classification, for at least a ten-year period. I have excluded South Africa and Portugal (1911–1925) as having overly restrictive franchises. Czechoslovakia is not included because external intervention was the major factor in the destruction of democracy in that nation in 1938.

21. On the First Austrian Republic, see Alfred Diamond, *Austrian Catholics and the First Republic: Democracy, Capitalism and Social Order, 1918–1934* (Princeton: Princeton University Press, 1960); and Simon, "Democracy in the Shadow." On Estonia, Tonu Parming, *The Collapse of Liberal Democracy and the Rise of Authoritarianism in Estonia* (Beverly Hills: Sage Publications, 1975). On Ceylon, S. Arasaratnam, "The Ceylon Insurrection of April 1971," *Pacific Affairs* 45 (Fall 1972): 356–371; A. Jeyaratnam Wilson, *Politics in Sri Lanka 1947–1973* (London: Macmillan, 1974). On India, Richard L. Park and Bruce Bueno de Mesquita, *India's Political System*, 2nd ed. (Englewood Cliffs: Prentice-Hall, 1979); Robert Hardgrave, *India: Government and Politics in a Developing Nation*, 3rd ed., (New York: Harcourt, Brace, Jovanovich, 1980).

22. On the intervention against the Turkish government in 1960, see Walter F. Weiker, *The Turkish Revolution 1960–61* (Washington: Brookings Institution, 1963), and Richard D. Robinson, *The First Turkish Republic* (Cambridge: Harvard University Press, 1963); on subsequent military involvement, see Ahmad, *The Turkish Experiment* and Sayari, "The Turkish Party System." On France, John S. Ambler, *The French Army in Politics, 1945–62* (Columbus: Ohio State University Press, 1966); Edgar S. Furniss, *DeGaulle and the French Army: A Crisis in Civil-Military Relations* (New York: Twentieth Century Fund, 1964); Claude E. Welch, Jr., and Arthur K. Smith, *Military Role and Rule* (North Scituate, Mass.: Duxbury Press, 1974), pp. 205–234. On Greece, Stephen Rousseas, *The Death of a Democracy: Greece and the American Conscience* (New York: Grove Press, 1967); and *Keesing's Archives,* 1967, 1968. An excellent introduction and overview of the Chilean crisis is Arturo Valenzuela, *The Breakdown of Democratic Regimes: Chile,* vol. 4 of Linz and Stepan, *Breakdown of Democratic Regimes.* On the Philippines, see the references in note 8, above.

23. Alfred Stepan, *The Military in Politics: Changing Patterns in Brazil* (Princeton: Princeton University Press, 1971). On the same general point, see Samuel E. Finer, *The Man on Horseback: The Role of the Military in Politics* (New York: Praeger, 1962); Huntington, *Political Order,* ch. 4; Nordlinger, *Soldiers in Politics,* ch. 3; Lloyd E. Rudolph and Susanne H. Rudolph, "Generals and Politicians in India," *Pacific Affairs* 37 (Spring 1964): 5–19; Welch and Smith, *Military Role and Rule,* pp. 246–249.

24. On the Venezuelan military in the period after the overthrow of the dictatorship in 1958, see Gene E. Bigler, "The Armed Forces and Patterns of

Civil-Military Relations," in John D. Martz and David J. Myers, eds., *Venezuela: The Democratic Experience* (New York: Praeger, 1977), pp. 113–133.

25. Nordlinger, *Soldiers in Politics*, pp. 65–78.

9. Democratic Performance: Liberty, Competition, Responsiveness

1. See for example Carl Cohen, *Democracy* (New York: Free Press, 1971), ch. 10, and Robert A. Dahl, *Polyarchy: Participation and Opposition* (New Haven: Yale University Press, 1971), ch. 1 for discussions of the relationship between civil rights, particularly freedom to inform and persuade, and democracy.

2. Raymond D. Gastil, ed., *Freedom in the World: Political Rights and Civil Liberties, 1978* (New York: Freedom House and G. K. Hall, 1978); p. 19.

3. Ibid., pp. 10–13.

4. Charles Taylor and Michael Hudson, *World Handbook of Political and Social Indicators* (New Haven: Yale University Press, 1972); and Charles Taylor and David A. Jodice, *World Handbook of Political and Social Indicators*, III (New Haven: Yale University Press, 1982).

5. Douglas A. Hibbs, *Mass Political Violence* (New York: John Wiley, 1973), p. 112.

6. These correlations are with log transformed sanctions.

7. Using log transformed variables for population, GNP/capita, riots, deaths, and sanctions, the standardized coefficients for 1958–1967 are as follows: population + .28, GNP/capita − .10, majoritarian electoral laws − .01, presidential executive + .22,* fractionalization of legislature + .32,* extremist vote − .16, riots + .76,** deaths − .02. In 1967–1976 the equivalent coefficients are similar, but deaths are significant and presidential executives are not.

8. On the problem of permanent minorities in democracies, see Cohen, *Democracy*, pp. 74–75, and the reference to ethnic politics in Chapter 3 above.

9. The problem that emerges in a multiparty system where the parties represent special configurations of interests may approximate some form of the famous Arrow paradox. See Anthony Downs's discussion of the problem of the "coalition of minorities," in *An Economic Theory of Democracy* (New York: Harper and Row, 1957), pp. 55–60; and the general problem created by the Arrow paradox, discussed by Downs, pp. 60–62, and originally developed by Kenneth J. Arrow in *Social Choice and Individual Values* (New York: John Wiley, 1951). For a general analysis of implications of the Arrow paradox for democracies, see William H. Riker, *Liberalism against Populism* (San Francisco: Freeman, 1981).

10. I have developed this analysis more thoroughly, tracing the emergent rules connecting election outcomes and the formation of governments in response to them under different party systems, in G. Bingham Powell, Jr., "Party Systems as Systems of Representation and Accountability" (Paper delivered at the 1981 Annual Meeting of the American Political Science Association, New York). The special clarification created by pre-election coalitions is discussed in that paper.

11. The sources used were Mackie and Rose, *International Electoral Almanac, Keesing's Archives,* and various individual country studies, particularly those in the American Enterprise Institute's "At the Polls" series, edited by Howard R. Penniman.

12. Some parties that are here considered excluded, such as the Swedish Communists, the Italian Communists 1976–1979, and the Danish Socialist People's party, did play important roles in supporting minority governments. In some cases they certainly won policy concessions. Even the long-excluded British Liberals played such a role in 1977–1979. But information is not systematically available on the roles and rewards of such parties.

13. Again, the formation of pre-election coalitions can greatly clarify the role of elections in shaping government coalition formation. The rules of connection are clearer and voters seem to be encouraged to penalize governments for poor performance where such pre-election coalitions are presented to the electorate. See Powell, "Party Systems as Systems of Representation and Accountability."

14. See ibid. for further discussion of this problem and its effect on voters.

15. Needless to say, this characterization is a time-bounded one. In the nineteenth century differences between right and left in Western Europe were defined primarily by religious policy. In the future, new policy conditions and theories may alter the present associations in various ways. Here, however, I am using these characterizations to link citizens and policies through party policy alternatives offered in the time period in question.

16. Douglas A. Hibbs, Jr., "Political Parties and Macroeconomic Policy," *American Political Science Review* 71 (March 1977): 467–487. David R. Cameron, "Inequality and the State: A Political Economic Comparison" (Paper delivered at the 1976 Annual Meeting of the American Political Science Association, Chicago); and David R. Cameron, "The Expansion of the Public Economy," *APSR* 72 (Dec. 1978): 1243–1261. Edward R. Tufte, *Political Control of the Economy* (Princeton: Princeton University Press, 1978).

17. On the historical development of public policy in the United States and Western Europe, see Richard A. Musgrave, *Fiscal Systems* (New Haven: Yale University Press, 1969); Arnold Heidenheimer, "The Politics of Public Education, Health and Welfare in the USA and Western Europe," *British Journal of Political Science* 3 (July 1973): 315–342; Anthony King, "Ideas, Institutions and the Policies of Government," *British Journal of Political Science* 3 (July 1973): 291–314.

18. See Harold Wilensky, *The Welfare State and Equality* (Berkeley: University of California Press, 1975). Also, Robert W. Jackman, *Politics and Social Inequality* (New York: John Wiley, 1975).

19. Percentages of Gross Domestic Product (GDP) are used rather than Gross National Product (GNP) because of source availability. The differences are not too great for these countries. Sources for inequality data are Hollis Chenery et al., *Redistribution with Growth* (New York: Oxford University Press, 1974), pp. 8–9; and Felix Paukert, "Income Distribution at Different Levels of Development," *International Labour Review* 108 (Aug.–Sept. 1973): 97–125. The two estimates are averaged where available for the same country.

20. See Musgrave, *Fiscal Systems;* Wilensky, *Welfare State;* and Arnold Heidenheimer, Hugh Heclo, and Carolyn Adams, *Comparative Public Policy* (New York: St. Martin's Press, 1975).

21. As Sawyer has demonstrated, most effects of income equalization do come from government transfer policies, such as social security and welfare, rather than from tax policies. See Malcolm Sawyer, "Income DIstribution in OECD Countries," O.E.C.D., *Economic Outlook, Occasional Papers,* July 1976.

22. Cameron, "Inequality and the State."

23. However, the multivariate analysis below suggests that the effects of class voting on total revenue increases are weak after a measure of international economic vulnerability is introduced. Left-bloc success continues to be a powerful factor; see Cameron, "Expansion of the Public Economy."

24. Data on marginal tax rates of average workers are from O.E.C.D., *Economic Outlook* 74 (March–April 1975): 39. The data estimate how much tax the average worker pays when his earnings increase by 10 percent; both income tax and social security are included; returns in transfer payments are not included; the average worker is assumed to be married with two children.

25. See Cameron, "Expansion of the Public Economy," p. 1255, for some evidence on over-time changes in Britain, Germany, Denmark, and Norway, 1961–1975, in relation to leftist control of government.

26. The source is Sawyer, "Income Distribution." Sawyer also supplies an excellent account of the problem encountered in using and comparing income inequality data in general.

27. Cameron, "Expansion of the Public Economy." Perhaps surprisingly, a similar measure, foreign trade as a percentage of GNP (provided by Charles Taylor and Michael Hudson, *World Handbook*), does not give nearly as strong results.

28. See note 24 above.

29. My analysis was carried out using a measure of the relative restrictiveness of abortion laws in 1972 developed by Marilyn J. Field, "Determinants of Abortion Policy in the Developed Nations," *Policy Studies Journal* 7 (summer 1979): 773. Field's own analysis using 29 contemporary developed nations, including a number of Eastern European nondemocracies, found a + .51 correlation between Socialists in the legislature and liberal policies; the coefficient drops to + .13 controlling for percentage Catholic in the population. However, her analysis of policy liberalization between 1920 and 1974 suggests the great importance of leftist parties, including their role in changes in the 1970s in Austria, West Germany, France, and Italy (over Christian Democratic opposition). For a discussion of various empirical studies of the effects of elections on policy, see Anthony King, "What Do Elections Decide?" in David Butler, Howard R. Penniman and Austin Ranney, eds., *Democracy at the Polls* (Washington: American Enterprise Institutes, 1981), pp. 293–324, and Richard Rose, *Do Parties Make a Difference?* (Washington: American Enterprise Institute, 1980).

30. For some American studies indicating that broad changes in citizen preference tend to be reflected in programs offered and executed by both

political parties, see Benjamin Ginsberg, "Elections and Public Policy," *American Political Science Review* 70 (March 1976): 41–49; Alan D. Monroe, "Consistency between Public Preferences and National Policy Decisions," *American Politics Quarterly* 7 (Jan. 1979): 3–20; Gerald M. Pomper, *Elections in America: Control and Influence in Democratic Politics* (New York: Dodd, Mead, 1974), chs. 7, 8, 10. A complete comparative analysis of responsiveness must take account of these "anticipatory" tendencies, which seem to be a very important element in democratic politics.

31. It might be suggested that multipartyism is itself an indicator of good representative performance—allowing the preferences of citizens more direct and complex representation in the legislature. Having no data on citizen preferences, I cannot address this issue here. We have already seen (in Chapter 5) that representational parliamentary systems do encourage more direct reflection of votes into seats, as had been shown by Rae and others: Douglas Rae, *The Political Consequences of Electoral Laws* (New Haven: Yale University Press, 1967).

Representation of preference is a fascinating problem, but its exploration must await more adequate comparative materials. For comparative analysis of the role of parties in preference representation in 50 communities in Austria, see G. Bingham Powell, Jr., with Lynda W. Powell, "The Analysis of Citizen-Elite Linkages: Representation by Austrian Local Elites," in Sidney Verba and Lucien W. Pye, eds., *The Citizen and Politics* (Stanford: Greylock, 1978), pp. 197–218. Also see Christopher H. Achen, "Measuring Representation," *American Journal of Political Science* 22 (Aug. 1978): 475–510; Samuel H. Barnes, *Representation in Italy* (Chicago: University of Chicago Press, 1977), chs. 8 and 9; Warren E. Miller and Donald Stokes, "Constituency Influence in Congress," *American Political Science Review* (March 1963): 45–56; Lynda W. Powell, "Issue Representation in Congress," *Journal of Politics,* in press; Sidney Verba and Norman H. Nie, *Participation in America* (New York: Harper and Row, 1972), pp. 267–285, 299–308.

32. I include only Switzerland and pre-1967 Uruguay as having fully institutionalized the collective executive. However, many countries use a variety of consultative practices in special policy areas or as informal mechanism for limiting political tension. See especially Arend Lijphart, *Democracy in Plural Societies* (New Haven: Yale University Press, 1977), ch. 2, and Chapter 10 below.

33. Pearson correlation based on 18 industrialized countries: in the 10 countries with low class voting correlation between left success and growth of government 1960–1970 is +.10; in the countries with high class voting, r = +.89.

34. The simple correlations between leftist governmental success and growth of government were +.49 for 8 countries with usual single-party majorities and +.70 for 10 countries with usual minority election outcomes; +.45 and +.75 for the majoritarian (and presidential) versus representational constitutions. However, when the "openness of the economy" variable is entered in the equations, the regression coefficients change to +.57 and +.58 in the party-system comparisons and +.47 and +.69 in the constitutional

comparisons. These coefficients are based on 16 cases, because "openness" data were not available for Australia and New Zealand (a fact that limits notably the variance on the leftist-success variable). In the analysis of the relationship between leftist success and income tax increases, the regressions show stronger coefficients in the countries with high class voting ($+.79$ versus $+.69$), but *weaker* coefficients in the multiparty systems and representational constitutions. Again, data for Australia and New Zealand are lacking, and the small number of cases compels us in any case to regard the results as merely suggestive.

10. Conclusion: Constraint and Creativity in Democracies

1. The new data on protests, riots, and deadly violence (as well as on many other variables not studied here) will be published in Charles Taylor and David A. Jodice, *World Handbook of Political and Social Indicators,* III (New Haven: Yale University Press, 1982). The events were collected from a wide range of newspaper sources and published materials. I am grateful to David A. Jodice and Charles Taylor for permitting me to use these data for comparison before publication of the new *Handbook.* Appreciation is also due to Karl Deutsch and the International Institute for Comparative Social Research, Science Center Berlin, for support of data collection for the new *Handbook.*

2. Because of the complexities of the modeling involved, and some instability in the coefficients, these analyses are not reported in detail, and should be considered only suggestive at this point. But addition of the voting turnout variable to the best equations predicting extremist-party vote, from Chapter 5, does yield a significant regression coefficient, at least in the more economically developed countries. The data suggest that higher turnout may be especially related to greater support for diffuse "protest" parties, rather than for "ideological contenders." (The standardized regression coefficient was $+.22$ for 27 cases.)

3. Edward Tufte, *Political Control of the Economy* (Princeton: Princeton University Press, 1978).

4. Ibid., p. 12.

5. See especially Harry Averch, John E. Koehler, and Frank H. Denton, *The Matrix of Policy in the Philippines* (Princeton: Princeton University Press, 1971). Also see Thomas C. Nowak, "The Philippines before Martial Law: A Study in Politics and Administration," *American Political Science Review* 71 (June 1977): 522–539.

6. Arend Lijphart, *The Politics of Accommodation* (Berkeley: University of California Press, 1968).

7. Ibid., and Arend Lijphart, "Typologies of Democratic Systems," *Comparative Political Studies* 1 (April 1968): 3–44.

8. Arend Lijphart, *Democracy in Plural Societies* (New Haven: Yale University Press, 1977); Val Lorwin, "Segmented Pluralism: Ideological Cleavages and Political Cohesion in the Smaller European Democracies," *Comparative Politics* 3 (Jan. 1971): 141–175; Gerhard Lehmbruch, "A Non-competitive Pattern of Conflict Management in Liberal Democracies: The Case of Switzerland, Austria and Lebanon," in Kenneth McRae, ed., *Consociational*

Democracy: Political Accommodation in Segmented Societies (Toronto: McClelland and Stewart, 1974), pp. 90–97; Eric Nordlinger, *Conflict Regulation in Divided Societies* (Cambridge: Harvard Institute for International Studies, 1972); Jurg Steiner, *Amicable Agreement versus Majority Rule: Conflict Resolution in Switzerland* (Chapel Hill: University of North Carolina Press, 1974). An interesting and (usually) creative debate has developed about the idea of consociationalism. Among the contributions are Hans Daalder, "The Consociational Democracy Theme," *World Politics* 26 (July 1974): 604–621; Brian Barry, "Political Accommodation and Consociational Democracy," *British Journal of Political Science* 5 (Oct. 1975): 477–505; Jurg Steiner, "The Consociational Theory and Beyond," *Comparative Politics* 13 (April 1981): 339–354; Arend Lijphart, "Consociational Theory: Problems and Prospects," *Comparative Politics* 13 (April 1981): 355–360.

9. Arend Lijphart, "Consociationalism and Federalism: Conceptual and Empirical Links," *Canadian Journal of Political Science* 21 (Sept. 1979): 499–515. Federalism is worthy of some comment here, as it is a constitutional dimension that has loomed large in the theoretical literature, but which I did not examine in Chapter 4. Federalism means the presence of constitutional arrangements designed to provide a degree of regional autonomy and systematic national representation for geographically distinct units. Often federal constitutions represent the compromise that was necessary to get member units, formerly autonomous states, to sacrifice their independence in the search for military security or economic advantage. Federalism and consociationalism can be seen as different, but comparable, bargains under which groups and parties give up some freedom of action in order to gain security for other goals. An elegant discussion of these relationships has recently been presented by Bruce D. Berkowitz, "Stability in Political Systems: The Decision to Be Governed," (Ph.D. diss., University of Rochester, 1981), esp. ch. 8. Federal arrangements of guaranteed local autonomy and explicit national representation of constituent units help provide some security to citizens and provincial leaders in their relationship with the national government.

Eight of the democracies that I have discussed have federal constitutions: Australia, Austria, Canada, West Germany, India, Switzerland, the United States, and Venezuela. In addition, Great Britain long allowed great regional autonomy in Northern Ireland. More recently, Belgium has moved in a direction of increasing federalism in response to the pressures of linguistic separatism, and as part of the set of compromises for dealing with that issue in the 1970s. Italy has also taken some steps toward implementing the federalist provisions of its constitution, and various countries have seriously considered federalist arrangements for some regions.

In a statistical sense, federalism is not as consistently important in its impact on democratic outcomes as the major constitutional variations I have discussed. Much depends on the viability of the regional forces in comparison to national ones and the expression of these in party systems. In Austria, for example, the very strong national parties have taken away most of the independent significance of federal arrangements. In Canada and the United States the most distinctive regional forces (Quebec and the South) have for most of this century been closely tied to one of the major national parties and made this tie a major part of their political positions. As Riker and Lemco suggest, the number and balance of the federal units may also be of critical importance, although we have too few cases of federalism in this study to explore this variable with any confidence. (See the argument and data in William H. Riker and John Lemco, "The Relation between Structure and Stability in Federal Governments," in *The Future of North America: Canada, the United States and Quebec,* II (Cambridge: Harvard Center for International Affairs, 1981). Federalism can certainly be important, under some circumstances, for defusing issues that might be intensely divisive if confronted nationally. There is little doubt that the potentially divisive effects of linguistic issues have been defused in Switzerland in part because the great importance of cantonal government means that the critical decisionmaking units are usually linguistically homogeneous. The Belgian efforts at developing federalism have been designed to achieve the same end. (See James A. Dunn, Jr., "Consociational Democracy and Language Conflict: A Comparison of the Belgian and Swiss Experience," *Comparative Political Studies* 5 (April 1974): 9–16. Lijphart's estimate of consociational practices, used in the text analysis, seems to include federal practices of this kind. On the other hand, federal arrangements can also allow local majority exploitation of regional minorities (as in Northern Ireland) or provide a site for the organization of resistance to the national government, as in the American Civil War. On federalism in general, see William H. Riker, "Federalism," in Fred I. Greenstein and Nelson W. Polsby, eds., *Handbook of Political Science* vol. 5, (Reading, Ma.: Addison-Wesley, 1975,) and the references cited therein.

10. Lijphart, *Democracy in Plural Societies,* pp. 119–129, 180–181.

11. On Austrian consociational practices, see Frederick C. Englemann, "Austria: The Pooling of the Opposition," in Robert A. Dahl, ed., *Political Oppositions in Western Democracies* (New Haven: Yale University Press, 1966), pp. 260–283; Kurt Steiner, *Politics in Austria* (Boston: Little, Brown, 1973); and Rodney P. Steifbold, "Segmented Pluralism and Consociational Democracy in Austria," in Martin O. Heisler, ed., *Politics in Europe* (New York: David McKay, 1974), pp. 117–177.

12. See David Eugene Blank, *Politics in Venezuela* (Boston: Little, Brown, 1973); Daniel H. Levine, *Conflict and Political Change in Venezuela* (Princeton: Princeton University Press, 1973); and the excellent essays, especially by Baloyra, Martz, and Myers, in John E. Martz and David J. Myers, *Venezuela: The Democratic Experience* (New York: Praeger, 1977).

13. See Dunn, "Consociational Democracy"; Val R. Lorwin, "Linguistic Pluralism and Political Tension in Modern Belgium," *Canadian Journal of History* 5 (March 1970): 1–23; and James A. Dunn, "A Revision of the Constitution in Belgium," *Western Political Quarterly* 27 (March 1974): 143–163.

14. See Steiner, *Amicable Agreement,* p. 33. However, Steiner points out that the Social Democrats were not given fully proportional representation on the collective executive until 1959.

15. For Lijphart's own analysis of problems of consociationalism, see

Democracy in Plural Societies, pp. 47–52. Also see the essays cited in note 8 above.

16. See the excellent brief account by David E. Schmitt, *Violence in Northern Ireland: Ethnic Conflict and Radicalization in an International Setting* (Morristown, N.J.: General Learning Press, 1974); also see Richard Rose, *Northern Ireland: Time of Choice* (Washington: American Enterprise Institute, 1976); and Lijphart, *Democracy in Plural Societies,* pp. 134–141.

17. I did not include Venezuela here, as it is not covered by Lijphart. Adding it to the regression model does not substantially change the results shown in table 10.3. Thus, the coding is based simply on Lijphart, "Consociationalism and Federalism," p. 513. One reason that this analysis must be treated as merely suggestive is that substantial timing problems are involved. Lijphart identifies Austria and the Netherlands as fully consociational up to 1966 and 1967, respectively; yet, it is clear that many consociational practices continued in these countries at least well into the 1970s. The difficulties reinforce the general need for much more careful and systematic study of the full range of leadership practices in bargaining, consultation, and the institutionalization of mutual veto powers in various policy areas. Given the absence of such studies, the safest practice here seemed simply to use Lijphart's attributions as a general means of indicating those countries in which some regularized consociational practices are known to have been present.

18. See Harry Eckstein, *Pressure Group Politics: The Case of the British Medical Association* (Stanford: Stanford University Press, 1960); and J. J. Richardson and A. G. Jordan, *Governing under Pressure: The Policy Process in a Post-Parliamentary Democracy* (London: Martin Robertson, 1979).

19. See the excellent recent discussion of such changes in Italy and Israel by Sidney Tarrow and Ariel Levite, Legitimation from Right and Left" (Paper presented at the 1981 Annual Meeting of the American Political Science Association, New York).

20. This is a point well discussed by Robert A. Dahl in *Political Oppositions in Western Democracies* (New Haven: Yale University Press, 1966), and is one of the points upon which Steiner ("The Consociational Theory") and Lijphart ("Consociational Theory") agree. Expanded conceptualizations of decisionmaking modes may also be a fruitful avenue for research, as suggested by the interesting and provocative analysis of "decision by interpretation," in Jurg Steiner and Robert H. Dorff, *A Theory of Political Decision Modes: Intra-Party Decision Making in Switzerland* (Chapel Hill: University of North Carolina Press, 1980).

21. See G. Bingham Powell, Jr., "Party Systems as Systems of Representation and Accountability" (Paper presented at the 1981 Annual Meeting of the American Political Science Association, New York), and Chapter 9 above.

22. See especially Sidney Verba and Norman H. Nie, *Participation in America* (New York: Harper and Row, 1972), chs. 17–20; Sidney Verba, Norman H. Nie, and Jae-on Kim, *Participation and Political Equality: A Seven-Nation Comparison* (New York: Cambridge University Press, 1978), and the appendices summarizing other studies of varieties of participation; and Samuel H. Barnes and Max Kaase, et al., *Political Action: Mass Participation in Five Western Democracies* (Beverly Hills: Sage Publications, 1979).

23. For some initial work along these lines, see G. Bingham Powell, Jr., "Social Progress and Liberal Democracy," in G. A. Almond, M. Chodorow, and R. H. Pierce, eds., *Progress and Its Discontents* (Berkeley: University of California Press, forthcoming), and the references therein, especially C. H. Huang, "Democracy, Competition and Development: The Political Economy of Inflation and Growth in Developing Countries" (Ph.D. diss., University of Rochester, 1979).

Appendix

1. Charles Taylor and Michael Hudson, *World Handbook of Political and Social Indicators* (New Haven: Yale University Press, 1972).
2. Charles Taylor and David A. Jodice, *World Handbook of Political and Social Indicators* III (New Haven: Yale University Press, forthcoming).
3. Douglas A. Hibbs, *Mass Political Violence* (New York: John Wiley, 1973), p. 10.
4. Thomas Mackie and Richard Rose, *The International Almanac of Electoral History* (New York: Free Press, 1974).
5. Douglas Rae, *The Political Consequences of Electoral Laws* (New Haven: Yale University Press, 1967), p. 56.
6. In addition to accounts of the parties and their activities in *Keesing's Archives, Europe Yearbook,* and other general sources, a number of specific studies were helpful in forming judgments about characterization of parties as extremist during this time period. I should emphasize, however, that although these accounts were of great value, not all of their authors would agree in designating the parties as extremist. Robert N. Kearney, *The Politics of Ceylon (Sri Lanka)* (Ithaca: Cornell University Press, 1973); A. Jeyaratnam Wilson, *Politics in Sri Lanka 1947–73* (London: Macmillan, 1974); Calvin A. Woodward, *The Growth of a Party System in Ceylon* (Providence: Brown University Press, 1969); Frederico G. Gil, *The Political System of Chile* (Boston: Houghton Mifflin, 1966); Arturo Valenzuela, *The Breakdown of Democratic Regimes: Chile,* vol. 4 of Juan Linz and Alfred Stepan, *the Breakdown of Democratic Regimes* (Baltimore: Johns Hopkins Press, 1978); *Costa Rica: Election Factbook,* no. 2 (Washington: Institute for Comparative Study of Political Systems, 1970); Robert J. Alexander, *Latin American Political Parties* (New York: Praeger, 1973); Charles F. Denton, *Patterns of Costa Rican Politics* (Boston: Allyn and Bacon, 1971); Sten Berglund and Ulf Lindstrom, *The Scandinavian Party System(s)* (Lund: Studentlitterature, 1978); Hans Jorgan Nielsen, "The Uncivic Culture: Attitudes toward the Political System in Denmark and Vote for the Progress Party," *Scandinavian Political Studies,* 11 (1976): 147–163; Jerrold G. Rusk and Ole Borre, "The Changing Party Space in Danish Voter Perceptions, 1971–73," in Ian Budge, Ivor Crewe, and Dennis Farlie, *Party Identification and Beyond* (New York: John Wiley, 1976), p. 137–162; Paul R. Brass and Marcus F. Franda, *Radical Politics in South Asia* (Cambridge: MIT Press, 1973); Norman D. Palmer, *Elections and Political Development: The South Asian Experience* (Durham: Duke University Press, 1975); D. L. Sketh, ed., *Citizens and Parties: Aspects of Campaign Politics In India* (New Delhi:

Allied Publications, 1975); James W. White, *The Sokagakki and Mass Society* (Stanford: Stanford University Press, 1970); Philip Converse and Henry Valen, "Cleavage and Perceived Party Distances in Norwegian Voting," *Scandinavian Political Studies,* 6 (1971): 107–152; Henry Valen and Stein Rokkan, "Norway: Election to the Storting in September, 1973," *Scandinavian Political Studies,* 9 (1974): 205–217; Ronald Inglehart and Dusan Sidjanski, "The Left, the Right, the Establishment and the Swiss Electorate," in Budge, Crewe, and Farlie, eds., *Party Identification,* pp. 225–242; Henry Kerr, Jr., *Switzerland: Social Cleavages and Partisan Conflict* (Beverly Hills: Sage Publications, 1974); Feroz Ahmad, *The Turkish Experiment in Democracy 1950–1975* (Boulder, Colo.: Westview Press, 1977); Ergun Ozbudun, *Social Change and Political Participation in Turkey* (Princeton: Princeton University Press, 1976); Sabri Sayari, "The Turkish Party System in Transition," *Government and Opposition,* 13 (Winter 1978): 39–57; Ronald H. McDonald, "Electoral Politics and Uruguayan Political Decay," *Inter-American Economic Affairs,* 26 (Summer 1972): 25–46; Martin Weinstein, *Uruguay: The Politics of Failure* (Westport, Conn.: Greenwood Press, 1975); David Eugene Black, *Politics in Venezuela* (Boston: Little, Brown, 1973); John D. Martz and Enrique Baloyra, *Electoral Mobilization and Public Opinion: The Venezuelan Campaign of 1973* (Chapel Hill: University of North Carolina Press, 1976).

Index

Abortion laws, 198, 267
Agricultural minorities, 94–96, 102–105, 126, 131, 156
Ahmad, Feroz, 263, 264, 274
Alford, Robert R., 88, 253, 257
Alignment between parties & social groups, *see* Party-group linkages
Almond, Gabriel A., 238, 239, 240, 241, 243, 244, 247, 249, 259
Alt, James, 253, 254, 255, 257
Aristotle, 243
Australia, 56, 113, 135, 184
Austria, 115–116, 167–168, 171, 194, 213
Averch, Harry, 253, 269

Baloyra, Enrique, 38, 245, 271, 274
Banks, Arthur, 238, 239, 247, 248, 264
Barnes, Samuel H., 258, 260, 268, 272
Bayley, David, 124, 257
Belgium, 25, 113, 139–140, 214
Benjamin, Roger W., 252, 254
Berglund, Sten, 252, 254, 255, 273
Black, David Eugene, 271, 274
Bracher, Karl Dietrich, 26, 78, 242, 251
Brazil, 173
Bueno de Mesquita, Bruce, 259, 264
Butler, David, 4, 239, 250

Cameron, David R., 188, 191, 195, 266, 267
Canada, 213
Catholicism, 81, 85, 89, 196–197, 245
Ceylon: violence, 23–24, 157, 162; executive-legislative relations, 56, 135, 140, 147, 259; censorship, 172; attempted coup, 173
Chenery, Hollis, 246, 266
Chile: violence, 24, 165–166, 167; over-throw of democratic government, 49, 173; compulsory voting, 113; executive-legislative relations, 152, 220
Civil liberties, 3, 175–176
Coalitions: minimum winning coalitions, 136, 137, 141, 145–146; connectivity of, 137–138, 141, 146; oversize coalitions, 137, 138, 140, 141, 147; multivariate analysis of durability of, 147–151; limited manipulation of economic cycle by coalition governments, 209–211. *See also* Preelection coalitions
Cohen, Carl, 239, 240, 262, 265
Comparative analysis, limits of, 226–228
Compatibility of dimensions of performance, 25–29, 64–66, 201–208
Compulsory voting requirements, 13, 38, 113–114, 121
Consociational practices, 212–218
Constitutional setting, 54–73. *See also* Majoritarian-parliamentary system; Presidential system; Representational-parliamentary system
Converse, Philip, 250, 256, 274
Costa Rica, 113–114, 152, 220
Coups: military, 163–166, 173–174; executive, 165, 167–168, 170–172, 174
Crewe, Ivor, 250, 253, 254, 255, 256, 257
Criteria of democracy, 3–7, 200

Daadler, Hans, 250, 270
Dahl, Robert A., 4, 9, 238, 242, 243, 245, 249, 251, 265, 272
Deaths from political violence, 21–25; population size and, 33–34, 50–52; modernization level and, 40–41, 50–53; ethnic cleavages and, 44–47, 50–

275